PRAISE FOR *SELLING BLUE ELEPHANTS*

ACADEMIA

"*Selling Blue Elephants* promises to change the way we think about developing products. Over the years there have been a lot of books that deal with what the business person faces—most written from 20,000 feet. They're big on perspective but not on real 'how to do it.' Moskowitz and Gofman have written a book that tells the business person, anywhere in the world, how to compete effectively, no matter how small (or how large) the enterprise."

—**Professor Eugene Galanter, Director, Psychophysics Laboratory, Columbia University**

"The title of Howard Moskowitz's and Alex Gofman's engaging book, *Selling Blue Elephants: How to Make Great Products That People Want BEFORE They Even Know They Want Them*, almost says it all. *Selling Blue Elephants* lays out for the reader the ways that the general approach, dubbed Rule Developing Experimentation or RDE, makes it possible to design and test products, packages, messages, and services in ways that will appeal to consumers—even when the consumers are not able to articulate what it is that appeals to them. RDE is largely grounded in Moskowitz's formal training in the quantitative discipline of psychophysics, and in *Selling Blue Elephants* the authors lucidly and brilliantly give many examples of the ways they have applied this sophisticated psychophysical approach to the marketplace. Read, enjoy, and learn!"

—**Professor Lawrence E. Marks, Professor of Epidemiology and Psychology, Director, John B. Pierce Laboratory, Yale University**

"*Selling Blue Elephants* convincingly demonstrates the value of systematic experimentation in the design of new and improved products, be they coffee, pickles, or graphic designs. It also shows how it pays to focus on individual differences in consumers when optimizing many of these products. And it does all this with an engaging and entertaining set of real-world examples from the authors' own extensive experience.

It is as fun to read as it is educational."

—**Gary Beauchamp, Ph.D., Director and President, Monell Chemical Senses Center**

"*Selling Blue Elephants* will indubitably appeal to the global community of marketers and product developers. Moskowitz and Gofman have clearly laid out a set of knowledge-building techniques for discerning consumer minds that may change the way companies do business. Traditionally and all too frequently, business decisions are made using methods that are powerful but time consuming and cumbersome. *Selling Blue Elephants* solidly paves the way to change that by providing reliable, easy-to-use, affordable techniques and tools. In the hands of business practitioners, these methods might be of a tremendous value to the corporations and delight the customers by meeting their 'wants and needs' better and faster."

—**Professor Vijay Mahajan, Professor of Marketing, The University of Texas at Austin**

"This book is indeed an excellent masterpiece from two prominent authors and practitioners. It is an absolute 'must read item.' It provides practical insight to business leaders who wish to create the oft-wished 'thinking society and organization' among their fellow employees. The book provides a way to deal with new opportunities in a risk-conscious culture. Even more important and enjoyably so, the book shows how the organization can become far more efficient in its tasks. As a professor specializing in financial services and risk management, I am delighted to see these issues taken up, approached solidly, and solved to the corporation's benefit."

—**Professor Hj Mohd Rasid Hussin, Department of Financial Services and Risk Management, MARA University of Technology, Malaysia**

"Whether you are an optimist or a pessimist, Moskowitz and Gofman demonstrate how the use of a technique called Rule Developing Experimentation (RDE) can turn average products into amazing products!

This book is well written with plenty of interesting stories and case studies from pickles to politics! We are introduced to Allison-the-Entrepreneur, the Lara Croft of the business world, who adopts RDE and uses it to develop a successful business. Following her adventure is a fun way to learn about the benefits of RDE.

Selling Blue Elephants is a must for any marketer or product developer who wants to learn the art of success!"

—Iain Bitran, President, The International Society for Professional Innovation Management, UK

CORPORATIONS

"*Selling Blue Elephants* is a must read for anyone wanting to understand the DNA of a consumer's mind—how to create products that people must have even before they know it."

—Mark Thompson, co-author of the international bestseller *Success Built to Last* (*Wall Street Journal* and *BusinessWeek* bestseller, the Top 3 of Amazon's Best Books of 2006 Editors' Picks: Business)

"*Selling Blue Elephants* is a must-read for anyone in business—whether you are an entrepreneur, an employee of a privately held company, or a member of a billion-dollar multinational corporation. Moskowitz and Gofman introduce readers to the world of Rule Developing Experimentation (RDE) and illustrate its applicability and value through a number of beautifully explained real-world examples ranging from pickles, pretzels, and pasta to credit cards, magazines, and presidential elections!

I can't imagine that there will be a single reader who does not get something of value out of this book."

—Phil Perkins, Senior Vice President and Director of Research, Development and Innovation, Bush Brothers & Company

"Moskowitz and Gofman have opened up to the business world a new dimension for creating innovation from the consumer's perspective. Up to now, consumers often told us their feelings about innovations *after the fact*, when it was already too late. Now we can implement the consumer's ideas early in the innovation process in order to create new products that have a greater chance of succeeding. It looks like Moskowitz and Gofman's powerful development tool can be a welcome addition to your innovation portfolio.

It can provide a blueprint for the future success of your product. Essentially the tools make the consumer your invention partner."

—Sven Gohla, Vice President, R&D, The La Prairie Group, Switzerland

"You will know (and use to your benefit) more about your competitor than he knows about himself. More about his advertising, his brochures, and the flaws in his marketing. What you do need is the breakthrough called Rule Developing Experimentation (RDE).

Read this book. Experiment. And discover the biggest competitive advantage you've ever had."

—Jerry Lee, owner, WBEB Radio Philadelphia

"Again, Howard Moskowitz has manifested with this book that he is truly the leading personality in the consumer research world. It is one thing to write a meaningful book for the market research community—it is quite another thing to write it in such a fascinating and comprehensive style as he and Alex Gofman have done. The reader will get more than just an intellectually appealing learning experience. He will enjoy the journey, discovering how wonderfully this book has been written."

—Johannes Hartmann, Vice President Consumer Insight Foods, Unilever, Netherlands

"Engaging and powerful product success stories. Not for the fainthearted or the linear minded. The Prego story is particularly close to my heart as I lived the intensity of the planning and design sessions, the various tastings, and the logistics of getting the product, the pots, the pans, and the ladles to the right cities. The rich results from this study provided 'focus' for new product development, and 'broke the paradigm' by looking beyond 'texture' and 'color' as key drivers of consumer liking.

Bravo to the authors for bringing this story and their approach to the business world, and to readers in general."

—**Cecille Feliciano, former Gravies and Sauces Research Manager, Campbell Soup Company**

"RDE is an intuitively compelling, powerful concept, but somehow that simple powerful elegance was lost in the academic treatment of the subject. Finally, there's a book that explains how RDE can be applied to marketing and product development in simple, clear, and (dare I say) entertaining terms.

A breath of fresh air!"

—**Jeff Ewald, founder, Optimization Group, Inc.**

"Moskowitz and Gofman take us through the commercial beginnings of RDE with a series of case studies in consumer packaged goods that are still exciting today. They then lead us through later applications in the area of services, communications, design, and packaging. But where the rubber really meets the road is when they lead us into the 'algebra of the consumer mind' and Mind Genomics. RDE comes alive as a powerful social, political, and commercial tool as it is applied to the construction of It!^{TM} databases that have the capacity to become an amazing library of insight into the consumer mind for marketers, politicians, and social engineers alike.

One of the most original marketing books in decades."

—**Simon Chadwick, partner, Cambiar LLC**

"*Selling Blue Elephants* is a refreshing, user-friendly approach to explaining to business and marketing folks something they need to know but find hard to understand: how consumers really make choices. We are creatures who communicate most about our inner preferences when we can just compare options or select alternatives, rather than attempting to analyze and explain our own behavior or beliefs. *Selling Blue Elephants* helps us see how apparently complex questions can be scientifically resolved through a mixture of everyday examples and light stories. I both enjoyed and learned from the read."

—**Tony Cowling, President, TNS, UK**

"This book is both deep in content and surprisingly easy to read. The book's ability to convey scientific information in a down-to-earth and even enjoyable medium is a tribute to the authors' enthusiasm and vision. I cannot wait to give a copy to my co-workers and friends so they can appreciate the role and contribution of market research to business success."

—**Roseanne Luth, President and CEO, Luth Research**

"I have seen firsthand the dramatic impact that the creative use of RDE/IdeaMap can have on a business. Beyond this incredible technique to which Moskowitz and Gofman have dedicated their professional career, they personally bring unparalleled experience and insight into the realm of accurately predicting human behavior and preference. Anyone who believes that marketing research is limited by the current imagination of the consumer—that it cannot be helpful in divining emerging or completely new categories of consumer or business products or services—is sadly mistaken.

Those who use RDE wisely will not only leave their competitors in the dust, but will get to the future much more quickly and profitably, and enjoy lasting competitive advantage."

—**Don Lowry, Vice President, SEI Wealth Network (former Marketing Executive, Campbell Soup Company)**

"Using RDE, Howard helped us grow the Prego brand to twice its size. The optimization and category assessment methods of RDE led to the launch of the highly successful Prego Extra Chunky line and the double-digit growth of the base Prego business. In the spaghetti sauce market, we did a category audit. RDE uncovered a huge untapped niche that existed in the marketplace. We developed products for this niche and grew our market share to twice its original size by following the insights identified in the RDE-based category audit and optimization. This brilliant identification of a food segment was largely responsible for the success of the Prego brand in the market."

—Monica Wood, Vice President, Global Marketing Research Head, Novartis OTC
(former Director, Market Research, Campbell Soup Company)

"Moskowitz and Gofman managed to give a twist of storytelling to methodologies, crafting their highly informative case histories into good stories that cover a wide array of industries, from food to electronics, from advertising to stock markets. Beyond the unequivocal value of their actionable Rule Developing Experimentation, this book is in itself an enjoyable opportunity to read and learn."

—Marco Bevolo, Director, Foresight and Trends at Philips Design,
Royal Philips Electronics, Netherlands

"Howard and Alex don't beat around the bush. *Selling Blue Elephants* gets to the heart of the matter by Page 2, and never lets up. Executives will appreciate the accessible discussions. Analysts will love the plethora of actual examples and their lucid conceptualization. Five stars from me for this punchy, thought-provoking read for anyone in R&D, brand management, new market strategy, or just plain old marketing research."

—Shashank Tripathi, Regional Director, Asia Pacific, Universal McCann, Singapore

MEDIA

"Seldom does a book come along from exceptional minds that combines whit, whimsy, savvy, and intellectual rigor, while at the same time being extraordinarily useful. *Selling Blue Elephants* is such a book. Having coached some 12 thousand people over the last three decades, I have learned that people can seldom accurately articulate the reasons for their preferences and choices. This book tells you how to solve this problem and develop profitable products.

If marketing matters to you, you have to read this book!"

—Stewart Emery, co-author of international bestseller *Success Built to Last*
(*Wall Street Journal* and *BusinessWeek* bestseller, the Top 3 of Amazon's Best
Books of 2006 Editors' Picks: Business)

"Intellectually rigorous, hugely entertaining, always thought-provoking: this is one great book."

—Roger Tredre, Editor-In-Chief, Worth Global Style Network, UK

SELLING BLUE ELEPHANTS

HOW TO MAKE GREAT PRODUCTS THAT PEOPLE WANT BEFORE THEY EVEN KNOW THEY WANT THEM

HOWARD R. MOSKOWITZ, PH.D.
ALEX GOFMAN, PH.D.

Vice President, Editor-in-Chief: Tim Moore
Editor: Yoram (Jerry) Wind
Acquisitions Editor: Martha Cooley
Editorial Assistant: Pamela Boland
Development Editor: Russ Hall
Associate Editor-in-Chief and Director of Marketing: Amy Neidlinger
Publicist: Amy Fandrei
Marketing Coordinator: Megan Colvin
Cover Designer: Alan Clements
Managing Editor: Gina Kanouse
Project Editor: Michael Thurston
Copy Editor: Krista Hansing
Proofreader: Water Crest Publishig
Indexer: Erika Millen
Senior Compositor: Gloria Schurick
Manufacturing Buyer: Dan Uhrig

© 2007 by Pearson Education, Inc.
Publishing as Prentice Hall
Upper Saddle River, New Jersey 07458

Prentice Hall offers excellent discounts on this book when ordered in quantity for bulk
purchases or special sales. For more information, please contact U.S. Corporate and Government Sales,
1-800-382-3419, corpsales@pearsontechgroup.com. For sales outside the U.S., please contact
International Sales at international@pearsoned.com.

Company and product names mentioned herein are the trademarks or registered trademarks of their
respective owners.

IdeaMap®, IdeaMap®.Net, StyleMap® and StyleMap®.Net are registered trademarks of Luxton
Enterprises. US Patent 6,662,215. Other patents pending Moskowitz Jacobs Inc. © 2007. All rights
reserved.

Printed in the United States of America

Third Printing May 2010
ISBN-10: 0-13-338164-1
ISBN-13: 978-013-338164-1

Pearson Education LTD.
Pearson Education Australia PTY, Limited.
Pearson Education Singapore, Pte. Ltd.
Pearson Education North Asia, Ltd.
Pearson Education Canada, Ltd.
Pearson Educatión de Mexico, S.A. de C.V.
Pearson Education—Japan
Pearson Education Malaysia, Pte. Ltd.

Library of Congress Cataloging-in-Publication Data is on file.
This product is printed digitally on demand. This book is the paperback version of
an original hardcover book.

I lovingly dedicate our book to the lights of my life. Thank you, Arlene, for being you and for all that you have done for me over these many years. Also to my children, Daniel and Yaffa Moskowitz, and David and Chavi Moskowitz. Finally, to Temima, Yosef, Ahuva, Hadassah, Shira, Meirah, and Noach. You are our seeds of the future.
—Howard Moskowitz

To my late father, to whom I owe my gratifying life-long pursuit in search of the answers to "why?" and "how?" about the surrounding world, and to my children, Alli and Matt, and my wife, Irene, who make this quest meaningful.
—Alex Gofman

CONTENTS

Foreword

Welcome to the brave new world, where science and knowledge meet, and perhaps give the *status quo* a run for its money.

This book is about Rule Developing Experimentation (RDE)—a business process with which a company can know more about customers than many think even possible. That information sheds light on what the company has to do to ride the wave, get the next set of customers, and then anticipate the future. Armed with these new information-gathering tools, a company can find out what turns on their current and potential new customers, insightfully create new products, successfully launch them, and happily grab market share from the competitors. Imagine this as the world for generations to come—where what you *are* means less than what you *can be* tomorrow, and what you can be tomorrow becomes increasingly simpler to achieve for a company so determined.

So with this vision of what the world's going to be like, let's return to *Selling Blue Elephants*. Moskowitz and Gofman are experienced in this world where in order to survive, businesses must understand the customers' needs, both current and not yet thought of. Translating them into successful business rules virtually overnight—and at the same time doing it inexpensively—is something that was unimaginable just a few years ago.

The authors have managed to systematize the approach so any business person can take advantage of it whenever needed. This is not one of those dreary handbooks or over-simplified manuals for people feeling challenged in marketing, product development, and so on. Howard and Alex have struck a beautiful balance; a readable scientific foundation free from mind-numbing and deep statistical excursions; a balance of hands-on experience without making the reader feel boot-camped or even coached; and principles plus case histories that are downright entertaining, informative, and educational. The book leads you on a captivating journey with each chapter introducing gradually more and more useful details about RDE widely applied from food product development to political campaigns, from advertisements to stock market predictions, from driving innovation to package and magazine cover design. And the list goes on. By the end of the book you realize you are ready to try it yourself. It is deep enough in details to let the reader jump-start RDE immediately, and at the same time general enough to stimulate a search for new applications.

When I started reading their work, I was amazed that companies could actually learn so much by systematic variation. It was surprising to me, who had grown up in a world of smart and systematic thinkers. We used some of these approaches when I worked closely with the founder of Schwab.com, but not to the extent, nor with the same rigor that our authors have done. We survived and grew, but we could have done things far faster and better than we did had we had the blueprint from experimentation. When it came time to apply this approach in our study and book, *Success Built to Last: Creating a Life that Matters*, we got a chance to use the systematic experimentation that our authors promote. It worked like a charm, and confirmed in two weeks of "scientific work" those insights that we had found in a couple of years of interviews. We authors were convinced, and in fact so convinced that we wrote up the chapter about RDE as the final "methods" chapter in our book.

One of the traditional questions of any foreword is *who is this book written for?* With *Selling Blue Elephants*, this is a tricky question. On one hand, brand managers, advertising specialists, product developers, marketers and market researchers, designers, communications professionals, and of course students will clearly benefit from reading this book and applying RDE to their respective fields. The general reading public will find much of this book fascinating. On the other hand, even the authors seem to be uncertain where the limits of the approach are. Who knows, maybe the biggest RDE success will come out of the areas only hinted at or not even touched in this book.

So, again, why is RDE so important? Quite simply, none of us in the business world really knows all the answers all the time. Oh, certainly there are some of us who can ride a winning streak, who may be connected to "what's going on right now." But as an investor and business builder, I think it's important to take a longer view. It's good to be right. And, I've learned over the years that nothing is better than knowledge. *Selling Blue Elephants* gives us the way to gain that knowledge about the customers' mind easily, anywhere, anytime, and for virtually any topic. The authors have, in effect, created a manifesto for change that will be equally powerful in the hands of the small business and the large corporations anywhere in the world.

Spending a big portion of my professional life trying to understand and explain to others what it entails to become successful, I feel that this book and RDE may be the most useful tools on the road to success for motivated businesspeople.

Howard and Alex have put together a really captivating book. They've woven together stories about business successes in a way that I as a businessman and investor find fascinating.

—Mark Thompson
Executive coach and management advisor, and co-author of the
international bestseller *Success Built to Last*

About the Authors

Howard Moskowitz is president and CEO of Moskowitz Jacobs Inc., a firm he founded in 1981.

Dr. Moskowitz is both a well-known experimental psychologist in the field of psychophysics and an inventor of world-class market research technologies. Dr. Moskowitz graduated Harvard University in 1969 with a Ph.D. in experimental psychology. Prior to that, he graduated Queens College (New York), Phi Beta Kappa, with degrees in mathematics and psychology. He has written/edited 16 books, has published well over 300 articles, and serves on the editorial board of major journals. His extensive speaking engagements span both scientific and market research conferences, as well as guest lectures at leading business schools and food science departments of universities.

Dr. Moskowitz has been the recipient of numerous awards, including the David R. Peryam lifetime achievement award by the American Society for Testing and Materials; the Charles Coolidge Parlin Award from the American Marketing Association, considered to be the Nobel Prize of market research, for his lifetime contributions to the field, ranging from product work to the optimization of consumer concept and package designs; and the 2006 ARF Innovation Award for the development of the most innovative research idea. For the past two years, Dr. Moskowitz appeared weekly as the Food Doctor on ABC NewsNow, where he anchored a 10-minute spot featuring young food and beverage entrepreneurs.

Alex Gofman is vice president and CTO of Moskowitz Jacobs Inc. Alex is well known as a co-inventor of world-class marketing and market research technologies as well as for his work in cross-science development in experimental psychology and computer science, and as the architect of the award-winning IdeaMap® family of products. He has been leading the development of new technologies, algorithms, and software applications since he joined the company in 1992.

Mr. Gofman previously worked with international high-tech and software development companies in the U.S. and Eastern Europe. He authored and co-authored more than 30 papers, holds 18 patents, contributed to a concept research book, and presented papers at multiple international conferences around the world that earned him several awards nominations. Born in an industrial region of the Ukraine, Mr. Gofman has an MS degree in Computer Science from Donetsk National Technical University, where he graduated summa cum laude in 1981.

Acknowledgments

No writers complete a book, or even an article, by themselves. It's just not possible. We have been blessed by the wonderful people who really deserve our thanks and acknowledgment.

At Moskowitz Jacobs, we are grateful to our very talented technology group—Madhu Manchaiah, John Ma, and Prasad Tungaturthy—who created the IdeaMap.Net tool for RDE and made sure, time after time, that the RDE programs could be accessed and used by anyone, anywhere in the world. This book really paints the flowering of your contributions.

We greatly appreciate our capable research team who consistently ensured that the RDE technology and application turned into actionable business information. Their efforts have helped hundreds of corporations around the world achieve development, marketing, and sales goals.

Our marketing support team helped us through the process. Suzanne Gabrione proofread the book, ably assisted by Joyce Mitchell. This dynamic duo found many errors that we made, and all through the editing process offered many 'reader-oriented' suggestions for style and language that we gratefully incorporated.

We are thankful to our friend and colleague, Marco Bevolo of Philips Design in Eindhoven, who was a continuing source of inspiration. Marco provided a unique, artistic, and often refreshingly different point of view for many of our business ideas. He is a wonderful and precious colleague.

We save our greatest acknowledgment for the Prentice Hall team, with whom we worked for two good, quite enlightening years. They offered a continuing source of ideas, inspiration, direction, education, and occasionally great fun in conversation.

Our grateful thanks go to three individuals in particular.

Dr. Jerry Wind, Lauder Professor at Wharton, was and continues to be our mentor, guiding us in both writing and indeed thinking of new applications. Jerry, we thank you for inspiration we could have received nowhere else.

Tim Moore of Prentice Hall provided ongoing encouragement, direction, and most of all a warm shoulder to lean on. You motivated us again and again as we struggled with the right language, balance, and direction. Thank you very much, Tim, for your never-failing guidance.

Martha Cooley of Prentice Hall became our guide, our vade mecum, through the intricacies of publishing. We could always turn to her for guidance, for a point of view, and for direction in this world of business. Martha, thank you for being there for us.

Of course, no acknowledgments would be complete without recognizing the people who actually put the book together, managed the publicity, and essentially kept us eager authors "in line" with their direction during editing and production. Our thanks go to Pam Boland, assistant to the publisher; Russ Hall, development editor; Amy Neidlinger, marketing director; Amy Fandrei, publicist; Megan Colvin, marketing coordinator; Michael Thurston, production editor; Alan Clements, cover designer; Bill Camarda, cover copy writer; copy editor Krista Hansing; and proofreader Sarah Kearns of Water Crest Publishing. Thank you all.

IN MEMORIUM

Kathleen MacDonnell (1949-2007) friend, colleague, early proponent, and staunch patron of RDE. It was Kathleen more than anyone who was responsible for giving us the chance at The Campbell Soup Company to create the success of Prego, which in turn inspired us to further evolve RDE to where it is today. Kathleen, we will miss you greatly.

INTRODUCTION

BUSINESS WISDOM FROM THE MOUTH OF DR. SEUSS

One of the most publicized stories of extremely aggressive development and marketing for a "revolutionary" food product is Dr. Seuss's *Green Eggs and Ham*.[1]

Like any good salesman, Sam-I-am, the marketer and indefatigable creator of the new product, is full of energy and passion. The story starts with a grumpy "customer" who leisurely reads his newspaper. Using stratagem after stratagem, Sam tries to get his customer to try his revolutionary product: green eggs and ham. The customer repeatedly refuses, claiming he simply does not like it. Sam tries multiple tactics to win the customer, but without success, which, in the end, lead to frustrating trial-and-error iterations, not particularly productive, always painful, and sometimes costly.

Sound familiar?

Sam randomly tests different ideas: a train meal ("on a train"), fast food ("in a car"), even an outdoor picnic ("in a tree"). None works. Then Sam tries a "home-made" message ("in a house"). Different packaging options still do not produce expected results ("not in a box"). Sam's emotional messages, playing on the appeal of friendly dinner situations ("with a mouse...with a fox") still fail to increase purchase intent. All those messages fall on deaf ears. Sam's clever insight was to manipulate color ("in the dark"), but by then, it was too late; his customer had already formed new and unwanted preferences, so Sam simply ran out of luck.

Although successful (the product was *finally* sold, with an ecstatically happy customer as a result), Sam's nonsystematic "trial-and-error" approach was simply too inefficient. Even worse, Sam might well have antagonized his customer during his pursuit, leading to the customer's complete rejection of the product—and possibly the rejection of Sam's whole brand.

What was wrong? Sam felt that he was doing his best. He was sincerely following a typical strategy: *seemingly haphazard, random experiments* to find a selling formula for his product. Sam wasn't particularly successful, expending lots of energy and going far out of the way to achieve his marketing goal. The missing critical part was the *systematic* nature of the experiments—or, more correctly, its absence.

Fast-forward. Meet Allison-the-Entrepreneur, a very ambitious and entrepreneurial recent MBA graduate fascinated with Sam's work. Armed with Sam's experience, as limited as it is, and dedication, Allison decided to put an even more revolutionary product, blue eggs, on the market. How would she design and promote her innovative food item in today's highly competitive market of egg-based products? Instead of random, haphazard efforts, we will see how Allison grabs hold of the full power of Rule Developing Experimentation (RDE). Allison-the-Entrepreneur will show how today's new development tools take her far beyond Sam, into a competitive world, with a lot less effort and a lot more success. Indeed, she will soon discover that RDE can help her create, market, and sell virtually any product better and faster. Even selling blue elephants will not be a particularly far-fetched business proposition for Allison!

WHAT IS RDE?

RDE is a systematized solution-oriented business process of experimentation that designs, tests, and modifies alternative ideas, packages, products, or services in a disciplined way so that the developer and marketer discover what appeals to the customer, *even if the customer can't articulate the need, much less the solution!*

You got an assignment to launch a new credit card for your bank. How do you make consumers pick your offer out of hundreds and hundreds of look-alikes? The marketing department suggested conducting a survey of a targeted group of consumers. What should customers read in a credit card offer to convince them to apply? Well, what if we just *ask them* what kind of APR, rewards, annual fees, appearance, name, and so on they'd like? Sounds like a very prudent way to obtain consumer insights to innovate. In fact, a very big chunk of consumer research is still done this way.

As you can guess, the results of this market research exercise turn out to be quite predictable. The consumers want 0% APR, no annual or transaction fees, and, of course, a bunch of meaningful, expensive benefits that are easy for them to earn and to redeem.

Wow! How "insightful" these findings are! But are they feasible? Can you act on them? Did you solve the problem or just identify it? Have you discovered rules as a result of this research, the way the world operates, so you can do far better? Can you even afford the solution?

The challenge is that, in many cases, consumers cannot articulate exactly what they need, want, or like. Is there a way to solve the problem? In focus group after focus group, developers and marketers are often stymied, despite their best efforts. However, the solution comes quickly, often blindingly so, when the developers and marketers take their time *to identify and experimentally explore the factors that could drive consumer interest*—whether features of a credit card, sweetener for a soft drink, color and picture for a package, or a specific message for an advertisement. Show the customers (or let them try) several *systematically designed* prototypes, and they will tell what they like, what they do not, and what does not make any difference to them. The experimental design used for the prototypes creation will "magically" return to you what each individual feature (option or ingredient) "brings" to the party. Now you have a clear way to create rules for winning offerings or new best-selling products by combining those features into the best possible combinations—even if no consumer ever tested these specific combinations. You will see this simple, structured process in many examples later in this book.

Different types of RDE are surprisingly similar to each other. You follow these straightforward steps:

Think about the problem and identify groups of features that comprise the target product (offering, etc.). For example, in the case of a soft drink formulation, the variables could be Amount of Sugar, Acid, and so on. In credit card RDE, the variables (categories of features) could be Annual Fees, APRs, Rewards Options, and so on. Every such variable (or a "bucket" of ideas) comprises several alternatives. For example, when you work with a beverage, sugar content may be 6, 8, or 10 units; when you work with a credit card, APR may be 0%, 4.00%, 9.99%, 15%, and 21.99%. *So the first step is to do your homework and structure the problem.* This is the most difficult part of your job. Here is where your expertise comes in. Be aware of the GIGO (Garbage In, Garbage Out) principle to appreciate the importance of the first step. The good news is that you can throw *many* ideas into the buckets for customers to test. The rest of the process is highly automated, virtually painless.

Mix and match the elements according to a special experimental design (a schema of putting together elements)[2] to create a set of prototypes. The second step is usually done automatically by a tool that creates a unique individual design plan for each respondent, resulting in individual models of utilities for each respondent.

Show the prototypes to consumers (or let the respondents taste them, in the case of products) and obtain their reaction (usually, purchase intent, liking, or interest in the idea). The third step is typically an automated Web survey or a taste exercise in a facility.

Analyze results[3] (build individual models) using a regression module. The magic of experimental design estimates the contribution of each individual element to the liking scores that a consumer would assign, whether the contribution is positive (so the liking is higher) or negative (so the liking is lower). Colloquially, analysis shows what everything brings to the party. This analysis is automated. Shortly after completing the survey, RDE tools provide a table of utilities (individual scores of elements), the building blocks of your new products.

Optimize. To uncover your *optimal product* or ideas, you just need to find (usually an automatic process as well) the best, or optimal, combination that has the highest sum of utilities. It is that simple!

Identify naturally occurring attitudinal segments of the population that show similar patterns of the utilities. The segments span demographically and socially among different groups of people. By creating rules for the new products or services using the attitudinal segments, it's possible to increase the acceptance by 10–50% or even more. You don't have to worry about creating modestly better products averaged for everyone when you can create superb products for selected people. The good part of the process is that it is (as you can guess by now) also an automated procedure.

Apply the generated rules to create new products, offerings, and so on. Want to have a credit card optimized for value-oriented middle-aged customers? Just "dial in" the parameters in the tool, and voilà! Here is the best possible offering! Want to offer a credit card for young professionals? You have the data already—just "dial in" what you want, and the rules are immediately generated.[4] This step is the most fun to use.

RDE *breeds* market success through knowledge by clearly and dramatically revealing how specific factors drive consumer acceptance and rejection. Best of all, RDE prescribes for business *what to do,* rather than just leaving the suggestions as hypotheses. RDE produces *actionable* rules (directions), even if there was no inkling or iota of direction about what to do at the start of the RDE process. And best of all, these rules can be the powerhouse for sustained competitive advantage because they *show how the world works.*

THE ROOTS OF RDE

Let's trace the origins of RDE. It has an interesting history, filled with dollops of experimental psychology, a healthy dose of business pragmatism, and the vision of a new branch of social science.

First, the tools of experimental psychology. RDE is founded on the realization that perception and behavior are linked in a two-way exchange. If you increase the level of sweetener in Pepsi Cola, it will taste sweeter. Liking can change as well—consumers can grow to prefer the sweeter cola. In fact, if you want to create an optimum Pepsi, one strategy changes sweetener level, measures sweetness, measures liking, and finds where liking reaches the highest or optimum level. This is a simple example of RDE. You change the stimulus, you measure the response, you find the pattern or the rule, you make the product, and, hopefully, you succeed in the marketplace more than you did before. So RDE is, in part, a branch of experimental psychology.

Second, the driving power of business. Businesses make products, offer services, and, for the most part, try to do so with some profit. With increasing competition, you are better off when your offering is "new" (at least, perceived to be a fresh idea), "better" (according to the people buying it), and "profitable" (at the end of the day, after all the costs have been factored in). You may be lucky to guess correctly about the product or message in business, if you are the so-called golden tongue, a maverick executive, one of the truly talented. For the other 99% of people, it's good to know how the world works and the rules by which to make the offering better and cheaper—of course, all the time doing it faster. Unless you are in that 1% of incredibly gifted or lucky predictors, business works better with rules. These rules will tell you how to create winning formulations that taste great, better messaging that grabs customers, better packages, or magazines that fly off the shelf. *RDE is about how best to perform each of these tasks. RDE produces results every time you use it. The process takes just days, not years.* In some cases, the results were obtained in just a few hours. That speed and accuracy are good for business.

Third, the world-view of social science. Formal, scientific experimentation in social science with the express objective of generating rules is just beginning. Not much has been done yet in the way psychologists and business-people do experiments. However, RDE is related to a field called adaptive experimentation (AE),[5] or adaptive management. AE tries to find answers to ecological or social problems through trial and error, using feedback to drive the next steps. At each step in this process, the researcher looks at the data, tries to discern a pattern that might exist, and adjusts the conditions. The most publicized cases of AE are very lengthy, large-scale, even monumental projects in ecology, theoretical science, or the sociology/environmental area. However, AE doesn't generate rules. Instead, AE searches for workable solutions using the process of experimentation. AE is not defined by a simple experimental structure with finite steps, nor is it governed by limited time frames. RDE comes into social science by using experimental methods to understand the algebra of citizens' minds.

RDE is not a new idea. Parts of it have been around a long time, but it takes a while to sink in. In some respects, RDE is obvious, in the same way that two well-known platitudes are evident:

- Every parent realizes this simple truth, handed down from mother to child, from mother to child: *Do your homework and you'll be promoted to second grade.*
- Most people in agriculture realize that the following well-known Irish proverb contains a lot of truth: *The best fertilizer is the farmer's footsteps.*

WHY RDE?

RDE evolved from other breeds of experimentation because companies recognized the nature of their competitive environment, knew that they had to be "better," and began to recognize the value of disciplined development. When a few years ago Hewlett-Packard faced a sustained erosion of its position in the market, despite the fact that its products were comparable or even superior to what its rivals offered, management decided to rethink the marketing strategy and build a decision-making structure based on evidence.

In a sense, RDE helped turn around Hewlett-Packard. (See Chapter 1, "Hewlett-Packard Shifts Gears," for details about the sustained use of RDE in high-tech companies such as HP.) When the goal was to create a better pasta sauce (as with Campbell Soup with its Prego), a good RDE strategy systematically explored the ingredient factors that made pasta sauce better, and soon afterward created a significantly better sauce. (Chapters 2, "Maxwell House's Calculus of Coffee," and 3, "Dialing Up Delicious: Major Discoveries fromVlasic and Prego," show several great examples of RDE use by major food companies.) When the very difficult goal was to create messaging for a better Playtex tampon so women would feel safe and discreet, that, too, was grist for RDE, which optimized the messages every bit as easily as it handled, say, the messaging for computers, credit cards, or cars. (Explore Chapter 4, "How to Make People Feel Good Even When They Pay More," for RDE use in message optimization.) When the goal was to create better package designs that jumped off the shelf for Swanson frozen dinners, RDE was beginning to be accepted in that world of design and did its job, again with a clear increase in sales. (Chapter 7, "Bridging Cool Design with Hot Science," demonstrates RDE use for package and magazine cover designs.) Of course, no one would ever claim that experimentation could replace artistry in design, in communication, or even in the technicalities of product creation. It was just that RDE *systematized* the process of discovery and development.

What about sustained innovation, political and social areas, and the stock market? RDE found its home there as well (see Chapters 6, "Rubik's Cube of Consumer Electronics Innovation"; 10, "RDE Defeats Murphy's Law and 'Bares' the Stock Markets"; and 11, "Asia Calling, Ltd.: The China Angle," correspondingly).

Sounds good, but shouldn't one have a triple Ph.D. in statistics, psychology, and social studies to use RDE? And be versed in long formulas with Greek letters? Perhaps, in the early days, but not recently. Now the answer is "Not at all."

At one time, to drive a car, you needed to intimately know the engine, transmission, and all those complex things under the hood and below the floorboards—and you were expected to fix your car yourself. With time, more people had to drive, and the cars evolved into something easy to use (albeit, much more technologically sophisticated). This, by itself, allowed even more people to drive. How many drivers on the road now even know where the transmission is located? The same is happening to RDE. *Something invented and designed by the most educated people in the industry is now ready to be used by any businessperson with the same ease that today's personal computer can be used.* More companies have used RDE on a sustained basis to survive and overpower their brutal competition. This need for RDE enticed the development of new tools that made it easier. In turn, RDE became easier to use, and often with a lot of fun. Applying Malcolm Gladwell's metaphor,[6] RDE is now reaching a *tipping point*.

FOX HUNTING PRODUCT DESIGN WITH RDE

Let's go to a game called "finding a fox in the forest." Fox hunting, or transmitter hunting (also known as T-hunting or radio direction finding), is a popular activity among amateur radio operators. We think that the skills acquired in the game might be very useful for the astute business leader or product developer. A skilled fox hunter can find the "fox"—a hidden transmitter—quickly, easily. Can the brand manager, product developer, or corporate C-suite executive learn to find his or her product "fox" as readily? Our quest takes us to the Albuquerque Transmitter Hunters competition.[7]

The transmitters—the "foxes"—are deliberately hidden somewhere and are "hunted" by participants using radio direction–finding techniques. The technique is quite simple. The hunter has a receiver with the large antenna and needs to experiment with the direction of the antenna. Even the smallest tilt of the antenna changes the strength of the signal (the antenna is very selective and has a very narrow angle of vision). Therefore, it is crucial to keep experimenting with the position of the antenna and adjust movements accordingly. Each new adjustment and move ideally brings the hunter closer to the target. Made a wrong step—and the victory is lost to a competitor who found the direction faster.

Sound eerily familiar to what you've experienced recently? Think of the last product, the last advertisement, the last package, and what it took to get there.

In one variant of the hunt, five transmitters send out the signals in sequence, each of them on for just a minute. The objective: to discover all the transmitters as quickly as possible before time runs out. Hunters need to adopt a working strategy and make a sequence of tactical decisions, not much different from what a developer or marketer does, but rather than competing for customers, the hunters are simply playing a game to discover the transmitters.

It's clear that the game of fox hunting parallels the game of business.

- Firms create new products or services, and, in many cases, they do so in completely new areas (our "wild" forest with hidden transmitters).

- There may be more than one opportunity, so a firm must create a priority list of ideas (a player's sequence of transmitter hunts).

- Little information is known about these new products or services (unknown location of the "foxes"). One has to listen carefully for weak signals from the customers, who might not even know that they are broadcasting a new opportunity (listen to the receiver).

- To find the new killer idea, the developer or marketer should try many new options, moving gingerly in measured steps to maximize learning and success (rotate the antenna in different directions).

- Sometimes the step is quite small but can produce huge results (the slightest tilt of the antenna can make a big difference in the assumed direction, so get it right).

If you think about this game, you might feel as if you've been hunting foxes your whole life. But, more important, how successful do you think you'd be in fox hunting if you were working with a badly tuned or outdated receiver or, even worse, playing the game without one? You'd see immediately that there would be little hope of winning.

The same applies to the business environment. Without the knowledge and power of RDE, it's likely that you—and just about any other businessperson—will wander around far longer in the search of the new product or message, and quite likely will miss the most valuable opportunities. In the best-case scenario, you will probably find one or a few good workable ideas, about the same time that your competition does. RDE changes those odds dramatically—and, of course, changes them in your favor.

COMPANIES ARE USING RDE, WHETHER THEY KNOW IT OR NOT

You don't always find what you're looking for—but you rarely find what you're not looking for.

Skeptics might say, "Heck, RDE is just a scientific name for trial and error, right?" Actually, yes and no. No, because a trial-and-error approach is usually completely random, and RDE is all the way on the other end of the spectrum. Yes, because you set the scene for profitable learning by astutely designing and executing the trials, by keenly observing the reactions of the customers, by shrewdly detecting what part works and what does not ("errors"), and, finally, by making educated modifications to the trials and iterating the process, if needed. You've set up the scenario to learn from your successes and your mistakes. More than likely, you will succeed simply because you have thought through the problem, that inner game so necessary for winning, and you have followed the process, making measurements that quickly yield the rules.

It is difficult to ignore the power of being able to know the algebra of consumer minds *before* they can even articulate the need. Many companies already use RDE to their advantage, in one form or another. *There is every reason for you to be up to speed, or even faster than them.*

TESTING NEW ELECTRONIC GADGETS WITH "OTAKU" IN JAPAN

Japan is the home of some well-known examples of product development experiments. Japanese society is less polarized in income compared to the West. People tend to buy products based not on their income, but on their taste. This variation in taste leads to a huge variety of products on the market, brutal competition, and, as you might expect, continual experimentation.

Tokyo is a vast market for testing new commercial ideas. Tokyo's great size, density, and diversity, and excellent transportation system make it an ideal setting for social experimentation. There are whole districts in Tokyo called *antenna districts*, where companies and consumers test out the newest product ideas, as well as deliberately start fashion trends.[8] These districts naturally attract *otaku* ("geeky fans") and professionals in fashions, electronic products, and so on.

Arguably, Japan's most dynamic sector is high-tech. In the Akihabara district of Tokyo, sometimes called the "Electric City," a visitor can buy virtually any product or gizmo that uses electricity. Just a few blocks of densely packed stores sell about 10% of the total electronics in Japan. Here *otaku* can find products that anticipate the market and that will not be available anywhere else in the world for months or perhaps even years to come.

Many products sold there will never find their way to the shelves of other stores because Akihabara, dubbed as Mecca for early adapters, is also the place for the marketers to test what "flies" with the consumers and what does not. One example is Seiko Corporation. *Annually*, Seiko develops more than 2,500 watch designs and introduces them in test markets. The winning designs are further improved, tested again, and only then launched in target markets.[9] Japan's icon, Sony, also develops, tests, and measures about 1,500 products annually. About 20% of them are completely new designs, and only a portion of those find their way to the global market.[10] Some believe that the global success of Japan's electronics manufacturers *begins* in Akihabara. In their race to be the first to market with the season's latest products, electronics manufacturers send prototypes of their new products to Akihabara to see if they will fly. The rivalry is fierce, with some product lifecycles reduced to a few months, turning Akihabara into a churning, self-renewing experimentation paradise. The sales and feedback are closely monitored by the companies for further modification and the ultimate launch decision. In a sense, it has been done at the expense of traditional market research. On the flip side of this Japanese innovation phenomenon is the fact that some of the most successful products in history, such as Sony PlayStation, have been developed against the corporate view.

KEEPING CUSTOMERS DURING "DOWN TIMES" IN BRAZIL

Could RDE be applied the same way in developing countries as in the U.S., Europe, and Japan? This story[11] in Brazil is a wonderful example of *retaining* customers by RDE-inspired communications, in a way that shows the importance of a systematic approach in a challenging business environment, where Unilever Brazil was riding the storm of economic uncertainty and massive competition. The Brazilian political and economic climate, seldom calm, had turned volatile in 2002. Consumers reacted by avoiding many premium brands, Unilever's brands among them. Times were tough in Brazil.

Unilever owned Brazil's market leaders in 14 product categories, distributed among foods, household cleaning, and personal care. These premium names in Brazil included Hellmann's, Knorr, Omo, Comfort, Lux, and the newly launched Dove. Despite the fame and admiration earned by its premium products, Unilever itself was not a well-known brand name in Brazil.

Unilever used RDE to drive messaging by having RDE reveal the "algebra of the consumer's mind." By doing so, Unilever discovered the hot buttons to keep the customers. RDE drove Unilever to create three alternative (versioned) executions of its newly developed customer magazine *DIVA,* and to distribute these to groups of high-value customers, the Unilever target. By monitoring the reactions of the customers, discerning what worked, and then modifying its communications, Unilever created new messages and tapped into the heart and soul of the Brazilian customer. This systematic approach, promoted by RDE, effectively *saved the Unilever business in Brazil.* The happy consequence was that, during a recession marked by heavy down-trading in virtually all consumer product categories (especially upscale ones), RDE-driven knowledge of the customer maintained and even increased market share of Unilever's premium products.

This book presents to you many other RDE case histories that have resulted in huge competitive benefits for their users. But the book does more than that. It also teaches you RDE. RDE successes are within reach of most companies and can be dramatic. Some examples that you will see later in this book range from the more than 200% increase in credit card acquisitions to the 42% increase in jewelry catalog response rate with a much higher average purchase at the same time, as well the creation of such iconic products as Vlasic pickles and Prego extra-chunky pasta sauce along with the aspects of the massive application of RDE in China and India. The examples abound.

BUYING IN AND GETTING STARTED

In a natural world, mutation and sexual recombination allow a species to thrive. The same is true for innovation in any type of business: Permanent mindful experimentation enables companies to survive the competition and succeed. Read on—you will see for yourself that RDE is the easiest, most affordable, and most manageable way to innovate.

What are the key points of RDE to keep in mind when you read on? The bottom line is simple:

- You create a culture of disciplined experimentation and learning that is critical for the competitive market that faces you today.
- You learn while doing. The benefit is simple. You optimize your development and communication over time. This should bring substantially more market success because you are delivering what your customers want, even before they know it—and before your competitors discover it (unless they're reading this book right now).

We're not alone in promoting this disciplined experimentation. Two icons in the marketing world, Jerry Wind and Vijay Mahajan, consistently promote the benefits of experimentation because of its "ability to continuously learn, added incentive to develop and test innovative strategies, making it harder for the competition to figure out what your strategy is and creating a culture of experimentation and learning...even more critical in the changing and turbulent...environment."[12]

RDE is practical; in many cases, it can be easily handled by a small team or even one person in a very reasonable time with a modest budget. *The beauty of the RDE process is that it does not require (nor even expect) deep knowledge in advanced statistical areas.*[13] RDE generates knowledge and business results at the same time, with relatively little effort, but with enormous payouts for years to come.

So why do you want to read about RDE and use it in your everyday business life? It is quite simple because RDE

- Solves problems instead of just identifying them.
- Generates rules—it's actionable.
- Needs no advanced knowledge—it's accessible.
- Promotes logic and learning. No more guesswork is needed when you can be right and "hit the nail on the head" far more often.
- Applies to a wide range of real-life problems. It's not limited to products or advertising only.

Read on and enjoy this new field of Rule Developing Experimentation. There's a lot here, and the road beckons.

ENDNOTES

[1] Dr. Seuss, *Green Eggs and Ham*, (Random House: New York, 1976). According to Luis Menand ("Cat People: What Dr. Seuss Really Taught Us," *The New Yorker*, 23 December 2002 and 30 December 2002), this book is the fourth-best-selling children's hardcover title of all time. The book originated with a wager between Theodore Geisel (Dr. Seuss's real name) and his publisher, Bennett Cerf. Dr. Seuss won the bet. Forty-nine of the words in *Green Eggs and Ham* are one-syllable words. Cerf made out even better than Menand realized: As Seuss himself noted 25 years later, "Bennett never paid!"

[2] See Chapter 4 for more details.

[3] In many cases (especially, more simple ones), Steps 4-6 are treated as one step.

[4] See, for example, Chapter 4 for Credit Card RDE that has increased new customers acquisition by more than 200%!

[5] *American Marketing Association Dictionary of Marketing Terms* defines AE as "an approach (and philosophy) for management decisions, calling for continuous experimentation to establish empirically the market response functions. Most common in direct marketing, it can and has been applied to advertising and other marketing mix variables. The experiment should reflect the needed variation in stimuli, cost of measuring the results, lost opportunity cost in the non-optimal cells, and management confidence in the base strategy." (Source: www.marketingpower.com)

[6] Malcom Gladwell, *The Tipping Point* (Little, Brown & Company: Boston, 2000).

[7] "What Is T-Hunting and ARDF?"; www.home.att.net/~wb8wfk.html.

[8] Kuniko Fujita and Richard Child Hill, "Innovative Tokyo," World Bank Policy Research Working Paper 3507, February 2005.

[9] Jerry Wind and Vijay Mahajan, *Convergence Marketing: Strategies for Reaching the New Hybrid Consumer* (Financial Times Prentice Hall: Upper Saddle River, NJ, 2001).

[10] Ken Belson, "Sony Again Turns to Design to Lift Electronics," *New York Times* (2 February 2003).

[11] K. Sapiro, M. Pezzotti, A. Grabowsky, A. Gofman, H. Moskowitz, "How Can Premium Brands Survive During an Economic Recession?" ESOMAR Latin America Conference 2005, Buenos Aires, 2005.

[12] Jerry Wind and Vijay Mahajan, *Convergence Marketing: Strategies for Reaching the New Hybrid Consumer*, referenced earlier.

[13] A big proponent of this approach, Thomas Schelling (Nobel Prize in Economics, 2005), has been known to say, "I think math is used too much to show off. It's a lazy way to write...[the much harder thing is to] write clearly and use analogies that people can understand" (Kim Clark, "In Praise of Original Thought: Tipping Points and Nuclear Deterrence Lead to the Nobel in Economics," *U.S. News & World Report* [24 October 2005: p. 52]).

PART I

Making Money

RDE was a best-hidden secret in the late twentieth century. In this section, you will see how some well-known companies discovered—and, in fact, actually invented—sound solutions for their problems using RDE. These are the stories that proved the RDE approach and moved it from the realm of pure science to the desk of the business manager.

1

Hewlett-Packard Shifts Gears

It is a truism in business that change is the only constant. And so it has been for Hewlett-Packard. At the dawn of the twenty-first century, Hewlett-Packard stood tall as an icon in the technology world, but an icon that was now encountering rougher waters than it had ever experienced. Competition was heating up, traditional sources of profits were being hammered by lower-cost Asian and American competitors, and in this increasingly brutal environment, HP's corporate culture was often perceived to be outdated, an impediment to performance.

At Hewlett-Packard, people knew how difficult it was becoming to predict the success of marketing such complex and fast-changing products as consumer electronics. The dynamics of the consumer electronics industry is notorious for its lightning speed and maddening unpredictability. It is quite easy, almost a fun sport, to analyze the success or failure of products *post mortem*. It's not that simple to do so in advance. There's a very long list of products that were superior to their competition but failed miserably in the market when consumers got their hands on them. Maybe marketing dragged behind? Other excellent products with enormous marketing budgets never caught up with the consumers, either. And vice versa.

The history of HP can be very instructive. During the last few years of the 1990s, HP faced a sustained erosion of its position in the market, despite the fact that its products were comparable or even superior to the products its rivals offered. HP faced its most daunting challenge among its future customers: teens and young adults, who were prime candidates for high-tech products. HP faced very strong competition from such rivals as Sony and Apple, who were gaining traction among the young with their lifestyle advertisements. Both Sony and Apple had successfully focused their creative energies to communicate how *cool and modern the person looks* when using their products. In contrast, argues author and trends observer Tim Macer,[1] HP was still using quite uninspired campaigns, concentrating on *what the product does,* and compounding the problem by dotting its campaigns with "clinical shots of hardware and bullet-point tech specs."

It appeared to HP that many product-development and marketing dogmas that had ruled the business world for decades just did not work anymore, despite ever-increasing budgets that marketers had demanded, received, and spent to the best of their abilities. Cognizant of the problem, HP decided to retool its development and marketing strategy to build a new *decision-making structure,* which they envisioned as follows:

- Based on evidence, not on supposition
- Applicable to a wide range of marketing issues
- Fast, streamlined, inexpensive, and accessible not only to the marketers, but also to engineers, designers, and just about anyone else involved in making decisions about products, markets, and promotions
- Capable of generating actionable rules to resolve the problem, not just state it

Rule Developing Experimentation (RDE) fit in perfectly with HP's new goals and became one of the "evidence-promoting" components. Hewlett-Packard embraced RDE on a wide scale with some "spectacular results."[2] Dvorak Franco, then head of the customer insight team responsible for HP's home range of products, admitted, "Our marketing programs lacked the relevance, vitality, and compellingness of other leading brands and weren't really doing anything in an impactful way. It was time to go back to basics and start looking at testing concepts with consumers."

At the beginning, HP planned to use the conventional, classic market research approach; batteries of *focus groups and surveys* to test all the elements of the marketing, from features to promotions, packaging, and pricing. This string of initial efforts would then be followed by so-called "traditional quantitative research" (such as surveys) to measure the effect of each factor in HP's marketing efforts. That stepwise, sequential, conventional plan promised to be overly expensive, maddeningly laborious, and slow, and, worst of all, not sufficiently rigorous.

It's worth a short digression to reflect on the whys and hows of HP's decision to move away from major reliance on focus groups and go more toward the RDE approach of disciplined knowledge development. It is not big news *now* that the focus groups are not as effective as one might have hoped and that many companies have started a cautious move away from relying on them in the way that they did before. Cammie Dunaway, chief marketing officer at Yahoo! Inc., announced at a Silicon Valley conference in September 2005, "My research department doesn't know it, but I am killing all our focus groups."[3] Dunaway wants to put the business of observing the people "like zoo animals" though one-way mirrors out of business. Yahoo! got very little useful information out of moderated focus groups. Instead, Yahoo! opted for "immersion groups," in which product developers talk to users freely, without the moderator intervening. Another giant, beverage icon Coca-Cola, publicly announced a similar opinion, albeit more strongly stated. Sergio Zyman, Coke's former marketing chief, reportedly said, "Focus groups are a waste of time, filled with people telling you what you want to hear so they can go home."[4]

With the help of design specialists at Ford & Earl, and following the guidance of the marketing research consultants from Optimization Group, HP began seriously adopting the *RDE-based approach* to test and optimize new concepts and ideas among its target consumers using a specially created proprietary Web panel. RDE, by then embodied in an easy-to-use and affordable Internet tool,[5] did all the "heavy lifting." The most important task facing HP was to identify specific problems, structure them, and then put these features into the RDE Internet tool (step 1 of the RDE process described in the Introduction). The rest of the RDE steps were guided by, as well as handled by, the tool virtually automatically, a blessing to any company that has to respond quickly in a competitive situation. The system performed on "automatic," "mixing and matching" the features of

HP's ideas to create new vignettes (step 2) and presenting these vignettes by Web survey to respondents for evaluation (step 3).

In its application just described for HP, RDE changed the way the company thought about answering the problem of "What shall we put into this product to make consumers want to buy it?" HP, as well as many other companies, had been accustomed in its previous experience to instructing consumers to rate one feature of an offering at a time. This rating scheme had never really produced actionable results on the scale HP needed because, in real life, customers are faced with more complex offerings comprising several elements. Furthermore, the traditional approach (now being replaced by RDE) appeared unable to deal with the difference between an idea and the way the idea is expressed. RDE pushed HP to see what was important (what to say) and the right language (how to say it). As we progress through the book, you will see in detail how RDE solves this critical business problem in industry after industry, application after application.

The results of the studies were analyzed practically immediately after completion of the interviews on the Web (step 4). At the end, the RDE tool automatically generated actionable rules about what consumers liked and what they did not, and advised what to say to consumers to trigger their interest in the product, how to say it, and to whom to say it (steps 5–7).

This RDE approach produced for HP's product designers and marketing specialists might best be called, in Franco's words, an "always-on intelligence system." *The technology company has brought the consumer to the table in every design initiative or marketing decision* in a way and scale that was unprecedented for HP.

This is how HP and their consultants described the process:

> The process is highly streamlined. Typically within 24 hours, Ford & Earl will have [the RDE project] online and have sent invitations to panelists ... within another 24 hours the target sample—typically 1,000 or more respondents—will have been reached.... By this time, [HP's internal designers, engineers, and product and program managers] will know whether the proposition is going to fly with consumers or not.... Although the usual turnaround time is 48 hours, urgent studies can be done even faster.

The first target for HP was to test and then *optimize* new promotions. Here, HP skillfully used the power of RDE to succeed in the continuing competitive market. Being able to paste on the meeting room wall the "dissected" consumer feedback on the relative value of the different elements of a proposition gave marketers confidence about their fact-based decision-making; as a result, they enjoyed substantially greater, more consistent successes.

By itself a classical case of RDE at work, promotions were just the beginning. Promotions sell what has been already developed. What about guiding RDE down to the innards of the organization, to the high-tech development laboratories and marketing groups? *The RDE challenge, the task to really brings RDE to the corporation, was to find that "something" that would differentiate HP from the rest of its competitors.*

Like everyone else, HP was captive to its past, to its way of doing development, to the "one-at-a-time" strategy that was strongly ingrained in engineers and had permeated the entire HP corporation. The customary one-dimensional view of problems can make developers, researchers, and marketers spectacularly unsuccessful or even misled. This seemingly straightforward approach fails to differentiate between *baseline* consumer interest in the product category and *specific* interest in the actual product being offered. Those neat, one-at-a-time investigations miss the patterns that separate the "good" from the "great." RDE avoids that comfortable one-at-a-time trap. RDE presents participants with many different vignettes or scenarios that they consider, does so rapidly and inexpensively, measures the participant's "gut feel" to each vignette, identifies "what works," and then synthesizes new, promising combinations of ideas comprising better ideas. In essence, RDE deconstructs the outside world to its units. RDE helped HP institute a rapid and inexpensive way to understand the algebra of its customers' minds.

At a time when the value of strategic planning is being questioned, Macer says, research that provides such a sharp and quantifiable focus on reality can be instrumental in counteracting arguments or ill-judged initiatives from senior management. HP did not stop at providing this sharper focus. Instead, HP extended RDE even further. Unlike the data from most ad hoc research projects, which varies in structure and topic, HP used RDE's discipline to uncover the broader "meta patterns"—patterns that reveal the bigger pictures, across products, across categories, across countries, and over time. HP was in a position to allow "nature" to reveal herself and, by doing so, moved the business ahead.

The accumulating library of RDE studies opened a *new, virtually effort-free* opportunity for the consumer insight team to integrate data across different knowledge-development tasks. The growing RDE database yielded the long sought-after patterns. It became clear that across its many different product lines, HP attracted two radically different segments of consumers, with drastically different mind-sets:

- **Segment 1**—*Technologically savvy individuals* who mix and match separate components, and who enjoy and occasionally even revel in the challenge of getting them to work together.

- **Segment 2**—*Individuals who prefer a complete package* with all the accessories that work straight out of the box.

This knowledge helped HP to focus and target its ongoing marketing efforts, making them more efficient and, as time would prove, far more profitable. RDE provided the specific numbers—what ideas compelled and just how compelling the ideas could become when properly framed. RDE revealed in clear relief what ideas to choose and how to communicate them.[6]

Beyond discovery, however, was RDE's gift of the long-desired and powerful new vision to HP's fact-and-knowledge-oriented culture. Positioned at the base of all HP activities, this technology and science orientation got the boost and reorientation it needed from RDE. Taking a cue from the engineers, HP marketers discovered that the RDE exercises identified what should be done *specifically* to *reverse-engineer their competitors' marketing, and thus find out what works.* How did it happen? HP ran images, slogans, and phrases from a competitor's brochures and Web sites through the RDE tool (IdeaMap.Net) and quickly discovered the impact of each of the competitor's phrases and pictures.[7] The surprising outcome—unexpected weaknesses in seemingly formidable opponents:

> "I [Dvorak Franco] find it fascinating that we can test our competitors in this way. The tool will tell you what's compelling and what's not working for them."[8]

As the result, RDE enabled HP to re-engineer its marketing in terms of pricing its consumer products, structuring offers, and making its rebate

2

Maxwell House's
Calculus of Coffee

The oldest known examples of Rule Developing Experimentation (RDE) come, probably not surprisingly, from food and drink. Food preparation is critical to our path of becoming human. "Cooking with RDE" proved to be critical for more business success in the competitive world that humans created.

Historically new, acceptable dishes emerged agonizingly slowly compared to what we're accustomed to today in our increasingly busy world. It likely took many generations to experiment and develop so-called "ethnic cuisine." Most of the natural experiments in cooking were really merely small and slow random tests, mixing together ingredients, cooking over a fire, and tasting. In these haphazard trial-and-error efforts, experimentation at some point ceased for the major aspects of foods. Yet experimentation continued for small changes, such as those distinctive nuances of flavor and appearance that are well appreciated as they were noticed and commented upon. Food culture matured and some products became "typical"; tribal leaders fought to preserve tradition, but experimentation proceeded, almost as if the search for "better" was embedded in the genes of the human being.

That's the story of food and culture. Nowadays, the development of many new packaged food products is only partially an art of great chefs. The new news is that rarely is development haphazard and slow. Business thinking simply doesn't reward and, more important, doesn't even allow that leisurely pace. The bigger part of the process is scientifically designed experimentation, our friend RDE. The process that took hundreds or even thousands of years for early *Homo sapiens* is now compressed into just a few weeks, with much more targeted results.

We ought to note up front that RDE with food products is still somewhat more involved and labor intensive than with concepts, messages, or ideas. The latter are much more automated and do not require food preparation and tasting, although when you prepare food, you make actual samples— which can be lots of fun.

This chapter and the next bring you inside the corporation's kitchen and thinking. We show you the results of experiments with food and beverage, illustrating RDE with examples from three great companies and their products. One of today's opinions summarizes what we're about to share: "The most important and visible outcropping of the action bias in the excellent companies is their willingness to try things out, to experiment."[1] And experiment our three companies did! Let's go see and, through reading, maybe get a taste of the RDE first fruits.

A TASTIER, MORE PROFITABLE BLEND: RDE COMES TO MAXWELL HOUSE COFFEE

The biggest difference between RDE and the random trial-and-error approach is the active, structured, thoughtful nature of the experiments. In our first example, you'll see how General Foods, Inc. (now part of Kraft Foods, Inc.), used RDE to understand coffee, how new rules about the tongue of the coffee drinker emerged, and how this disciplined—*and not always popular*—experimentation led to more profits and, of course, market success.

BY WAY OF BACKGROUND: THE ROMANCE OF COFFEE

The growth in consumption of the beverage and its variations, as well as the sheer number of new coffee shops, is astonishing. The Starbucks chain grew from 55 outlets in 1989 to well over 10,000 in 2006. The number of independent coffee shops in the United States is even larger. The last few decades introduced more changes into coffee making than all the previous history of the bean. To appreciate this fact, let's dive into a little bit of coffee history.

Recent research indicates that the coffee plant, *Coffea arabica*, originated in Ethiopia and somehow was introduced to Yemen, where it has been actively cultivated since the sixth century. Starting from coffee houses in Cairo and Mecca, coffee became a passion instead of just a tonic. By the thirteenth century, Muslims everywhere were drinking coffee religiously, splashing over into secular life. And wherever Islam proliferated, coffee went: North Africa, the Mediterranean, and India.

The further history of coffee becomes even more intriguing. Arabia successfully kept the monopoly—by making export beans infertile through parching or boiling—until the 1600s, when Indian pilgrim Baba Budan managed to smuggle out some beans and break the monopoly. Soon a merchant from Venice introduced coffee to Europe, and the race was on.

The Dutch founded the first European-owned coffee estate, on colonial Java, now part of Indonesia, in 1696. In the early eighteenth century, Louis XIV received a coffee tree for Paris's Royal Botanical Garden from his royal Dutch brethren. Some years later, clippings from this tree found their way (another cloak-and-dagger story) to Martinique; in the next 50 years, they grew to 18 million trees. From Martinique, coffee trees went to Brazil, giving a start to the world's greatest coffee empire. By 1800, Brazil's monster harvests had turned coffee from an elite indulgence into an everyday elixir, a drink for the people.[2]

FROM ROMANCE TO WHITE-COAT CHEMISTS: COFFEE TODAY

Our journey into RDE for coffee begins around 1950, some 1500 years after coffee was thought to be discovered.

Sitting around a table, we find about 6 to 10 people, each with a tray of cups brimming with coffee. The cups are numbered in a way that defies any pattern. We see numbers such as 473, 219, and the like. The cups are arranged in a certain order, definitely not a simple numeric progression. In front of the tray, we see sheets of white paper; we're told they're "ballots." A person in a white coat—probably a laboratory technician, although it might as well be a chemist or any of a dozen other types of "-ists"—is giving instructions. The instructions say to taste the coffee and write down a number from a scale to describe the intensity or strength of what is being perceived. At the end of a half-hour or so, the participants have gone through a half-dozen or dozen cups of coffee, looked at each cup of coffee, sniffed the coffee, tasted the coffee, and written number after number to describe their perceptions. Occasionally, a participant reaches for a glass of water, takes a sip, swirls the water around, and then *expectorates* (spits) it into a large funnel that leads to a big bowl underneath the table. Then the participant returns to the task, refreshed, once again to inspect, sniff, taste, and rate the next coffee. It all looks like great fun, yet everyone seems to concentrate so much on what he or she is doing. They are immersed in the experience, doing a "job."

So begins modern-day RDE in the food industry, in this room that looks like a laboratory, as our participants (or so-called panelists) dutifully evaluate their assigned samples of test coffees. Out of these humble beginnings, seemingly so far removed from the computers and models of today's marketing departments, grew this new and exceptionally productive approach to solving business problems. RDE led to more products, more profits, at a much faster pace.

What you just read about happened in the 1950s dozens of times and happens today, albeit in a modified form, thousands of times. The cups of coffee that the panelists evaluated are samples that the product developer *systematically varied*, hoping to discover that magic brew, that single product that appeals to the consumer more than any other coffee. The hope was then, as it is now, that there are breakthrough products waiting to be discovered.

All the hoping, all the wishing, all the well-written articles on trends don't really help the developer crack the coffee code. It is homework. When Starbucks, Folgers, Maxwell House, Lavazza, Dunkin Donuts, and the dozens of other coffee companies large and small want to create a new blend or flavor, they use test procedures that pretty much look like what we just described. Maybe the rooms are a bit more modern, better decorated, or equipped with computers instead of white paper "ballots," but, for the most part, we would be hard-pressed to say that there's much difference today from the test methods used a half-century ago. The difference is that in the coffee business 50 years ago, just a few competitors infrequently introduced only a handful of blends and flavors. Nowadays, with the ranks of competitors growing faster than you can count them, there's no longer the luxury of time to test, retest, test-market in a region of the country, and then roll out the product nationally—if it passes muster in the all-too-long test market.

Another difference, perhaps a more profound one, haunts the corporation and sets the stage for RDE. The times of the single "perfect coffee" are long gone. The modern social phenomenon of coffee-drinking culture and fierce competition has resulted in an ever-growing number of blends and flavors, such as, for example, Java Chip Frappuccino Blended Coffee, Bourbon Streusel Cake, or Vanilla Viennese Cinnamon flavors. Globalization has made the situation even more difficult to handle. The taste of the customers in every locality differs—sometimes just a little, sometimes dramatically. Is there a simple and efficient way to optimize the blends and flavors to please the different palates that human beings come equipped with?

If globalization is a problem, abundant choice can be its companion problem, equally difficult to deal with. Now some companies offer astonishing assortments of flavors. For example, San Giorgio Coffee Company sells more than 240 coffee types and flavor varieties.[3] Timelines are short for a company to identify the best offering, in light of consumer tastes and competitive threats. The number of competitors grows each day, chipping away at the company's core brand. Profits are harder to come by. Everyone competes with everyone else. To make matters even more difficult, coffee competes with other beverages that also enjoy their varied popularities, so it's not just one coffee against another, but coffee against tea, soft drinks, energy drinks and a variety of beverages that keep popping up, as if from nowhere, to grab the drinker's tongue and wallet.

The food business adapted the RDE method that statisticians originally created, but with the ever-pressing need for "performance," RDE morphed into a technology to launch "winners" and make a lot of corporate profit. Not to mention a lot of homework that kept people busy learning about their product, learning about what their consumers wanted, and, in the process, churning out winners.

MAXWELL HOUSE IMPLEMENTS RDE FOR A BETTER, MORE PROFITABLE BLEND

How do companies such as Starbucks, Maxwell House, Folgers, and Nestle create such wonderful products? And what happens when the company wants to make an even better product to get more of the market and to refresh its product in the face of competitors close at its heels? Anyone who has tried to mix coffee beans to make an individual roast soon realizes in dismay that it's not quite as easy as one thinks, although when the right combination is reached, the results can be "heavenly."

In the 1980s, the Maxwell House brand was the part of General Foods' stable of well-known, highly respected, generally successful brands of beverages and foods. Maxwell House Coffees, made famous by hostess Elsa Lanchester years before, was manufactured in Hoboken, New Jersey, by processes that began with the raw coffee bean. Beans were roasted at different temperatures for different times, depending upon the bean, and the process finished with a specific blend of these roasted beans. When correctly brewed, the result was a rich-tasting, satisfying cup of coffee.

With changing tastes and coffee beans varying, Maxwell House found itself looking for a *business-based system* to guide the coffee blender at the plant so that the product would be the same, highly acceptable, and profitable. It was not sufficient to rely solely on one particular combination of beans and roasts, slavishly following this recipe year after year. If the price of beans were to rise, the coffee purchasers would end up spending the year's profits on the volatile raw material. If the price of some of the beans in the blend were to drop, as was often the case, the coffee purchasers would miss an opportunity for substantial profits that might just as easily flow to the bottom line. Not only was price an issue, but availability of beans also became a problem; some beans simply became unavailable at certain times for reasons beyond the control of Maxwell House—or, indeed, of any company. Finally, a *system was needed to protect the corporation—it is the system that incorporates the knowledge, not just a few potentially hard-to-replace experts.*

The early work on coffee blending prior to RDE relied on elite experts with "golden tongues," the so-called coffee panels. These experts, trained to *describe* their perceptions of coffee with an elaborate set of terms such as *fruity, buttery, burnt,* and *caramel,* met regularly to evaluate coffees. Just like all the other coffee companies, Maxwell House would not stop at expert panels alone. After the experts had passed on a product, the consumer researcher submitted the final product to a consumer test, to ensure that the coffee just developed was sufficiently acceptable. No one, from president to brand manager to laboratory technician, dared to take any chance with the corporation's treasure, the Maxwell House brand and the actual coffee itself that was marketed under the Maxwell House brand.

During the mid-1980s, however, and for years afterward, the coffee business encountered a number of shocks. Bean prices followed somewhat of a yo-yo pattern, first increasing, then decreasing, then increasing, and so forth. The uncertainty of economics combined with the increasingly competitive market always portends a bad combination for business. Recognizing this volatility of price that would inevitably affect the bottom line, and, at the same time, becoming aware that RDE could protect and optimize the formulation in the face of this uncertainty, Maxwell House commissioned *one of the first major studies of coffee*—or, indeed, of any beverage—using RDE as a tool to maintain quality and keep price within bounds.

Now that you have a sense of the business situation, let's see how RDE helped Maxwell House develop new products. You will see how they increased the value of the brand, made far better-tasting coffee, and, in doing so, significantly increased the company profits on a sustained basis for the first five years following the RDE exercise. Although we present the system as a set of steps, remember that not all RDE exercises flow in such a smooth manner. Life and reality intrude, meaning that, in business applications of RDE, there is the inevitable back and forth. We will come to that later; it makes an interesting story in and of itself.

WHAT DID MAXWELL HOUSE DO, AND WHY?

RDE does not happen just by wishing. It takes planning.

STEP 1: RECOGNIZE THE PROBLEM AND DECIDE TO TAKE ACTION TO DISCOVER WHAT SPECIFIC PROBLEM THE COMPANY FACES

This sounds like a truism. Doesn't everyone recognize when product quality has dropped and the product is no longer quite as good as the specifications require it to be? In the ideal world of business, no product would ever be outside specifications. All products would maintain the quality that the developer specified at the start. Like other coffee manufacturers—and, indeed, like all consumer product companies playing in a competitive world—Maxwell House conducted regular head-to-head tests against other competitor products to identify when its products were out of specification and needed remedial action. One of these competitive audits revealed the problem. After purchasing Maxwell House coffee and testing it against other competitor coffees purchased at the same time, the bad news surfaced. Market research reported that some of the Maxwell House products did not perform as well as they should have. When consumers were instructed to choose the coffee they preferred, many of them did not choose the Maxwell House product (the coffees were disguised in the so-called "blind taste test"). Table 2.1 shows an example of these results. Typically, the data is presented in a simple table, similar to the type of report that a patient gets from laboratory tests. By themselves, the results are innocuous, but in the hands of a skilled interpreter, the results (whether from taste tests for a company or laboratory tests for a patient) can bring joy or dread. This is the type of data that sends alarm signals through management and inevitably leads to anxiety-filled meetings.

Table 2.1

Example of a report from a competitive product audit. Participants tasted both Maxwell House (MH) and one of two competitors (Brands A and B) on a "blind" basis. (Data was disguised to maintain confidentiality; the winning numbers are shaded.)

	Audit Test #1 MH Loses Dramatically to the Competitor		Audit Test #2 MH Performs about the Same as the Competitor	
	MH	**Brand A**	**MH**	**Brand B**
Overall Ratings				
Overall Liking	66	71	64	63
Purchase Interest (Top 2 Box %)	58	69	56	54
Appearance Attributes				
Like Overall Appearance	71	68	70	74
Like Color	76	70	78	80
Light vs. Dark Color	17	21	15	17
Aroma Attributes				
Like Overall Aroma	58	65	61	60
Strength of Aroma	58	67	55	50
Taste/Flavor Attributes				
Like Overall Taste/Flavor	59	67	63	65
Strength of Taste/Flavor	69	64	66	60
Smooth Tasting	51	59	47	46
Bitter Tasting	59	54	55	58
Burnt Tasting	55	52	54	59
Strength of Aftertaste	68	63	66	71
Preferred (%)	43	57	51	49

Most companies use some sort of competitive product audit, either formal or informal, so that product issues eventually surface. These audits are "early warning devices." Most such audits of the competitors reveal that the problem exists, although the audits don't prescribe the solution. The problem could be slipped product quality, an inevitable consequence of continual cost cutting. Or, as all too often happens, perhaps inevitably over time, consumer tastes have changed so that the product is out of sync with consumer preferences.

The audit results can be interpreted in different ways depending on the employee, his/her job, and their vested interests. The purchasing agent responsible for buying the coffee bean (procurement) argued that the problem was shifting consumer tastes, not a change in bean quality that came from trying to get the best deal for the bean at perhaps the risk of product taste. This trade-down of quality for momentary cost savings often happens, whether or not companies want to admit it. Just as vehemently, the product development manager argued that the product was okay and the bean quality was okay, but the production specifications were not tight enough. It was clearly necessary to create a new product or reformulate the current product to satisfy these evolving and emerging taste preferences.

Overseeing both purchase and R&D product development was marketing, which simply wanted to sell more coffee because that was the criterion for its performance rating. Marketing at Maxwell House did not know why the in-market product had scored poorly, but it was the marketers' responsibility to fix the problem and stem the decline of market share. If consumers clearly preferred one product to another on a blind basis, and if both products were equally advertised and promoted, then over time, the less-liked product would lose market share. The loss might be slow or quick, but the change would be inevitable. It was just a matter of time.

STEP 2: CREATE AND TEST MANY SYSTEMATICALLY VARIED TEST PRODUCTS

Simply being able to identify a problem does not solve it, no matter how well written the report is, how the results are couched, or who does the reporting in the first place. This truism is doubly true in product development. There are no ingredients for "good taste," and the advertising agency cannot really fool the consuming public more than a few times with a clever advertising campaign. People catch on; if the coffee does not taste good, sooner or later, the consumer will reach another four inches to the right or to the left on the shelf and choose another brand that "tastes better." The consumer might be lost forever, especially when the competitor's coffee really does taste better.

Product developers at Maxwell House realized that they had to discover what particular combination of beans and roasts would appeal to their consumers. The work would be *systematic,* not haphazard. The developer would generate rules. And the rules that emerged would guide Maxwell House, perhaps for years, in buying coffee beans, in blending, and even perhaps in positioning the coffee to the public based upon specific sensory characteristics that RDE revealed to be important.

So how does the product developer decide what to vary in the experiments? First, scope works. For best results, *the experiment base of prototypes should be wide, to encompass many of them.* Think for a moment about the Sony Walkman or Seiko watches. Sony introduced several hundred; Seiko tested several thousands of models just to find the right ones. Second, experience helps. If the product developer were new to the business of coffee, a prudent move might be to learn about the ingredients from textbooks, trade magazines, consultants, and other sources; buy some of the beans; combine them in various proportions; test these combinations with consumers; get ratings of liking; and finally identify what combinations "work." Working in product development means that the combination that the developer selects should be affordable, highly acceptable, and stable, to thus generate better market performance.

Maxwell House used a straightforward development strategy of testing, learning, and retesting until they "got it right." Coffee researchers had years of experience, so it was not necessary to start at square one. They already knew about the product from years of trial and error. *Both the consumer and the product needed systematized study.*

Just knowing the key variables to study was not enough. That hoped-for magic combination of beans was of interest. The most efficient RDE-based approach in product development requires that the developer *systematically vary* the physical formulation. Table 2.2 shows five of these combinations, as well as the current Maxwell House product. You can see that the four rows correspond to the four different beans (A, B, C, and D), which the developer has combined into different combinations (prototypes). Statisticians have developed plans or layouts for combinations of these variables. The product developer need only follow this experimental plan, using his knowledge of the coffee bean to give an ingredient "reality" to the plan. Furthermore, consumers who will taste the test products don't have to know what these combinations actually contain—they just have to taste the product and say how much they like (or dislike) the prototype. RDE thus defines the combinations and eventually shows the researcher how to analyze the results and adjust (adapt) the formulation to obtain higher consumer liking.

Table 2.2

Combinations and ratings for the Maxwell House RDE study. Consumers rated five different test blends in taste tests. The actual formulations are coded.

Product	Test 1	Test 2	Test 3	Test 4	Test 5	Maxwell House
% Bean A	15	15	55	35	35	NA
% Bean B	15	55	15	15	15	
% Bean C	55	15	15	35	15	
% Bean D	15	15	15	15	35	
Cost of the beans (units)	76	27	63	19	58	
Rating of Liking (0 = Hate, 100 = Love)						
Liking—total panel	47	64	56	48	58	53
Liking—"bitter seeking segment"	54	56	57	62	61	48

In a nutshell, make the different combinations that the design calls for, even if you believe some of these combinations just won't work. The requirements for successful RDE remain simple, concrete, and quite enlightening: Do the homework, don't be afraid to test many more prototypes, and contract out the repetitive, onerous work to subcontractors so you can concentrate on building a better product. Most of all, don't be quick to judge. The history of great products is full of examples of a winning idea that an executive initially rejected. *Do not throw out the baby with the bath water—test everything.*

STEP 3: TESTING THE PROTOTYPES WITH CONSUMERS AND COLLECTING THEIR RATINGS

Running the taste test with these different products is fairly straightforward, except that the people running the test must attend to lots of details, such as serving the coffee fresh, making sure each person gets the appropriate product at the right time, and, of course, checking that the session is run at a professional level with proper taste-test controls.

Maxwell House researchers ran the test. They brought the consumers into a central location; let each consumer taste a different randomized set of 8 coffee samples from the full set of 17 test products plus the current "blind-tested" Maxwell House and their competitors' coffees. The consumers then rated liking and other characteristics. Despite the emphasis on seriousness, this RDE exercise really turned out to be fun, as so many of them do. Consumers liked it, and Maxwell House staff, technical as well as marketing, realized that they were about to crack the coffee code.

We don't necessarily think of RDE and new product development as having much to do with human nature; instead, we think of the process as a rigid business and scientific process that's devoid of soul and individual idiosyncrasies. That's not the case here. The first thing the Maxwell House product developers did was rush through the different completed questionnaires to see whether the average ratings for their prototypes were high enough, and higher than both the two main competitor products and the current Maxwell House coffees. All three products had been included in the test as benchmarks. These little dramas in RDE product tests occur in project after project because the company professionals involved in developing and improving products are keenly interested in finding out whether they have succeeded. The consumer is the ultimate arbiter of this success.

For Maxwell House, the result was a data set that would be used for more than a decade. Look back at Table 2.2, with the five test blends and the current Maxwell House product at the time of the RDE project. The numbers in the first rows are the percentages of the four different coffees (A, B, C, and D correspond to the major coffees—Brazil, Central, Colombian, and Robusta). Clearly, consumers liked some of these combinations better than what Maxwell House was putting on the market.

STEPS 4, 5, 6: STACKING THE DECK FOR SUCCESS: DISCOVER THE DIFFERENT "TONGUES" IN THE POPULATION (ANALYSIS, OPTIMIZATION, AND SEGMENTATION)

The data in Table 2.2 tells us that the effort to create these different coffees showed Maxwell House a number of improved coffees that tasted better to consumers. But was that all? Some observations by the scientists at General Foods suggested that there are different "tongues" in the population—people with different preferences. To be sure, all the Maxwell House consumers said that they wanted a "rich, robust" taste. However, the data suggested something different. The data suggested different patterns of what people like. When the Maxwell House researcher plotted the data from this RDE exercise on a graph, it looked very much like Figure 2.1 for bitter versus liking. *That is, as the coffee tasted increasingly bitter, the coffee consumer appeared to like the coffee more, but only up to a specific point.* Beyond a certain bitter taste, the consumer liked the coffee less.

A deeper finding revealed a very big opportunity for General Foods. Dividing the consumers by the pattern of what they liked revealed *three clearly different segments of consumers.* Some people liked more bitter coffee, some people liked less bitter coffee, and others liked coffee with a moderate amount of bitterness (see Figure 2.2). Surprisingly for Maxwell House, *all three groups of participants in this coffee taste test said they wanted a rich, robust cup of coffee. In their minds, the coffee they wanted was strongly flavored, but their tongues were different. Their definition of "strong" was different.*

The results did not clearly reveal that consumers themselves actually understood what they wanted. They might have "known it when they tasted it," but they could not describe what they wanted. In the words of Malcolm Gladwell, who discussed in-depth RDE issues in his speech at the TED 2004 conference in Monterey,

> *"People don't know what they want...* It's a mystery and a critically important step in understanding our own desires and taste is to realize that *we cannot always explain what we want deep down."*[4]

This is a key learning from RDE. Management at Maxwell House concluded that it was not a product problem alone; it was a problem of changing tastes as well. In the words of Sherlock Holmes, "the game was afoot."

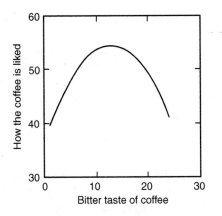

Figure 2.1 Bitterness versus liking for coffee averaged across all the coffee consumers. As the coffee tastes more bitter, the consumer likes it more, until the "bliss point" is reached, or the level at which the coffee tastes "best." Beyond that bliss point, the coffee simply tastes too bitter, and the coffee consumer starts to reject it.

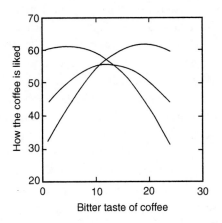

Figure 2.2 Bitter versus liking for the three coffee segments. RDE divides the consumers into different "tongues."

STEP 7: LEARN FROM THE EXPERIMENTS: DISCOVER RULES FOR BETTER COMBINATIONS OF BEANS THAT MAKE SUPERIOR COFFEE

Maxwell House tested the combinations, obtained the consumer ratings, and happened upon the "three coffee tongues." What happened next? How did the Maxwell House product developer make sense of these combinations and discover the *rules* for magical combinations that really work? We do not have to go into detail the way the statistician and researcher did and still do, but we ought to keep in mind some specific guidelines that they followed when they embarked on RDE with food:

1. **Create a "coffee model" using readily available statistical methods familiar to product developers and marketers alike.** The model is a set of equations (mathematical rules) that relate the four beans to the ratings assigned by the consumers who tested the products. Frequently, the researchers use computer programs to plot the combinations and the ratings, such as the surface we see in Figure 2.3. You will see shortly, however, that RDE is much easier to do with a user-friendly computer program that literally "dials a blend."

   The coffee model comprises a lot of information, beyond just the formulations and how much consumers liked each of them. Consumers also rated the coffee on different sensory characteristics (appearance, aroma, taste/flavor, mouth feel), giving each coffee product its own "sensory signature." The cost of goods comes from the procurement agent; the coffee model tells Maxwell House how expensive the coffee will be to produce. From the product developers and the buyers, the researchers obtained the "cost of goods" so they would know how much each cup of coffee would cost. The coffees differed in cost because some of the beans were expensive and some were cheap. Those costs play a very important role in RDE, allowing the developer to identify the improved coffee while at the same time ensuring that the coffee will be affordable and return a profit. Without this discipline of ingredient-costing, it might turn out that the coffee that performs well in these tests later turns out to be too expensive, forcing everyone back to square one. RDE's cost-based model tells the developer, marketer, and manufacturer *ahead of time* how much quality they want to put into the product, what it will cost them, and whether they want to set limits on cost for the best coffee formulation (or best blend of beans) they can possibly create.

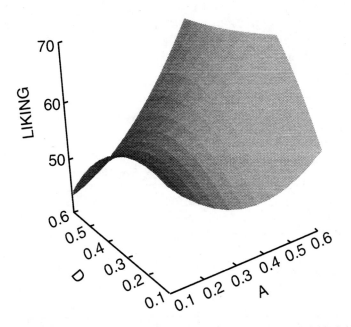

Figure 2.3 Three-dimensional surface showing how two of the four beans (Variable A, Variable D) together drive the rating of coffee. To find the expected rating, locate where Variable A and Variable D have their values, and then proceed upward to where that combination intersects the surface. The actual real RDE surface for the four beans is more complicated and can be explored by more user-friendly computer programs that give the company numerical formulations instead of pictures.

2. **Use the coffee model to synthesize the best new coffee ("dial a drink").** At the end of the day, RDE has a truly simple business objective: to identify the best coffee that the company can afford. For Maxwell House, that objective had to be restated a bit: to identify the best coffee defined as the specific combination that scores well among the three different taste groups of coffee drinkers (those who like strong and bitter, those who like rich aroma and moderately strong taste, and those who like weaker-tasting coffee). Synthesizing the coffee using the model is a desk job. When the developer has the equation, the rest is really *dialing for blends*.

You see a snapshot of a "dial a coffee" in Table 2.3, which shows three different alternatives. As with many of today's technologies, product models are run on PCs using fairly straightforward statistics. The developer or marketer uses the model to identify what particular combination of coffee beans at today's prices provides a high degree of liking, is affordable, and maintains the sensory signature of the product.

Table 2.3

"Dial a Coffee Blend" Using the Coffee RDE

Blend of Beans	Best for Total	Best for Total and More Affordable	Best for Bitter or Impact Seekers
A	20%	30%	33%
B	39%	30%	27%
C	20%	20%	20%
D	21%	20%	20%
Cost of the coffee beans (units)	65	50	46
Liking			
Total panel (all consumers)	59	56	55
Segment that likes bitter or impact	60	65	68

REVIEWING WHAT MAXWELL HOUSE LEARNED BY ITS RDE EFFORTS—ABOUT COFFEE, CONSUMERS, AND THE COMPANY

The management team at Maxwell House conducted its post-mortem on this very successful project. The actual efforts had been harder than they had realized. For sure, the project had started out to be rather direct. The early reports that there might be a product problem were true, but the nature of the problem was not clear until Maxwell House executed the RDE project.

The hardest part of the coffee project was the effort to make the product "right," to improve it so that the brand might survive to fight again another day. The information-gathering activities could all be described as "faultless." Indeed, for the most part, corporations already have perfected the process of finding out what is wrong with a product. Even with the language to describe the problems, an indirect description was clearly couched with many *ifs*, possibilities, emotional hemming and hawing, and ritualistic genuflections that accompany self-excusing phrases that seemed to make the problem almost a natural for the category.

In the end, RDE worked admirably, for it took the problem out of that unbearable situation in which the solution cannot be easily specified and instead prescribed a set of knowledge-building steps. RDE quickly, efficiently, and cost-effectively generated rules and prescribed knowledge-based actions leading to a better product. What was the ending of this story? In the words of Malcolm Gladwell,

> "If I were to ask all of you to try and come up with a brand of coffee—a type of coffee, a brew—that made all of you happy and then I asked you to rate that coffee, the average score in this room for coffee would be about 60 on a scale of 0–100. If, however, you allowed me to break you into coffee clusters, maybe 3 or 4 coffee clusters, and I could make coffee for each of those individual clusters, your scores would go from 60 to 75 or 78. The difference between coffee at 60 and coffee at 78 is the difference between coffee that makes you wince and coffee that makes you deliriously happy. ... most beautiful lesson of Howard Moskowitz is that in embracing the diversity of human beings, we will find a sure way to true happiness."[5]

Maxwell increased coffee sales by more than 15%, at the expense of the competitors.

Wow! This is exactly what Allison was looking for—a real-life RDE example for food product development. Allison grasped the idea immediately, although she still could benefit from some other examples and hands-on work. She will later realize that RDE for food products is a bit more difficult than RDE for ideas and messages. But this will not stop her. Allison has more energy and determination than her colleagues in many bigger corporations. And, unlike them, Allison cannot afford to hand off responsibility to sensory scientists and statisticians. So, using a structured RDE approach seems like her only chance to successfully develop a winning product.

We are quite confident that, along with you, Allison will become even more convinced with a further in-depth understanding of the approach in the next chapter. She will see how RDE gets out of a pickle—or, rather, how it works its wonders to find the best pickle.

The next chapter completes the story of RDE and food products, showing you how RDE goes *beyond better products to open entirely new business opportunities.* So, sit back, relax, and enjoy the world of Zesty Pickles from Vlasic, and Prego Pasta Sauce from Campbell's.

ENDNOTES

[1] Tom J. Peters and Robert H. Waterman, *In Search of Excellence: Lessons from America's Best-Run Companies* (New York: HarperCollins, 2004).

[2] Sources: www.nationalgeographic.com/coffee/ax/frame.html and www.coffeeresearch.org/coffee/history.htm.

[3] Source: www.sangiorgiocoffee.com.

[4] Malcom Gladwell. "What every business can learn from spaghetti." TED Conference, February, 2004, Monterey, CA, www.ted.com.

[5] Ibid.

3

Dialing Up Delicious: Major Discoveries from Vlasic and Prego

SO MANY PICKLES, SO MUCH OPPORTUNITY

Let's now switch from coffee to the world of pickles, that happy product of steeping cucumbers in a brine of salt water, peppers, dill, and all sorts of other flavor-giving ingredients. Pickles are not as glamorous as coffee. To be fair, some people are devoted to pickles and even organize such events as the Annual New York City International Pickle Day Festival.[1]

THE PICKLE THROUGH TIME

The history of pickles is much older than that of coffee. Pickles stretch so far back into antiquity that no definite time has been established for their origin, but they are estimated to be more than 4,000 years old. According to the New York Food Museum, pickles were adored by some of the most fascinating historical figures. To give the humble pickle the same center stage we gave to coffee, here is a bit of intriguing history and some peculiar facts.[2]

Cucumbers are mentioned at least twice in the Bible (Numbers 11:5 and Isaiah 1:8). History records their usage more than 3,000 years ago in Western Asia, ancient Egypt, and Greece. In 2030 B.C., cucumbers native to India were brought to the Tigris Valley, where they were first preserved and eaten as pickles.

Aristotle praised the healing effects of cured cucumbers. Cleopatra attributed a portion of her beauty to pickles—though we're not sure which portion. Some scientists believe that she used watermelons soaked in brine rather than the spicy cucumber/vinegar mix we know today—no matter, they're pickles all the same. The Roman Emperor Tiberius consumed pickles on a daily basis. Julius Caesar thought pickles to have an invigorating and health-promoting effect, so, naturally, he shared them with his legions. The enjoyment of pickles spread far and wide through Europe.

Queen Elizabeth liked pickles. And Napoleon valued pickles as a health asset for his armies, so much so that he offered the equivalent of $250,000 to anyone who could develop a way to preserve food safely. The man who won the prize in 1809 was a confectioner named Nicholas Appert, the first person to commercially pack pickles in jars.

What could a history of pickles be without some words of divine inspiration from William Shakespeare? Shakespeare peppers his plays with references not only to pickles, but new uses of the word as a metaphor:

- "Oh, Hamlet, how camest thou in such a pickle?" (*Hamlet*, Act 5, Scene 1)

- "Tis a gentle man here a plague o' these pickle-herring! How now, sot!" (*Twelfth Night*, Act 1, Scene 5)

- "What say you? Hence, Horrible villain! or I'll spurn thine eyes like balls before me; I'll unhair thy head: Thou shalt be whipp'd with wire and stew'd in brine, Smarting in lingering pickle." (*Anthony and Cleopatra*, Act 2, Scene 5)

A fondness for pickles has always been a national characteristic of the American people. It's a good thing, since our country's namesake, Amerigo Vespucci, was actually a pickle peddler in Seville, Spain. He supplied ships with pickled vegetables to prevent sailors from getting scurvy on long voyages. Whereas Columbus is credited with discovering America, Vespucci apparently had better PR skills; we are named after him. We became the United States of America instead of the United States of Columbus or even Vespucci. And that's probably a good thing, too.

George Washington was a pickle enthusiast. So were John Adams and Dolly Madison. Pickles inspired Thomas Jefferson to write the following:

> "On a hot day in Virginia, I know nothing more comforting than a fine spiced pickle, brought up trout-like from the sparkling depths of the aromatic jar below the stairs of Aunt Sally's cellar."

Many modern-day celebrities are reported to be passionate fans of pickles. Actor Bill Cosby, actress Fran Drescher (*The Nanny*), ex–New York Mayor Ed Koch, and Guardian Angel founder Curtis Sliwa are just a few recognizable names rumored to be pickle connoisseurs. Even Elvis Presley liked to eat fried pickles.

About 2.7 billion pounds of different types of pickles are consumed annually in the United States. That's nine pounds per person per year! There is a whole industry of pickles, professionally represented by the Pickle Packers International. There is a science behind pickles, and a host of professionals have spent decades refining methods for pickle making. And pickles are a big business. Look at any supermarket carrying a respectable array of condiments, and you will see all sorts of pickles, with many familiar variety names (Polski, Bread & Butter, Half Sour, Kosher, Low Salt, etc.). As a consumer, you are assaulted with different cuts of pickles, from full pickles to halves, spears, sandwich slices, refrigerator chips, and the like. Now, how to make sense of and money from this world of pickles?

THE PICKLE SHELF CONFRONTS THE CUSTOMER

For many years, pickles were home-made and usually sold locally, often with a strong heritage and the occasional folklore that made it a legend. Witness, for example, Gus' Pickles in New York. Vlasic is, in a way, the Gus' Pickles of the Midwest. The Vlasic Company, maker of pickles for decades, located in suburban Michigan, had begun to use modern principles of marketing to develop and sell their pickles. All was going according to plan. Vlasic built its new headquarters in suburban Michigan, hired talented marketers and product developers, and charged full speed into the fray of the consumer marketing jungle.

Vlasic had only one small problem: product knowledge and preferences. Most people eat pickles, but not particularly frequently—unless, of course, we are talking about a pickle addict. *Furthermore, no one is particularly brand loyal to a pickle the way they are to, say, coffee, cola, or cigarettes.* Pickles are pickles are pickles. Many pickles show up in meals eaten outside the home, and the eater doesn't know the type of pickle he is eating, much less the brand name. A pickle might taste great, and the eater would comment on the taste, but it is rare for someone to ask for a pickle by name. The pickle is simply not on center stage, no matter how great it tastes.

The brand manager and vice president of marketing at Vlasic, both pickle veterans, recognized a major opportunity. Not enough was known about the type of pickles people liked. As a group, they agreed to give RDE the chance to create a better pickle. The folks at Vlasic didn't make their decision cavalierly—they were breaking new ground in the world of pickles and had to be right. What the approach helped them to develop went far beyond a better pickle, to consequences that pleasantly surprised them.

As in the coffee case discussed earlier, this story commenced with competitor taste tests. This "due diligence" suggested that the Vlasic pickles were tasty but that "something" was missing. On a 100-point scale of liking, the pickles scored in the low and mid 50s, which, to the trained research eye, meant that pickles tasted good but not great. When the researchers looked at the data more closely, however, something interesting popped up that had escaped everyone before, except perhaps some pickle experts. Almost all of the commercially available, mass-merchandised pickles on the grocery shelf tasted either very weak or moderate, certainly not strong. Yet more than half of consumer taste testers across the three different test locations gave high liking ratings to the few commercially available strong-tasting pickles that had been included in the test, and low liking ratings to the weak-tasting pickles. Somehow the product developers and the marketers had inadvertently concentrated their efforts on producing a pickle that satisfied only about 40% of the market. The few very-strong-tasting commercially available pickles were the most highly rated by the other 60%. For reasons that are obvious today in retrospect, the developers chose to create "middle-of-the-road" pickles that would offend no one, but also not delight anyone, either.

Using RDE, the pickle developers at Vlasic *created 40 experimentally designed prototypes and tested them with the consumers.* They explored new "high-impact" pickles, pickles with "oomph," a strength that the other pickles on the market simply did not have. The experiments did not dictate what to put into the pickle brine to give the pickle "oomph"; that magic comes from years of working with pickles, knowing the ins and outs of brine and cucumbers, and developing a feeling about what customers will buy. RDE took the knowledge that it would be salt, garlic, pepper, other spices, and acid, and filled in the experimental layout of the test prototypes.

Before the consumer test, however, it seemed a good idea to try out the products—or, at least, the pickling brines—just to make sure that these pickles would taste different instead of being small variations of one another. An informal and now, in retrospect, unforgettable afternoon tasting the 40 liquid brines, conducted at the Admiral's Club in the Detroit Airport by the senior author (HRM) and three Vlasic professionals, marketers, and product developers quickly revealed that the project was on the right track. Some of these brines were weak; some had tremendous "oomph" and were downright delicious. To the four people tasting brine that October day in Detroit, it soon became clear that the project might hit pay dirt *because the RDE exercise had forced them to explore different products with radically different tastes—and some were quite good-tasting, to boot.*

And pay dirt was hit, in spades. Tests with the pickles a few months later showed clear evidence that customers wanted a better-tasting, stronger-tasting pickle. However, the RDE study revealed something even more important for Vlasic that, by now, is "old hat" if you read Chapter 2, "Maxwell House's Calculus of Coffee": There wasn't one pickle customer, but rather three distinct pickle customers, desiring pickles that were strong, medium, or weak but very crunchy. The proof was that, shortly afterward, Vlasic introduced its line of pickles varying from Low Salt to Zesty. The Zesty pickle, the highest impact of the lot, turned out to be *the best-selling pickle to date, and perhaps of all time. Using principles of RDE, working with the technologists and the consumer, Vlasic cracked the pickle code.*

It was also clear to Vlasic marketers that there had to be some way to imprint this new discovery of a taste continuum onto the mind of the customer that pickles ranged from weak to very strong. It's a simple idea now, but it is not that obvious when you are the first to recognize this sensory segmentation and new "rules" that really govern a product category. How do you communicate these discoveries to consumers, who are not waiting around for the next pickle? Vlasic marketers created a *thermometer scale,* which they put on every jar of Vlasic pickles to show how intense the taste was. Not only did Vlasic develop the pickle using RDE, but it also developed the packaging and the communications. This is still widely used in the food industry. Figure 3.1 shows an example of a modern variation of this scale, adapted for pepper "heat." The scale is pretty obvious and lets the consumer know exactly where you stand on "impact"—it's easy to remember, easy to convey, and proof that sensory differences mean corporate profits. The rest, as they say, is pickle history, and a bit of pickle legend.

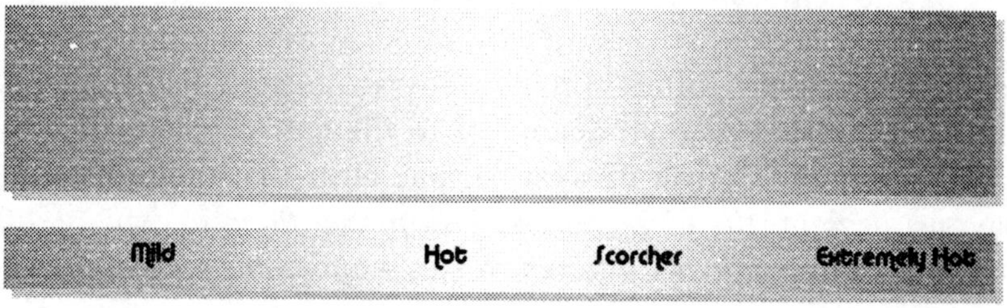

| Mild | Hot | Scorcher | Extremely Hot |

Figure 3.1 An example of a thermometer scale of spiciness originally developed by Vlasic, but now used widely for "impact" such as pepper heat. The color varies from green (mild, left) to yellow (in the middle) to red (extremely hot, right).

PASTA SAUCE, AS YOU LIKE IT: A STORY OF PREGO

Our last story on RDE-based food product development might well be the dearest to the authors' hearts because one result of this story is the shelf upon shelf of pasta sauces. The senior author was able to tell students at the Italian Gastronomic University in Pollenzo how to make pasta sauce *scientifically*, even if it is made not from Italian-grown *pomodoro*, or "golden apple," as the tomato is called in Italy.

SOME SAY "TOMATO"

Technically, a tomato is a fruit,[3] although, in 1893, the Supreme Court ruled in the case of *Nix* vs. *Hedden* that tomatoes were to be considered vegetables. According to the USDA, each American eats approximately 22 pounds of tomatoes yearly. More than half of the tomato consumption is in the form of catsup and tomato sauce.[4] In fact, Americans consume more tomatoes than any other single fruit or vegetable!

Originally cultivated by the Aztecs and Incas as early as 700 A.D., the tomato is native to the Americas, so the Italian expertise in tomato product really can be traced to an import. The expeditions of Columbus were the first to discover the fruit in 1493. Europeans were first made aware of the tomato when explorers brought back seed from Central America in the 16th century. Tomatoes quickly became popular in the Mediterranean countries but encountered resistance as they spread north. The British, in particular, considered the tomato beautiful but poisonous. This fear was shared in the American colonies, and it was years before the tomato gained widespread acceptance. In the early nineteenth century, Creoles in New Orleans chopped up tomatoes for gumbos and jambalayas, but elsewhere in America and in Europe, the tomato remained almost entirely a garden ornamental. Only by the middle of the nineteenth century did tomatoes slowly come into the widespread use across America.[5]

The story of RDE with pasta sauce begins like the other two: with a disappointing result on a taste test run by Campbell Soup. If anyone knows tomato, it's Campbell Soup, but at the time the project began, Campbell more strongly focused its attention on soup and was feeling its way in the world of tomato pasta sauce, then dominated by Ragú. Trying to create an authentic Italian pasta sauce in America was challenging. It wasn't just a matter of being truly authentic; one could develop products for pasta that were every bit as authentic as the sauces that, for decades, mothers and great chefs had made in Italy. The problem was the *taste of America*. It was not clear what customers wanted in a pasta sauce. You saw the same problem when we discussed Maxwell House and the Zesty pickle, probably for the same reason. We're dealing here with standards of identity, or what it means from a sensory viewpoint to be "authentic" as well as "good tasting" for pasta sauce, coffee, and, really, a whole bunch of products. Malcolm Gladwell got it right in his insightfully written article "The Ketchup Conundrum."[6] There are standards of identity, and sometimes we just don't know where to turn when we want a new product that keeps that standard, yet improves it a bit.

Following the Campbell taste tests, it seemed clear to the development team, many experts on tomatoes, that there was more to the pasta sauce than simply the tomato. But what, specifically? It was not clear what to add, what to do. When it comes to pasta sauce, there are *many, many alternatives*. This was not like coffee blends, with a limited set of, say, three to four coffee beans that one combines. Nor was it like pickles—once you've worked with acid, garlic, pepper, and a few other spices, you've done it the world of most pickles.

In the case of pasta sauce, observing consumers in their home (ethnography) and talking to them (focus groups) revealed a startling and somewhat disconcerting pattern to those expecting a quick answer. The finding was that many of the people in the study and focus groups said that they would not leave the product intact the way that the company made it. Each of these participants wanted to share personalized recipes. They all doctored the product somehow, some more than others, to the point that the product they served to their families at dinnertime bore little resemblance to the pasta sauce that they bought in the store. The pasta sauce that *they* served was a combination of what they bought and some part of themselves, *their own interpretation*.

"It may be hard today, fifteen years later—when every brand seems to come in multiple varieties—to appreciate how much of a breakthrough this was," wrote Malcolm Gladwell in 2004. "At Ragú and Prego, they had been striving for the platonic spaghetti sauce...[the way] it was done in Italy.... Once you start looking for the sources of human variability, though, the old orthodoxy goes out the window."[7]

The actual work with Prego began a little differently. Instead of working with known ingredients, the development group did its homework. Looking at what people did to the pasta sauces, they quickly realized that it was not a question of which four ingredients to vary. Nor, in fact, was it doing the preparer's homework and making a complete pasta sauce with all the ingredients—at least, not at first. The development strategy to create more complex and complete pasta sauces emerged years later, after the easy profits were made—but we are getting ahead of the story. *Instead, the real job was to identify exactly what to do—and only then do it.* The tough job was the thinking up front, especially in a world where there was nothing to copy. Coffee and pickles are simple, compared to pasta sauce; they have a much narrower range of sensory experiences that they create, no matter what experts may say, and neither coffee nor pickles features the range of ingredients that can be added. Pasta sauce presents a wider range, almost a *symphony* of characteristics, both those that the manufacturer can impart to the product and those that the consumer will add during preparation. Besides tomato flavor intensity, there's the texture, the types of particulates or inclusions, and their flavor notes, not to mention spiciness, sweetness, and acidity, all of which are quite different from the impact of the tomato taste itself.

The story proceeds rather directly, at least for the discovery phase, and with some pragmatic trade-offs of effort versus expected result. Product developers at Campbell quickly recognized the complexity of the problem, identified six ingredients that they believed to be drivers of liking, created the *45 different combinations* that the RDE design called for, and ran the study. The logic of RDE remained very simple. The goal was to uncover the best combination of pasta sauce ingredients, recognizing a simple rule that governed all sensory experiences; more is not necessarily better, and as the sensory intensity (say, of sweetness) increases, consumers first say that they like the product more, but eventually, with a middle level of sweetness, consumers like the product the most (this is their optimum, or "bliss," point). By the time this optimal sweetness is reached, further increases in sweetness generate less liking. To incorporate this curvature, which makes the sensory-liking relation look like an inverted U, the developer tests at least three different and distinct levels of each ingredient. With six ingredients in the pasta sauce, each at three levels, the total number of combinations to make is a staggering $3 \times 3 \times 3 \times 3 \times 3 \times 3$, or 729. Fortunately for the developer and for RDE, there are shortcuts. Not all 729 combinations need to be made. One could get away with 45 or even 29 with the right statistical design. The 45 pasta sauces were a lot to make, but as we will see, the payout was enormous.

An experiment of this size—taste testing the 45 pasta sauces—presents an entirely different type of problem to any developer, often a daunting one. How exactly should one test 45 different pasta sauces? It's nothing like testing coffees, which can be easily made with different coffee brewers, the way the Maxwell House developers tested their coffees. And it's nothing like unscrewing jars of pickles, cutting one of the pickles into four long slices, and apportioning one slice to each of four people. Pasta sauces have to be made quickly, with a lot of care taken to serve them fresh (in about two to three minutes) over warm pasta to a waiting panelist at the taste test. The picture the reader should paint in his mind is a group of three stoves, each with four burners, making five of the 45 pasta sauces at one time, serving them in batches to waiting individuals and repeating this exercise nine times.[8] Eventually, in different cities and with different orders of preparing the 45 pasta sauces, the field work was finished, the sauces served, and the data collected from more than 300 participants.

In any RDE work, everyone holds his or her breath until the results are in. Will the products do well? Is a new pasta sauce lurking in the wings? In the Prego case, the story was far stronger than anyone believed. The pasta sauces differed, all right, with some test products scoring better and others scoring worse than expected. However, the most exciting result was that there were *three clear segments of pasta sauce consumers,* and each could be won over by a sauce that scored 65 or higher on a 100-point scale. This was excellent news, the same type of excellent news that greeted both Maxwell House and Vlasic. But there was more, much more. When the consumers were asked what they wanted as the next generation of pasta sauces, many of them suggested pasta sauces with new ingredients.

To make a long story short, the rest is pasta sauce history. Prego introduced *a line of pasta sauces, not just one,* comprising one sauce that was regular/traditional; another that was spicy, to appeal to the "high-impact" segment; and a third, to appeal to the segment that wanted texture. These were radically different segments, with different wants. All three segments were ready for new sauces. And of those three, the last was the most important. Why? Because at the time, there was no extra-chunky pasta sauce in the supermarket. *And most people did not even know they liked it until they had tested it!*

Over the succeeding years, management and product developers at Prego used this RDE model to "dial up" new sauces, with new ingredients, just as management at General Foods "dialed up" coffees and management at Vlasic "dialed up" pickles. Indeed, the picture of "dialing a product formulation" is one of the outputs of RDE because the rules guide new products. The RDE model directed ongoing development and ensured profitability, while the consumer research continued to reveal acceptance for products with mushrooms, meat, garden vegetables, and eventually an increasingly complex array of ingredients.

Competitors also recognized the value of Prego's RDE testing. Not to be outdone, the competitor brands quickly latched on to the Prego strategy, and they themselves began to introduce products to appeal to these segments, in some cases, reverse engineering the Prego products so that they themselves could enjoy some of this burgeoning category. Today the competition is fierce, fueled by the RDE experience that produced Prego's market success. According to Mintel International, the pasta sauces market grew to $1.6 billion in 2004 and is expected to increase 6% by 2007.[9] Just look at the original "owner" of the pasta sauce category, Ragú, which had watched Prego invade its territory. Prego's success changed Ragú from a few sauces to many sauces, just to stay competitive. Today Ragú offers 36 *varieties* of Ragú pasta sauce, under six general subbrands, all similar to the types of consumer taste segments that Prego discovered through RDE. The dizzying assortment includes Old World Style, Chunky Garden Style, Robusto, Light, Cheese Creations, and Rich & Meaty, which means that there is very nearly an optimal pasta sauce for every man, woman, and child in America.

The sector that had a few choices just 15 to 20 years ago has grown into a burgeoning industry by itself. With a proliferation of sauces fighting for prime shelf space, retailers are seeing significant expansion in pasta sauce facings and sales. "We have 64 linear feet devoted to specialty pasta sauce—double from last year," says Joe D'allessandro, general manager at Verducci's Food Market in Ringoes, New Jersey. "There is a vast selection of high-quality specialty sauces now. Customers are trying multiple varieties and buying more." Turco's, in Hartsdale, New York, stocks more than

20 brands of sauces, including its own fresh brand made in-house. Priced at $5.99 for a quart container, the fresh sauces sell approximately 500 gallons a week.[10]

The proof is in the eating, or in the merchandising. Today, when you walk down the aisles in any supermarket, you can see dozens upon dozens of varieties of pasta sauce, many of which have been developed using first, second, and third generations of the RDE data. Many of them are delicious, some of them are delightful, and still others represent the further edges of vision for this segmentation, making you think about new vistas, such as seafood in the pasta sauce—something unthinkable when the category was young and Prego was the first to break the boundaries.

And why is it important for the rest of us? Malcolm Gladwell, who discussed RDE issues in his speech at the TED 2004 conference in Monterey, California mentioned in Chapter 2, answered the question this way:

> "It is in fact enormously important... Howard [Moskowitz] fundamentally changed the way the food industry thinks about making you happy. Assumption #1 in the food industry used to be that the way to find out what people want to eat, what will make people happy is to ask them. And for years and years, Ragú and Prego would have focus groups... And for all those years, ... no one ever said they wanted extra chunky. Even though at least 1/3 of them, deep in their hearts, actually did. *People don't know what they want.*"[11]

What was the bottom line of this story for Prego? Over the next decade, that new category proved to be worth *hundreds of millions of dollars* to Prego. Monica Wood, who was then the head of market research for Campbell's, recalls: "Here there was this third segment—people who liked their spaghetti sauce with lots of stuff in it—and it was completely untapped. So in about 1989–90, we launched Prego extra-chunky. It was extraordinarily successful."[12]

WHAT WAS ACCOMPLISHED BY RDE AND HOW WAS IT REALLY DONE?

It should be pretty clear by now that RDE is more than an afternoon's feel-good session in a business therapy office, where the participants unload their business-relevant shackles and constraints and adopt a new and creative attitude. If an outside observer were to look at this RDE process, what would he say? There aren't any magical exercises; there's no "aha" experience. It's more like the grind of studying for an exam or, even better, the tortuous process that athletes go through to condition themselves before a big, long, effort-filled race.

The three stories you read in this chapter and the previous chapter—about Maxwell House Coffee, Vlasic Pickles, and Prego Pasta Sauce—didn't come about because a maverick executive suddenly had a vision of the next generation of coffee, pickles, or pasta sauces sitting on the supermarket shelves, willing themselves to jump into the shopping carts, homes, plates, cups, and, hopefully, hearts of consumers. The three products emerged because of a little corporate discomfort and their willingness to experiment. An ordinary evaluation of the product revealed in its very ordinary way that the product was not as good as everyone thought it would be. No magic interloper came into the picture and suddenly changed everything. There was no time zero, no "big bang" when everything changed forever because a new coffee, pickle, or pasta sauce strode onto the scene. Instead, over time, people changed. They always do. People get tired of what they always buy. In a choice economy, where a dozen suppliers are waiting to sell to the wavering, wandering customer, the inevitable happened. The consumers found other coffees, other pickles, other pasta sauces, and their taste preferences simply shifted.

And what did RDE do? We can see no evidence of massive changes in the corporations. There was no Manhattan Project for pickles, nor a truly large-scale effort for coffee or pasta sauce. Quite the contrary—it was business as usual. The only difference was that, this time the parties involved decided *to solve the problem by understanding how their product worked, creating multiple prototypes based on an experimental design covering a very wide range of options, conducting relatively large-scale experiments, and trying to learn and adjust their strategy accordingly.* The bottom line was that RDE was done orderly, simply, with discipline in design, execution, and data analysis. The real excitement came when the data turned from a set of numbers to averages, from averages to results of different groups with distinct sensory preferences, and finally from those well-defined groups to equations. At the end, the most palpable excitement came from the new company's ability to "dial a product" using the RDE-based model or equation of the results and put it into the hands of a junior product developer or assistant brand manager, with no more than two to three years of experience. These were the future guardians of the product, thoroughly enjoying their first experiences with the tangible fruits of the experimentation. And what a journey it would be for years to come.

PRACTICAL HINTS AND BUSINESS LEARNING

No business story should be without some coda, some words of wisdom given to you after reflection. So what should we say here? That the process was, *aw shucks, simple*? That it was just science applied to foods? That we owe it to our mothers? Not really. If we were to say what we learned, it would be this: Do not prejudge, do not pull the budget, and, for heaven's sake, stop trying to bury the idea of experimentation because it sounds so risky. Instead, follow the scientific method and try to experiment—the more, the merrier. It is not risky. Sure, hours were spent making coffees, pickles, and pasta sauces that produced some crummy-tasting products. But the companies were after the pattern, the map and guide that allowed them to dial the products. If anything, they learned that they knew less when they judged more.

Perhaps the most important thing that we can learn is NOLF: No one lives forever, and making some poor products in the process of experimentation will neither ruin the company's financial statements nor hound the developer or marketer for a lifetime. IDEO, one of the most innovative companies in the U.S., has a saying in the office: "Fail often to succeed sooner."[13] Failure is the flip side of experimentation and risk taking. And if you do not take risks, chances are you will never succeed. Charles Schwab, for example, failed a number of times before hitting on a successful formula for e-Schwab. The whole history of his company has been a series of risks, failures, corrections, more risks—and hits. After so many failures, Schwab himself coined the term "noble failures," which kept the business on the cutting edge pushing the barriers. The idea of multiple prototypes removes the mental barrier of fear to make mistakes. Most of the prototypes *have to be* on the edges of acceptability (and beyond) in order to find the "peak" in liking!

Perhaps the most unexpected thing the companies learned was that development could be lots of fun. Nothing could beat that palpable excitement of "hitting the home run" based upon product rules discovered in the study. The awesome regularity of nature, the fact that one could build great products with this disciplined exercise that seems so rigid and so scientific, was part of the magic that came through those days. It's a magic that stays with the RDE participant for a lifetime and often becomes part of his or her self-selected stories in a life history—as well as the topic of many elaborated business-war stories.

A WORD FROM THE BLOGOSPHERE: WHAT DOES SPAGHETTI SAUCE HAVE IN COMMON WITH THE IPOD?

Eugene Wallingford looks like a typical professor, even in his picture on the front of the box of Wheaties Cereal placed on his Web site ("After the Chicago marathon, they let us be photographed next to this huge cereal box," he told Alex Gofman in a soft but energetic voice when Alex called him at the office.) Wallingford is an associate professor and the head of the Department of Computer Science at the University of Northern Iowa, as well as an avid marathon runner. To be sure that he is not confused (which is almost impossible anyway) with an athletic department coach, Wallingford has placed the Rodin Thinker picture next to his photo on the Web site. He is a big proponent of extreme programming (XP, one of the most effective but more inspirational and *experimentational* types of programming, as opposed to highly planned, more bureaucratic, and, in most cases—at least, if you do it outside Bangalore—more expensive and much slower software engineering).

Once, while waiting for a basketball game to start, Wallingford wrote a blog that caught our attention. In the blog, named "What Does the iPod Have in Common with Spaghetti Sauce?,"[14] he analyzed Malcolm Gladwell's article "The Ketchup Conundrum," mentioned earlier, together with Paul Graham's essay *Made in USA*,[15] which Graham wrote for the Japanese edition of his book *Hackers & Painters*.[16] Graham's book tries to explain why Americans make some things well but make other things quite poorly.

In his essay, Wallingford "was surprised to run across the same Big Idea in both papers," albeit it in different forms: "Design, well done, satisfies needs users didn't know they had."

The first approach to creating a great design is exemplified by the Steve Jobs iPod example. Graham relates how he felt after buying an iPod (formatting is ours):

> "I just got an iPod, and it's not just nice. It's surprisingly nice. For it to surprise me, it must be *satisfying expectations I didn't know I had. No focus group is going to discover those. Only a great designer can.*"

Another way is exactly the opposite of the Steve Jobs approach, which relies on a genius designer to assess the state of the world and create a product that scratches an itch no one quite knew they had. The Prego optimization approach, according to Wallingford, is more in the philosophical tradition of Art and Fear:[17] to produce and experiment with a lot of artifacts. Many will have no shelf life, but in the volume, you are more likely to create something of value.

But there is another hidden potential benefit of the RDE approach in the example of Prego, argues Wallingford: *In producing lots of stuff, designers overcome the fear of creating, especially things that are different from what already exists. Even better, such designers can begin to develop a sense of what works and what doesn't through voluminous experience.*

Graham tries to understand why the U.S. is good at designing some things, such as software, and bad at others, such as cars. Graham's diagnosis for problems with car design: Instead of relying on a sense of good design, American auto manufacturers rely on focus groups to tell them what people want.

So why is the U.S. good at designing other products, such as software? Americans are driven by speed, continues Graham, and some products are done better when done quickly without undue emphasis on getting it "right."

"If you work slowly and meticulously, you merely end up with a very fine implementation of your initial, mistaken idea. Working slowly and meticulously is premature optimization. Better to get a prototype done fast, and see what new ideas it gives you."[18]

Graham: "Do multiple experiments, do them fast, do them to learn."

One of the key learnings from the examples of this and the previous chapters is that *most people did not even know they like it until they tested it.* Allison-the-Entrepreneur learned it earlier from her book hero but was glad to get a scientific confirmation. So what else did she acquire from this chapter in her quest to promote her cherished new product? Allison neither has the resources to do a comprehensive time- and money-consuming qualitative research, nor believes that her niche business can afford random experimentation or a few focus groups. What if her idea is wrong and, after spending months of work and a small fortune (which she does not have yet), she ended up creating an "optimal" version of an unsellable product—that is, the best of the worst?

To improve her chances for success, Allison should create a range of prototypes of the product comprising different characteristics. She should not be afraid to use wide ranges of these features. For example, she could vary the color from very light blue color to rich and very dark in combination (according to a simple experimental design), with different patterns. A quite simple analysis at the end would yield the combination the consumer liked best. With RDE, Allison might well discover that she could sell the resulting product with far less hassle, and perhaps with greater profit as well.

ENDNOTES

[1] *New York Times*, 30 September 2005.

[2] Sources: Kenneth F. Kiple and Kriemhild Coneé Ornelas, *The Cambridge World History of Food* (Cambridge: Cambridge University Press: 2000); Don Brothwell and Patricia Brothwell, *Food in Antiquity* (Baltimore: Johns Hopkins University Press, 1998); www.nyfoodmuseum.com; www.mtolivepickles.com; www.ilovepickles.org; www.foodtimeline.org.

[3] It is the ripened ovary of a plant.

[4] See www.fsa.usda.gov.

[5] Maguelonne Toussaint-Samat, *History of Food* (New York: Barnes & Noble Books, 2003); and James Trager, *The Food Chronology: A Food's Lover's Compendium of Events and Anecdotes from Prehistory to the Present* (New York: Henry Holt and Company, Inc., 1995).

[6] Malcolm Gladwell, "The Ketchup Conundrum," *The New Yorker* (6 September 2004): 128–135.

[7] Ibid.

[8] Each individual tasted one sauce per each round (total 9 prototypes out of 45 per each respondent).

[9] Mintel Reports, "USA, Food and Foodservice: Pasta Sauces," April 2005.

[10] Nicole Potenza Denis, "Pasta Sauce Goes American," *Specialty Food Magazine* Nov/Dec 2004: 44–48; www.specialtyfood.com.

[11] Malcom Gladwell. "What every business can learn from spaghetti sauce." TED 2004 Conference, February, 2004, Monterey, CA, www.ted.com.

[12] From Malcolm Gladwell's "The Ketchup Conundrum," referenced earlier.

[13] Tom Kelley, *The Art of Innovation: Lessons in Creativity from IDEO, America's Leading Design Firm* (NY: Currency, 2001).

[14] Wallingford, Eugene. "What Does the iPod have in Common with Prego Spaghetti Sauce?" Blog: November 22, 2004 (http://www.cs.uni.edu/~wallingf/blog/archives/monthly/2004-11.html#e2004-11-22T09_45_54.htm).

[15] Paul Graham, "Made in USA," November 2004, www.paulgraham.com/usa.html.

[16] Paul Graham, *Hackers and Painters: Big Ideas from the Computer Age* (Sebastopol, CA: O'Reilly Media, 2004).

[17] David Bayles and Ted Orland, *Art & Fear* (Eugene, OR: Image Continuum Press, 2001).

[18] Paul Graham, "Made in USA," referenced earlier.

4

How to Make People Feel Good Even When They Pay More

From Alfa-Bank News Release (Moscow, September 19, 2006):

> Alfa-Bank and Aeroflot Programme win the MasterCard 2006 European Co-Brand Partners of the Year Award—Moscow, Russia. MasterCard in Europe named the winners of the 2006 European Co-Brand Partners of the Year Award. The Aeroflot–MasterCard–Alfa-Bank programme was acknowledged as the "Best Launch in 2005/2006."[1]

When a bank launches a new credit card, its executives do not necessarily announce their goal to make their project into a Hall of Fame or reveal the innards in news releases. The business objective is to make the card *successful*. The rest is directly correlated to the number of zeros the card generates.

The market for credit cards is huge and growing every day with the influx of a newly minted middle class in Asia and in other developing countries. In any given month, Americans owe more than $800 billion[2] to bank credit card issuers, an amount exceeding the gross domestic product (GDP) of Australia.[3] Americans are not alone. Brits owe $97 billion to bank credit card issuers (close to the GDP of New Zealand), and Aussies owe $19 billion to bank credit card issuers (similar to the GDP of Panama). Based on the population figures of 2004, Americans owe $2,311, the Brits owe $1,616, and the Aussies owe $950, for every man, woman, and child in their respective countries.[4]

The competition to acquire spending customers is fierce among the card issuers. How can you make a new card successful? What do you say to someone to get him or her to apply for and use a credit card? What type of rewards do you offer in a category that has become pretty much of a commodity, with bank after bank coming up with credit card ideas and advertisements? Ultimately, most efforts fail.

Switch gears for a moment. If you're selling jewelry instead of credit cards, how do you understand what tugs at the heart so your mail piece "sings"? In this chapter, we explore two of these communication problems to which RDE was applied, along with the approach, the discoveries, the offerings, and some happy and surprising results. RDE encouraged both MasterCard and Kay Jewelers to do the necessary homework that they had not done before. The rewards were delightfully tangible within just a few weeks.

As you saw in the examples in the gastronomical world in Chapters 2, "Maxwell House's Calculus of Coffee," and 3, "Dialing Up Delicious: Major Discoveries from Vlasic and Prego," RDE is not magic. RDE is, instead, a disciplined way to structure development to ensure success, especially when your customers are not even aware yet that they need, want, and like the products. The discipline to create multiple prototypes (either actual products or concepts) according to an experimental design, to test the prototypes with a wide range of customers (respondents), to detect distinct groups of customers based on their response pattern (segmentation), and finally to generate the rules to hit the home run applies to a wide range of message (offerings) optimizations across almost all industries that serve customers.

CREDIT CARDS IN HONG KONG: HOW HSBC FIGURED OUT THE RIGHT OFFER

Credit cards do not just appear out of nothing in the industry. They are usually the results of deals made between a credit card company such as MasterCard and different banks.

A few years ago, on a cold, early November evening, the co-branding group, headed at that time by Robert Wesley and assisted by Mava Heffler, assembled in the basement of MasterCard, Inc., the credit card giant that went public in 2006 and whose claim to fame is the MasterCard. Both leaders were marketing veterans assigned to creating a deal between MasterCard and the Hong Kong Shanghai Bank (HSBC).

The deal on the table confronting MasterCard was to issue a co-brand or affinity card connected with the upcoming World Cup in soccer. MasterCard looks for these topic-based opportunities to create a new credit card. The affinity-based card, tied in to the upcoming World Cup, was only one of a group of credit cards slated for that year. However, this Hong Kong story is of particular interest because MasterCard used RDE to great advantage, generating many times more card acquisitions than expected at the project's outset.

COMBINING IDEATION AND RDE TO CREATE A WINNING OFFER TO HSBC

With a two-week window, it was clear that the MasterCard group doing the deal had to move quickly. It was not enough to go to focus groups in Hong Kong, talk to a few consumers on Monday and Tuesday, and by Friday plan the credit card. That standard sequence had been followed before but had not yielded any breakthrough results.

It came as probably not too much of a surprise that MasterCard used RDE to create the HSBC credit card tied with the World Cup. It is the *how* that interests us here because RDE was then used as a blueprint for many other successful projects. Let's follow the steps to see how a bank used RDE in a highly competitive, nerve-wracking situation that called for quick, solid, results-oriented thinking and messaging.

STEP 1: IDEATION STAGE: IDENTIFY THE PROBLEM, GET IDEAS, EDIT THEM, AND PUT THE MODIFIED IDEAS INTO SILOS[5]

RDE forces thinking. Fundamentally, RDE made MasterCard and HSBC identify what they could offer and what they could say, and then forced them to put these ideas into "silos" or "buckets." Table 4.1 shows the basic arrangement of the silos for credit cards and both winning and losing elements. RDE produces a lot of rich data. You can get a sense of the range of ideas tested by RDE, in both strategy and execution, in basic ideas, and in ways to express the ideas.

Keep in mind that, with an RDE study, the more elements MasterCard tested, the more likely it was that the results would create a card that customers wanted. It does no good to launch a credit card based on testing a limited number of card ideas. The customers are unlikely to be excited about it if the messaging does not convince, if the graphics are wrong, and if the ideas have no pulling power. Therefore, this first step is essentially homework, something that is not always popular but is usually productive and always crucial.

Table 4.1

Performance of some winning (high utility, in bold font), losing (high negative, in italic), and neutral (in normal font) elements for the HSBC credit card. The utility shows the percentage of participants who change their vote from "not interested" to "interested" in the card, when the element is used. The additive constant is the basic percent of customers interested in the card, without any other communications.

Code	Messages/Visuals	Utility (Impact)
	Additive constant (a measure of base interest)	14
Visuals		
VS7	Bank logo, White World Cup logo, white soccer ball	**6**
VS12	Picture of Pele	4
Endorsers		
SP2	Endorsed by Pele	4
SP3	Endorsed by Au Wai Lan	−3
Ongoing Benefits		
ON5	As a card holder, you get to accrue points to get free phone cards.	**8**
ON10	As a card holder, you get a discount subscriptions to a sports magazines.	−1

Code	Messages/Visuals	Utility (Impact)
Emotional		
EM4	Every time you use the card, you show your support for the World Cup and get free gifts for yourself.	6
EM5	Every time you use the card, you show your support for the World Cup and make a donation to local youth sports programs.	3
General Benefits		
GE9	Bonus points program—use points to redeem for reduced annual fee/discounts on travel package/air miles/cash rebates/merchandise	13
GE5	Purchase protection against loss, theft, or damage up to HK$ 30,000 within 30 days of purchase	11
GE6	Special discounts at Hertz	–2
Name		
MA8	Introducing the "Sports Fan Privilege Card"	3
MA2	Introducing the "98 World Cup Commemorative Card"	3
Application		
AP4	With your application, you get a World Cup commemorative watch.	13
AP7	With your application, you get a restaurant cash voucher worth HK$20.	–6
Acquisition		
AQ17	Participate in a Lucky Draw—25 winners get an all-expense-paid trip for two to a World Cup early-round match in France.	13
AQ18	Participate in a Lucky Draw—5 winners get an all-expense-paid trip for 2 to the World Cup opening match in France.	12

One of the key responsibilities of MasterCard is to create the actual look of the credit card, an activity that involves the artist. Figure 4.1 shows the artist's renderings of what the front of the card might look like. MasterCard works with a group of artists who specialize in these card designs. The group created renditions of the new card. It was not clear to anyone on the development team exactly how important the actual look of the card would be or even what the card should look like. That's why the group tested 15 different looks, some with more complex visuals, some with less complex visuals. As you will see, these renditions turned out to be just another set of elements.

Figure 4.1 Three representative visual designs used in the RDE credit card study

STEP 2: COMBINE THE ELEMENTS INTO SHORT TEST CONCEPTS (MIX-AND-MATCH) AND INSTRUCT CUSTOMERS TO RATE THESE DIFFERENT COMBINATIONS

You will explore in more detail the idea of systematic variations later in this chapter (see the upcoming sidebar) and in Chapter 5, "Discover More About Your Competitors Than They Themselves Know—Legally," which gives an example of a teen ezine. For now, this is a systematic way to vary the combination that allowed MasterCard to estimate the impact or customer interest of each element of the combination. Simply keep in mind that *RDE systematically varies the combinations.* This systematic approach is the key because out of it will come the ability to identify what each individual element actually contributes to the odds of acquiring the card—and does so at the level of each participant.

The specific RDE experimental design comprised card advertisements similar to the solicitations that come by mail. Each card advertisement or test concept contained one element from up to five of the different silos. In the ideation stage, the group had come up with eight different silos, but the RDE experimental design used in this project selected a specific three, four, or five silos for a particular combination and presented one element from each selected silo.[6] Over time, respondents tested all the elements; the statistically based experimental design made sure of that.

One of the inevitable results of globalizing RDE is the need to have all the test materials in the appropriate languages so that all the parties can understand what they are doing. This concern applied to the credit card project as well. MasterCard translated the elements for the different concepts into Chinese and then had another group of translators "back translate" the Chinese phrasing into English. In any RDE, this strategy works wonders because it reveals whether the ideas in the concept elements are really sufficiently clear to withstand translation. If the "back translation" comes out in gibberish, this is a quick warning that somehow the ideas are not getting through.

You can see what a concept about the World Cup Card looks like in English in Figure 4.2 and another concept in Chinese in Figure 4.3. The computer created all of these combinations on the fly in Hong Kong during the course of the RDE interview.

Figure 4.2 An example of the World Cup concept for credit cards executed in English by a computer program that mixed and matched the concept elements according to the design specified by RDE

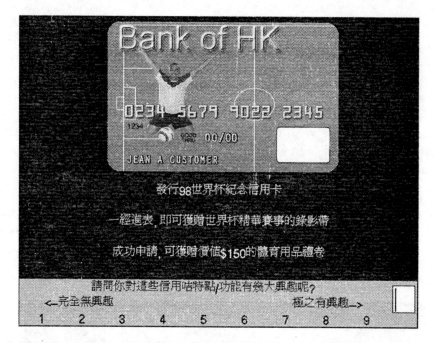

Figure 4.3 Another example of the World Cup concept for credit cards, this time executed in Chinese

TECH TALK: ADDITIONAL INFORMATION FOR THE "TECH READER"

Note: The rest of the information in step 2 is for the readers who want to understand the RDE process better. It is not necessary for you to comprehend it to harness the power of RDE—the process has been already automated with a Web tool. If you decide to spend a few minutes looking through it, you might find that it is not that complicated and, in a sense, is even elegant.

We illustrate the approach with an easy-to-understand, standard project, comprising 36 elements. The specific experimental design comprises six silos and six elements per silo,[7] which constitutes a *fixed structure*. Each time the design is chosen (a design can be applied to each individual respondent more than once, depending on the total number of the elements), the RDE tool selects a *different set*[8] of silos and elements per silo. This basic architecture is maintained, but each person tests a different permutation or arrangement of this basic architecture.[9] The 36 elements generate

48 unique[10] combinations for each person. Table 4.2 shows this basic architecture (partial) for one participant. For example, B5 refers to element 5 in silo B. Empty cells mean that the concept has only three elements. We show only the first 10 rows of this design, to give the reader a sense of what a design looks like.

Table 4.2

Example of an experimental design structure comprising six silos (letters A–F) and six elements per silo (numbers 1–6)

Concept Number	Elements			
1	A5	B5	D3	F6
2	A2	B5	D4	F4
3	B2	C3	E4	
4	A4	B1	E1	
5	A1	C5	D6	F3
6	A5	B1	D2	F3
7	A3	B4	C1	F6
8	A3	B3	C4	F2
9	B2	D3	E4	
10	A3	C2	D2	E1

STEP 3: EXECUTING THE STUDY IN HONG KONG AND COLLECTING CONSUMER DATA

The nice thing about RDE is that once the design is selected and the interviews set up, the process is automatic, rapid, and productive. Our credit card study ran quickly in Hong Kong, taking only three days, with a minimum of effort; computer-based interviews ensure this type of simplicity.

STEPS 4–7: SO WHAT DID WE LEARN AND WHAT WAS THE OUTCOME?

The outcome was a credit card launched in time for the World Cup. The credit card achieved year 1 expectations in month 1 and did more than twice as much in acquisition as was planned. At that time, six banks launched different World Cup cards; only the HSBC card survived, thanks to the fast, simple, and inexpensive RDE exercise.

Let's look at what was learned and what made this project such a success. Let's summarize key findings, generate rules, and make specific recommendations (the real benefits of RDE):

1. The data was obtained quickly from many local credit cards users. Only part of the participants were HSBC customers. This happy finding meant that the newly developed card could attract new customers from other banks and add to HSBC's core of satisfied customers.

2. The additive constant was very low, 14, meaning that, *for these potential card customers, the mere idea of a credit card was not important at all.* Only about one out of seven people (14%) thought that the card—without messaging—would receive a rating of 7–9 (very interested in the credit card with the benefits/characteristics listed). *It had to be the right messaging, or the card offer would be discarded.* The same thing happens routinely in the U.S. Credit cards are a commodity; the mail piece or take-one at the bank are thrown away, almost automatically, with nary a passing thought.

3. Two credit card mind-sets emerged from segmentation—and with them, of course, two classes of motivating messages—*shopper stuff* and *lifestyle*. HSBC could use the right combination of these ideas as the "hook" for its new card. Three of these segmenting ideas do well for both the shopper and lifestyle segments and also for the total panel (utility values of 13 just by themselves). RDE suggested these as "must haves" somewhere during the offering cycle:

Bonus points program—use points to redeem for reduced annual fee/discounts on travel package/air miles/cash rebates/merchandise.	13
With your application, you get a World Cup commemorative watch.	13
Participate in a Lucky Draw—25 winners get an all-expense-paid trip for two to a World Cup early-round match in France.	13

4. Our Hong Kong participants seemed to be talking out of two minds. The first element, promising bonus points, talks to the desire for something free. The second and third elements (commemorative watch and trip to France) combined both "stuff" and a desire to somehow participate in the World Cup. As we have

mentioned already, when MasterCard *segmented the people by the patterns of their utilities*, these two segments emerged very clearly. About half of the participants belong in the Stuff segment, and the other half belong in the Lifestyle segment. Clearly, the Buyer/Stuff segment will accept some of the Lifestyle ideas, and vice versa. Therefore, the *strategy has to merge messaging for these two different groups because they are not opposite to each other* (see Table 4.3).

Table 4.3

The ideas for credit cards that float to the top in Hong Kong and two major mind-sets discovered

	Total	Buyer Stuff	Lifestyle
Constant/"Basic Interest"	14	16	9
Winning Elements, Buyer/Stuff Segment			
With your approved card, you get a branded household electrical appliances worth HK$300.	11	16	7
Bonus points program—use points to redeem for reduced annual fee/discounts on travel package/air miles/cash rebates/merchandise.	13	16	11
With your application, you get a World Cup commemorative watch.	13	15	11
Winning Elements, Lifestyle Segment			
Participate in a Lucky Draw—25 winners get an all-expense-paid trip for two to a World Cup early-round match in France.	13	9	19
Participate in a Lucky Draw—5 winners get an all-expense-paid trip for two to the World Cup opening match in France.	12	9	17
With your approved card, you get a gift certificate to local sporting goods stores worth HK$300.	12	8	16

5. The segmentation turbocharged both the immediate launch of the credit card and the later follow-up communications with customers. The happy outcome was a set of messages that hit hot buttons for both segments, not just one, and, as time showed, an exceptionally profitable credit card that drew consumers to it rather than being perceived as yet another nuisance card.

6. In Figure 4.4, you can see the *"optimized" credit card launch visual (representative) and launch messaging that emerged from the MasterCard study.* Note that the visuals play a minor role in driving the HSBC card. It is really the messaging—specifically, the correct type of messaging. It pays to be sensitive to the language and specifics of the segments, not just to look at the total data.

Figure 4.4 The optimized credit card launch (English version), showing the messaging and a representative visual

JEWELRY FOR MOTHER'S DAY: HOW KAY JEWELERS ADDED ALMOST $500 PER SALE TO ONE TYPICAL MOTHER'S DAY JEWELRY PURCHASE

If credit cards bring out the *homo economicus* (economic man) in all of us, then jewelry brings out our other side, that which responds primarily to emotion. Jewelry expresses affection, achievement, and sometimes power. People have conquered, plundered, killed, and done much more in the name of acquiring jewels. Yet at the same time, a piece of jewelry can express one's most tender sentiments.

Tom Kelley of IDEO, who is frequently referred to as the man who has unlocked the magic box of innovation for corporate America, believes that "products today are becoming more about experiences and that services are encouraging relationships."[11] How do we unlock this treasure chest of customers; what messages engage them emotionally and create lasting relationships?

With this somewhat daunting introduction, let us turn to our second example about messaging, which combines the emotional and the economic into one story. Shaw's is one of the jewelry companies owned by Sterling Jewelers, Inc, and part of the Signet Group, the world's largest retail chain specializing in fine jewelry. Sterling operates 12 logos in the U.S. (Kay Jewelers, JB Robinson, Belden, Friedlander's, Goodman, LeRoy, Marks & Morgan, Osterman, Roger's, Shaw's, Weisfield, and Jared, the Galleria of Jewelry). Furthermore, Sterling owns approximately 1,100 retail stores in the U.S.; its U.K. parent operates more than 600 stores in the U.K. (including H. Samuel, Ernest Jones, and Leslie Davis).

After the boom of the late 1990s, when the jewelry industry enjoyed a double-digit increase in sales in some years, growth had started to stall.[12] Competition became even fiercer. Profitability suffered as well.

The objective of the RDE jewelry project was to develop a set of messages that would increase the likelihood that a Shaw's customer would buy a *significant piece* for Mother's Day. The secondary objective was to increase the monetary size of the purchase. Our story has an environmental undertone as well. Almost everyone in the United States over the age of 18 is solicited daily by different offers. It has been estimated that nearly 17 billion catalogs are mailed to consumers every year—roughly 59 catalogs for every man, woman, and child in the United States, or almost 190 per household per year. Victoria's Secrets alone prints more than *one million catalogs a day.*[13] The direct marketing industry consumes 3.6 million tons of paper annually, over 13 percent of all printing and writing paper. Like credit cards, offers for merchandise generally go unanswered, so that the money spent on printing goes right to the bottom, but this time not only to the bottom line but rather to the bottom of the discard bin. *How can a businessperson make her catalog offerings or promotions more successful?* Are there magic *"Open Sesame!"* words to tap into the minds of consumers? Are there different messages for different people?

RDE MEETS THE JEWELRY CATALOG

By now, the approach should be familiar: Create a set of silos or basic categories, and within each silo, develop simple messages. The silos for this RDE were Customer Perception, Emotional Benefits, Brand Recognition, Display Descriptors, Jewelry Descriptors, Customer Service, Inventory, Assurance, Value, and Promotions, with a total of 167 elements. The art of RDE in messaging is creating these elements. You can see examples of elements from these silos in Table 4.4 for text and in Figure 4.5 for visuals.

Table 4.4

Example of silos and elements for jewelry

Emotional Benefits
For celebrations that are truly special
This is the place I will come back to for my next jewelry purchase
I feel good when others notice the jewelry I am wearing
Brand Recognition
America's most trusted jewelers
Certified jewelry headquarters
Jewelry Descriptors
Diamonds, when nothing else will do
Classic jewelry with an on-trend look
Jewelry with a classic look

Figure 4.5 Representative visuals: These visuals stress more emotion and feeling, rather than product features. For product shots, the visuals attempt to give an overall sense instead of pointing out specific features.

Running an RDE evaluation with jewelry follows virtually the same choreography as running an RDE evaluation with credit cards. Only the topic and, of course, the participants differ. But the approach is the same. The participants were contacted from lists of customers and came into the site, where they looked at the different concepts on the computer screen, such as the concept shown in Figure 4.6. The rating scale was easy to use; the process was a lot of fun. The goal was not to sell the participant a piece of jewelry, as much as to discover what messaging would bring the customer into the store.

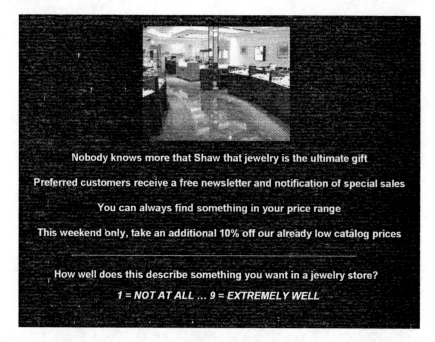

Figure 4.6 Example of a concept about a jewelry store (visual is representative). The concept presents messaging designed to drive a customer to visit a jewelry store rather than focusing on products.

The real "meat" of the RDE project for jewelry was to create messaging and sell more jewelry. In jewelry, as in credit cards, there are at least two radically different mind-sets. For the sake of our discussion, we call them Optimists (Segment 1) and Pessimists (Segment 2). You will see later how these mind-set segments are identified. In marketing, when we give names to segments, it helps fix in our minds something concrete about the segment.

The importance of RDE here is not simply to identify these two different mind-sets. Probably other methods might generate similar segments. Instead, Shaw's was interested in what *specific messaging* would drive purchase. That is, once we know the segments, we know what to say, how to say it, and to whom to say it.

You can see the radical differences between these segments in Figure 4.7 (best offer for the Optimist) and Figure 4.8 (best offer for the Pessimist).

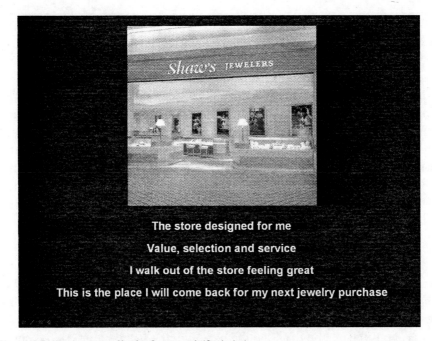

Figure 4.7 Jewelry store offer for Segment 1 (Optimist)

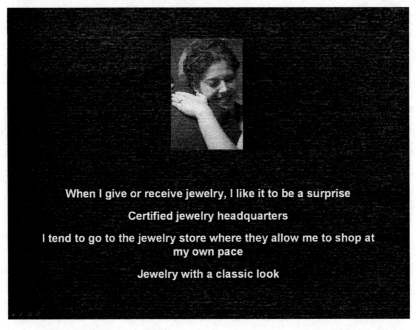

Figure 4.8 Offer for Segment 2 (Pessimist)

SO WHAT'S THE BOTTOM LINE? DID IT MATTER WHETHER THE MESSAGING WAS RIGHT?

Kay Jewelers put the results of the RDE to a stringent test. This validation of results followed a protocol that many direct marketers use. In many respects, it was very similar to the Unilever (Brazil) experience you read about in the Introduction. The first step in the protocol gathered additional information about the 169 participants. This was not very private information; most direct marketers have the information, including the number of people in the household, their ages, their sex, their income range, and the like. Such information is commonly available from companies and is considered public (whether we like it or not).

The second step created a "decision rule" or method by which to classify each participant as belonging to one of the two segments. It was important to develop this rule and validate it so that any new person could then be assigned to the most likely segment based on this decision rule. That is, if any new person were to come along, the decision rule would use this public information about the person to assign the person to the segment. Of course, such assignments are not perfect, but they are often far better than chance.

The third step created two mailing pieces, one optimized for the Optimists and the other optimized for the Pessimists.

The fourth step set up four target groups, two groups of so-called Optimists and two groups of so-called Pessimists:

- **10,000 Optimists** who received a brochure designed for **Optimists**
- **10,000 Optimists** who received a brochure designed for **Pessimists**
- **10,000 Pessimists** who received a brochure designed for **Optimists**
- **10,000 Pessimists** who received a brochure designed for **Pessimists**

The results of this controlled experiment dramatically validated the idea of RDE for messaging. Historically, the typical mailing generated about a 1% response rate (1 out of 100 people who got the mailing actually bought something) and an average purchase of $1,339. Sending the right brochure (the right creative) to the right segment dramatically increased the number of people buying (*42% improvement* for Optimists and *27% improvement* for Pessimists). Just as important, the sizes of the purchases *increased by several hundred dollars*. You see the happy results of this project in clear detail in Figure 4.9.

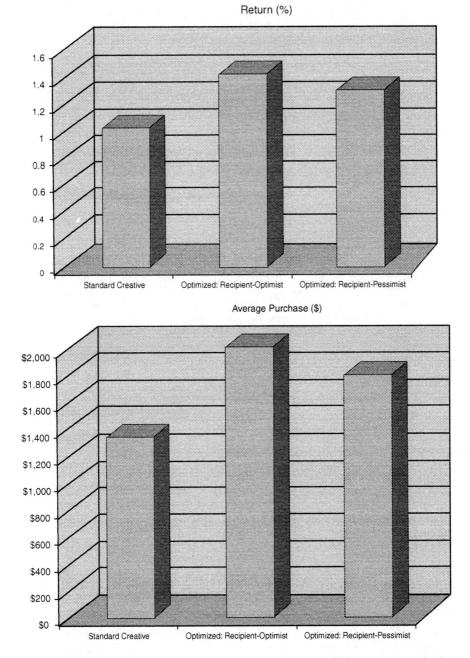

Figure 4.9 Results of the direct-mail experiment with jewelry, using RDE and segmentation into different mind-sets. The top graph shows the percentage of customers actually visiting a store after receiving a catalog. The bottom graph shows the average dollar amount of their purchase.

SUMMING UP: HOW RDE WORKS FOR MESSAGING

RDE applied to messaging identifies *what to say, how to say it, and to whom to say it.* In the communications industries, especially those in which creativity is prized, such as in advertising, one often hears that it is impossible to systematize the messaging, that messaging is an *artistic endeavor.* RDE in communication belies that emotion-filled argument. It could well be that developing specific phrases for communication is an art. However, *identifying what elements drive customer interest and maximize response is perfectly feasible using scientific methods.* It looks quite familiar by that time: Do your homework, create a lot of messages to test, don't be afraid to put in even crazy ideas, test all the messages using an experimental design with consumers—and the results may surprise you. Our example with credit cards shows that such experimentation can work quite well in the world of *homo economicus.* Our example with jewelry shows that such experimentation can work equally well in the world of emotions, where feelings are paramount.

In Chapter 2, Allison-the-Entrepreneur discovered how to create some winning products with the help from RDE, working with multiple prototypes of her innovative goods. Now, how is she to offer them to the customers? For obvious reasons, Allison-the-Entrepreneur could not possibly extend the individual passionate sales practices to a wide audience of consumers. This is not scalable. She considers offering her products using some type of media—perhaps through catalogs, for example, as in the case of jewelry. Another option is to mail postcards or e-mail invitations (much more affordable and massive), as in the case of credit cards. Even a more radical idea (possibly for later) is a co-branded credit card (say, which gives discounts at restaurants and stores). Allison should do her homework carefully to achieve good sales results. Allison cannot just assume that her only experience from reading the inspirational book can be extrapolated to every possible potential customer out there. Her customers do not even know they want this product. What Allison-the-Entrepreneur should do is *create a range of possible messages (offerings)—the more, the better—test them with a wide range of potential customers using the RDE approach, identify their mindsets, and create targeted optimized messages.* Essentially, this is very similar to her work done during the product-development stage, but applied to messages/offerings. It is that easy!

In the next chapter, you will see how this approach can be extended to cyberspace on the example of an ezine for teens. We deconstruct competitors' sites and see what works and what does not. (Yes, we're about to embark on a completely legal way to do commercial espionage! Sometimes this way, you learn more about your competitors than they know themselves.) Is there an opportunity for Allison-the-Entrepreneur as well?

ENDNOTES

[1] Alfa-Bank News Release, "Alfa-Bank and Aeroflot Programme Win the MasterCard 2006 European Co-Brand Partners of the Year Award," Moscow, Russia, 19 September 2006.

[2] Source: www.cardweb.com.

[3] Source: www.cia.gov.

[4] Source: www.cardweb.com.

[5] Groups of similar ideas (*elements* or *messages*), such as interest rates or logos. These groups are also called *bins* or *categories*.

[6] To make the respondents' jobs easier, RDE limits the number of silos in a concept. In this case study, it was five. In others, it might be a different number (three, four, or six, for example, depending on the specific RDE design).

[7] A large number of different designs is readily available.

[8] And/or in different order.

[9] C. Marketo, A. Gofman, H. R. Moskowitz, "A New Way to Estimate Interactions in Conjoint Analysis," Proceedings of 7th Sensomentrics Conference, Davis, CA, 2004.

[10] Up to the statistical limits. It is possible that a particular combination of elements is never repeated across a set of respondents.

[11] Tom Kelley, *The Art of Innovation: Lessons in Creativity from IDEO, America's Leading Design Firm* (Currency: NY, 2001).

[12] "Jewelry Sales Stay Even for 2002," *Professional Jeweler* (October 13, 2003); www.professionaljeweler.com/archives/news/2003/101303story.html.

[13] Daniel Farey-Jones, "U.S. Environmentalists Target Victoria's Secret over Catalogue Waste," *Brand Republic* (April 18, 2005); http://www.brandrepublic.com/login/index.cfm?fuseaction=Login&resource=BR_News&articleType=news&article=471049.

5

Discover More About Your Competitors Than They Themselves Know—Legally!

This chapter is not about "cloak-and-dagger, mission-impossible" type of commercial espionage, although the results might be much more exciting to the business professional. Let's change our *mis en scene* to the often-frenetic, generally frazzled content programming and marketing department of a Web-based broadcaster specializing in teen *ezines* (teen-based newsletters on the Internet). Unlike the scientists in the first chapters, there's no test tube in sight; the mere mention of statistical modeling makes the more creative of the group wince with pain, real or affected; and even in the most optimistic case, the deadline is always yesterday. Pain or no pain, technology-driven or artistically driven, its important to know what content and messaging works and what does not. And this time, it has to be done on "Internet time"—a.k.a., in no time at all (well, almost).

Before we go into a new application of RDE, let's try to clarify some terms. The term *ezine* is an *electronically* delivered *newsletter.* The idea of ezines might be straightforward enough in today's Internet-savvy, Google-enabled world, but getting to the origins of the word *ezine* itself is not that easy. At the time of this writing, that icon of the English language, *The*

Encyclopedia Britannica, did not even have an entry for "ezine." So how was the word *ezine* born? The most popular school of thought is that ezine' is short for the words *electronic* and *magazine*. Put them together, and you get *ezine*. Yet although this has become the almost universally accepted explanation, it is probably *not* actually true!

The real story is more interesting. First, an ezine is an electronic newsletter, *not* an electronic magazine. And, of course, the *z* that ostensibly comes from the word *magazine* doesn't even exist in the word *newsletter*. Here is a rival theory.[1] A *fanzine* was a publication with a small number of subscribers (perhaps from 5 to maybe 1,000). Fanzines were targeted publications geared toward specific interests, such as sci-fi, fantasy, and football clubs. They were frequently run by committed supporters. The ezine might obtain cult status, and the fans would contribute articles, usually in their nonprofessional, talkative, in-group style. Those printed publications were called fanzines but were frequently referred to as "zines" instead. Adding an *e* to the beginning brings us to the word *ezine,* and this offers us a much more logical explanation for the creation of this new word in the English language.

The proliferation of ezines has been dramatic. According to ezine and newsletter expert Michael Green, as of 2005, there were more than 500,000 different ezine titles vying for the consumer reader.

Whereas ezines were originally published in the fanzine tradition (enthusiasts writing about a subject they *love*), nowadays most ezines are published for *profit*. A renowned scholar in the field of ezines, Dr. Mani Sivasubramanian, points out, "An ezine is accepted to be the most effective online marketing tool, one with the highest return on investment. In simple terms, ezine marketing gives the biggest bang for your buck."[2]

EZINES AND COMPETITIVE INTELLIGENCE: WHAT WORKS FOR TEENS?

We now look at the set of steps that many companies use *to understand a competitive product category*—in this case, the teen ezine. The same structured approach, by the way, is used by car manufacturers to understand competitive advertising for automobiles, by computer companies to understand competition about the newest laptops, by food companies to understand what specific competitor messages about health foods really work to convince the resisting customer, and what messages are simply discarded as not being relevant.

The strategy of *deconstruction* is simple and quite straightforward. To deconstruct means to look at what everyone is doing, to discover what works and also what doesn't. A fast search on Google reveals many hundreds of different ezines and links to other similar material. It is quite simple to acquire many of the legitimately public pieces of information about the topic that competitors publish. The assiduous collector of such information might end up with hundreds of these screen shots, each with its own "look" and each with a series of different features and messaging. The question for the Internet publishing company is, "Which one of these different ideas works, and how well?" It's also important to keep in mind that the material put out by the different ezine publishers is their best guess. Looking at the competition means looking at what competitors *think* will work, rather than just wild guesses about what *might* work.

Realistically, what is so special about knowing what the competitor offers? After all, we cannot really control what the rival does. To those new to RDE, it seems that what the competitors are saying in their print advertisements is fixed, and we can learn whether the competitors are doing well or doing poorly only in the most general sense—sort of like an overall report card. These novices do not yet realize that by *deconstructing the competition, piece by piece, and systematically testing these ideas*, it is pretty easy to discover what the competition communicates well or poorly. To those new to the world of competitive intelligence, the very notion of learning from the competition beyond simply overall performance has not yet become part of their way of thinking. For them, experience with a systematic approach turns out to be a real eye-opener. Competitive intelligence thus gathers presumably good ideas, like a bee gathers nectar, from people who have already spent time and money putting forward ideas that they think teens will like. Why not use this rich source of information?

RDE goes beyond assembling the information. After collecting what competitors are doing, the next step discovers the "why" and the "how strong." RDE cuts these competitive Web sites into their components (called *content analysis of the ideas*) and then determines which of these component ideas really works. We don't really have to use the company's ideas; we could create our own from focus groups and invention sessions.

But the *goal here is not to create new ideas, but rather find out whether the competitors—and, indeed which specific competitor—actually got it right*. Often RDE surprises us with what it uncovers, occasionally quite pleasantly.

DISSECTING THE EZINE

The best way to approximate the RDE effort is to think of a large Excel-type file. Each row of the file contains one of the statements that a competitor ezine featured, edited down to be a reasonably short, single-minded idea. The editing cuts the complexity of the idea but remains true to the tonality of the language.

At the end of the exercise, the participants put together different messages or *elements* (36, in this case, but it could have been a much higher number, if needed). These deconstructed snippets of competitors comprised 30 text elements and 6 front pages (for the look). These elements presented a range of features and benefit statements, spanning the rational and the emotional aspects. Table 5.1 gives a sense of the richness that you can get just by doing the content analysis. However, the real "meat" comes in the RDE analysis, just ahead.

Table 5.1

Examples of different test-based messaging for teen ezines

Code	Silos/Elements	Ezine Source
Visuals		
A5	Home page screenshot of Teenvoices.com	Teenvoices.com
Trends/Style/Media		
B3	Give your opinion of the latest movies…music…video…	TeenInk.com
Features		
C1	…the hippest, hottest information from our editors…	YM.com
Fun/Play		
D4	Read all about the "lipslip"…Embarrassometer	React.com
Discussion/Chat		
E5	The hottest talk of teenagers on the Web	InSite ezine
Education/Career		
F3	Plan for a successful future	Studentcenter.org

One strategy might be to have teens rate these simple phrases and pictures of Web site front pages one at a time. Rating or ranking produces an *order of merit*, showing which ideas are best and which ideas are worst. A lot of marketers are satisfied with a rating/ranking exercise because they're looking simply at the "good vs. poor" ideas. If that is all, then the exercise solves the momentary problem, and the business moves on. But if the goal is to construct new ezines, identify segments, and *develop rules* for these new offerings, then the one-at-a-time effort is deceptive—it just can't do the job. The reason is simple. Participants answering questionnaires are almost always prodded to be rational and consistent when they answer. When you ask them to compare two very different ideas, they might or might not have an easy time. Here are two examples of ideas that call for the teen to self-express:

Experiment with your look...check out our digital makeover demo.

versus

Everything you need to move yourself to college.

The decision about which is the more interesting comes fairly quickly. Now let's try to compare the messages with a content element, where the idea is a well-known performer or personality:

Indigo Girls, Shanice, and more.

So which element is better, "Experiment with your look...check out our digital makeover demo" or "Indigo Girls, Shanice, and more"? Give this comparison to a teenager—or, in fact, to anyone—and the odds are that they will look at you as if you are crazy. The question does not make sense. Yet each of these different ideas, self-expression vs. teen idol, has its own utility, its own impact. It is simply hard to compare them *directly* when asked to. If you ask to rate all three, it is likely that most teens will comply but will not understand—or, at least, will not tell you the criteria that they used.

The same comparability problem haunts us in the simplest situations, such as understanding the relative impact of price, brand, and benefits in a deconstructed set of ideas. Typically, consumers will pick the lower price as being more desirable, although there are a number of occasions when the price communicates quality, so that participant picks the higher price. Participants can choose between two messages about product features, sometimes being aware of why they chose one over the other, and sometimes not being aware.

However, when you start testing prices, product features, brand names, and even pictures in a sequential list comprising examples of each of them in some randomized order, you will quickly discover that most of your willing participants certainly have a very hard time choosing between a product feature and a brand name. Consumer participants and also seasoned professionals might be good at some things, but they need to focus on lists of similar elements to feel comfortable ranking ideas.

The key to success in RDE is to give the consumer participant a meaningful stimulus and get their "gut feel" reaction, not an intellectualized response, the same way they react to real-life advertisements, and so on. There is absolutely no reason for the consumer participant to dissect his feelings and identify what part of the product or communication is working for him. Odds are, he will not know, or he might get it wrong. Nonetheless, his intuitive feeling for the entire product or communication is usually quite correct and reliable because that is what a person does all day long. People respond to combinations, not to components.

Let's follow the project from start to finish. We have already been through the deconstruction part of the exercise and saw how to gather information. Now we join the project in midstream as the project director takes this information from raw "idealets" (our own word), or little ideas gleaned from the competition, and proceeds all the way to the interview, analysis, and beyond.

> **NOTE**
> Don't be discouraged by a bit more mathematical references in some of the following steps. The good news is that the process can be easily automated (and already has been) with available, easy-to-use Web tools,[3] as we will show later in this chapter.

STEP 1: GATHER AND CATEGORIZE THE MATERIAL INTO SILOS

A. This exercise generates lots of competitive material, often a lot more than one would have guessed. Woody Allen has been attributed as saying "Success is 80% showing up." Success in RDE deconstruction of the competitive frame is 80% getting the right raw materials in the first place.

B. Define *silos or buckets* of related ideas (a.k.a. categories, such as price, service, and merchandising), and then put the different elements into these silos. The idea of silos and elements is really for bookkeeping purposes. The consumer participant will never even realize that these silos exist.

C. Edit the raw material so that the ideas within each of the silos differ from each other and make sense to a reader. Consumers are not analytical machines that respond simply to the content of messages; feelings are very important. All too often, deconstruction boils down the ideas into a bit of bone and flesh, with no real feeling. *Avoid that at all cost, or you will discover little that is not already obvious.*

STEP 2: CHOOSE AN RDE DESIGN (MIX AND MATCH ELEMENTS)[4]

You can find experimental designs in many textbooks or built-in in tools. In most cases, you do not need to understand the statistical details of the design, beyond the number of silos and elements in each. For those who still insist on seeing what is hidden under the hood, see the "Tech Talk" sidebar later in this chapter.

STEP 3: COLLECT RESPONDENTS' RATINGS

A. Invite the participants (for example, by e-mail). The best way to get interested participants is to offer a reasonable reward and make the study interesting. You do not have to pay each participant, but it is a good idea to seed the invitation letter with a fair chance to win some prize.

B. Begin the interview with a simple, engaging description of what the project is about. Experienced experimenters know that a participant who does not care or does not know what he is doing often provides incorrect and occasionally misleading results. A good thing to do at the start of the interview is to thank the participant and describe the project in simple terms. With RDE, the participant need only read the concept and rate it in its entirety.

C. Execute the interview on the Internet. The RDE tool creates each combination as prescribed by the design, presents that combination to the participant, and acquires the data. Each participant evaluates 48 different combinations (in the ezines case). The process is fast and fun (see the sample combinations in Figure 5.1).

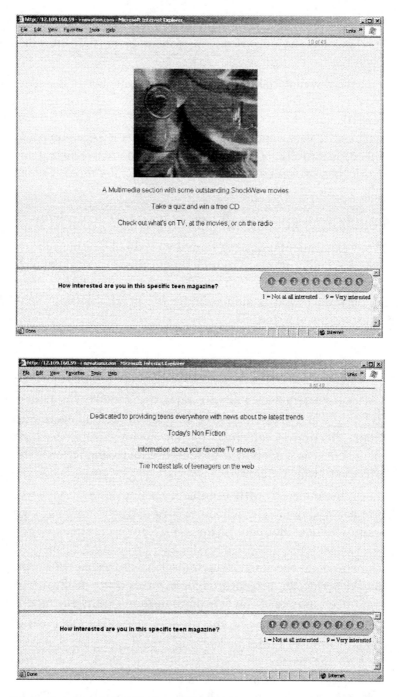

Figure 5.1 Two test concepts from the teen ezine project

D. Find out more about the participant in the same interview. At
the end of the RDE evaluation of concepts, the participants
answered a set of additional questions about themselves and
their attitudes toward ezines. *Linking the mind and the "who"
creates stronger communications and better ideas, sent to the
right people.* Note that a conventional consumer researcher
would obtain answers to *only* these types of questions about
ezine reader. Conventional research tells us all about how the
participant describes himself; RDE tells us all about how the
participant responds to the idea or the product, what is important, and what combinations really pique interest. Right here,
we see the dramatic differences between *describing oneself*
and *reacting to stimuli*, with the goal of developing "rules"
about the mind.

STEP 4: ANALYZE THE DATA

First, RDE creates a large set of data,[5] so we need not live with the simple,
not particularly insightful results of what is typically called a beauty
contest—"Which of these two concepts is better?" The Internet application and the Web server did all the heavy lifting, presenting the concepts
or vignettes, getting the answers (ratings), and, as you will see shortly,
doing the analysis automatically.

TECH TALK

The fact that you are reading this section suggests you prefer to know what
you drive. Here's a quick glimpse under the hood of conjoint analysis; it is
less intimidating than you might think.

Conjoint analysis is a statistical method rooted in mathematical psychology
and developed into a real-life marketing technique by the Wharton School
of the University of Pennsylvania. On a statistical level, RDE utilizes conjoint
analysis methods, although in a modified way. Later we review the approach
on a bit more technical level than the rest of the book.

We have a general idea about experimental design (a component of conjoint
analysis) from Chapter 4, "How to Make People Feel Good Even When They

Pay More" (see Table 4.2). The details of the design can be also summarized pretty simply.

Let's look at the data as a large spreadsheet file. Each row of the spreadsheet corresponds to one of the test concepts. We had 386 different experimental designs (one for each of our 386 teens). Each of those 386 designs comprises 48 test concepts. This means that we have a very large data set of 386 × 48, or 18,528 rows of data. Don't worry about entering all the data manually; everything is done automatically if you are using a program such as IdeaMap.NET, which we used to collect the data.

Each row has columns corresponding to the elements (36 of these columns, corresponding to the 36 elements that we tested in the project). You can follow along and look at Table 5.2, which shows a few of the 18,528 rows of data:

1. If the element appears in the concept, let's put in a 1 in the corresponding column.

2. If the element does not appear in the concept, let's put in a 0.

3. You will see a lot of 0s because most of the elements don't appear in a concept, but you'll see a few 1s, corresponding to elements that do appear.

4. The next column is a rating for the concept, showing how interested the participant was in the concept. This rating goes from 1 (not interested) to 9 (very interested).

5. Finally, let's do one transformation, changing ratings 1–7 to 0, and changing ratings 7–9 to 100. The reason for this change from the rating to a binary value (0 or 100) comes from the way people like to interpret the data. Although our teens rated degree of interest on a scale, we're really interested in whether the teen actually liked the idea (rating it 7–9) or whether the teen disliked the idea (rating it 1–6). The value of 100 also helps us to interpret the "output" of the regression analysis as a percentage of respondents. You'll see this interpretation later in this chapter. These new interest values appear in the column Rating in Table 5.2.

6. Now the matrix is ready for a very straightforward analysis, using the method of regression.[6] Regression analysis, a very popular and widely available statistical tool, relates independent variables (elements) to a dependent variable (rating). What we really try to

do here is relate the presence/absence of each of the 36 elements in our teen ezine test concepts to the participant's rating of not interested/interested (0 or 100, respectively).

7. The numbers that come out of this regression analysis show the odds or so-called *conditional probability* that a person will find the concept interesting.

Table 5.2

What the experimental design and some data look like: partial data.

Concept	Silo A						Silo B							Silo D						Rating	
	1	2	3	4	5	6	1	2	3	4	5	6		1	2	3	4	5	6	1 - 9	0 - 100
1	0	0	0	0	1	0	0	0	0	0	1	0	...	0	0	0	0	0	1	4	0
2	0	1	0	0	0	0	0	0	0	0	1	0	...	0	0	0	1	0	0	6	0
5	1	0	0	0	0	0	0	0	0	0	0	0	...	0	0	1	0	0	0	8	100
6	0	0	0	0	1	0	1	0	0	0	0	0	...	0	0	1	0	0	0	7	100
13	0	0	0	0	1	0	0	0	0	0	1	0	...	0	0	0	0	0	0	3	0
21	1	0	0	0	0	0	0	0	0	0	0	0	...	0	0	0	1	0	0	2	0
22	0	0	0	1	0	0	0	0	0	0	0	0	...	0	0	0	0	0	1	7	100
23	0	0	0	0	0	0	0	0	0	1	0	0	...	0	0	0	0	0	0	6	0
25	0	0	0	1	0	0	0	0	0	0	0	0	...	0	0	0	0	1	0	3	0
26	0	0	0	0	0	0	1	0	0	0	0	0	...	0	1	0	0	0	0	9	100
47	0	0	0	0	0	0	0	0	1	0	0	0	...	1	0	0	0	0	0	3	0
48	0	0	0	0	0	0	0	0	0	0	1	0	...	0	0	0	0	0	0	5	0

SO JUST WHAT DID RDE REVEAL ABOUT HOW TEENS THINK?

Let's follow the folks who are looking at the results. The ratings have been collected, the regression analysis run for each person, and the results tabulated. Now we jump into the data, just as the marketer, ad agency, or media planner might do.

The first number that emerges from the analysis is the *additive constant*, the conditional probability of a teen being interested in the ezine if there are no elements in the concept. This additive constant tells us how interested our teens really are in their ezines. The constant is a paltry 25; *without any additional information*, only about 25% would say that they are interested in ezines. We have already learned something important: The basic ezine idea needs more to snag a teen's interest. By the way, the additive constant comes out from the regression modeling. We don't need to have the teens tell us their general feeling; it will all come out from analyzing the relation between their rating and the elements or idealets that are put into the project.

RDE slices and dices the data from our 386 teens, using criteria based on the self-profiling classification questionnaire, or how teens describe themselves. For each groups of teens, we develop the RDE model showing the additive constant (baseline) and the part-worth contribution of each of the 36 elements. *Almost any way that we slice the data, we find that the general idea of ezines is not particularly interesting by itself.* It is the *content* that makes a difference.

The regression analysis produces a number for each of the 36 elements. The number (actually, coefficient, in the regression model, which is frequently referred to as a *utility value*) shows the *conditional probability or odds of the particular element driving interest*. In other words, the number approximates the incremental (positive values) or decremental (negative values) percentage points change in the number of interested teens. We look at only the highest-scoring elements—that is, those with the greatest utility or impact—so that putting them into a concept or a Web site really increases the number of teens who say that they are interested. This is the "gold" of RDE—what specifically to do to win (see Table 5.3).

The first finding is that the range of utilities is very narrow. The best-performing element generates only 6% of additional teens interested in the idea—pretty paltry. In fact, none of the elements really do well at all. The ezine should have utilities of +10 or more, meaning that if the element were put into a concept, an additional 10% or more of the teens would say that they are interested in the ezine. *This mediocre performance could either be because the teen ezines just missed the boat or perhaps because our teen participants fall into groups with different mind-sets that cancel each other.* What we might see, perhaps, are two or more groups who are very different from each other, even if they look the same from their self-defined profiles.

Table 5.3

The best winning elements for the total group of 386 teens

Ezine elements	
Take a quiz and win a free CD	6
Understand yourself	6
A Multimedia section with some outstanding ShockWave movies	6
Get a guy's perspective on your boy woes	5
Check out what's on TV, at the movies, or on the radio	5
Take our Techie Trivia Test	5
Find jobs that match your personality and interests	5

A natural question is, just how good is a +6? Is this a good score or a poor score? Table 5.4 gives a sort of rule of thumb. The ranges are not fixed and the descriptions are approximate, but you can get a general idea of where important elements begin.

Table 5.4

How to interpret utility values (when actual ratings have been converted to 0–100 ratings)[7]

Utility Value Range	Interpretation
15 and above	Superb! High interest.
10–15	Very good.
5–10	OK, adds something.
0–5	Why is it here? It does not do much— you can drop it.
Below 0	Bad. Detracts from interest. You want to avoid this, if you can.

The second finding is that there are very few negative performers. It is worth mentioning here that, in our experience in deconstructing such commercial materials, whether ezines or advertisements, we very rarely happen upon negative performers. *Businesses almost always screen out the obviously bad ideas.* However, at the same time, we also don't come across very many high performers, probably because the same screening effort that removes bad ideas gravitates toward the middle, truly pleasing no one.

The third and most interesting finding comes from looking at how well the different ezines perform. Do any of the ezines "get it," with consistently high utility values? Conversely, do any of the ezines simply miss time after time, so they have utilities close to 0? Looking at Figure 5.2, where each circle corresponds to an element taken from that particular ezine on the left (ordinate), we ought to be struck by the fact that most of the ezines are in the middle. No ezine does consistently well or above average.

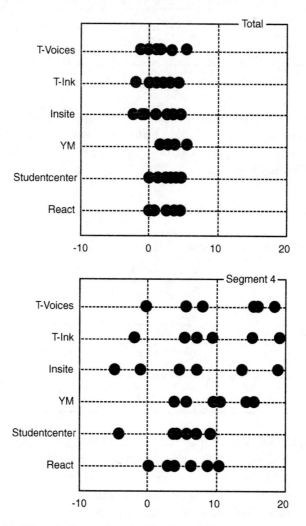

Figure 5.2 How the different ezines perform for Total Panel (top) and for a more targeted audience (Segment 4, bottom—see later in the chapter). Each circle corresponds to an element with the utility values that came from the regression model.

IF EVERYTHING IS MEDIOCRE, MAYBE WE CAN DISCOVER DIFFERENT MIND-SETS

It looks like the teens really do not care about what is in the ezines. Can this be true? If the basic interest level (the additive constant) is only 25%, and if none of the elements does much beyond an additional 6%, then what are we to make of the proliferating ezine and, in general, Web-based communications? Has everyone missed the boat?

That is pretty unlikely. We need to *divide the teens by the patterns of what they like.* When we cluster the teens by their utility patterns, we come up with four different groups or segments (as we have mentioned before, the process of segmentation is automatically done by the RDE tool, so the segments are automatically discovered when they exist). We do not know exactly what these segments are from our statistical work. Rather, we look at these groups discovered for us automatically and then see which particular elements float to the top—that is, which particular elements do well.[8] *Those "winning ideas or elements" define what the segment is all about.*

Presumably, these mind-sets are more homogeneous, meaning that *inside a segment, teens are generally thinking the same and reacting the same because they have the same mind-set.* We could look at each of the four different discovered segments—this is what we might do if we were in the ezine business. We don't need to go into details. Just look again at Figure 5.2 (second panel, for Segment #4). Suffice to say that it is very enlightening and somewhat unexpected to see utilities skyrocket to well above +20 for this large segment of teens that can be best labeled "I want to talk and express myself."

SUMMING UP: NOW THAT WE KNOW WHO THEY ARE AND WHAT THEY LIKE, HOW DO WE PROCEED?

The objectives going into the RDE exercise were to use the competitor ezines to identify what works and what does not. The ezine publisher was quite successful—*simply knowing what the competitor was actually saying made clear what messages worked and among whom.* But RDE teaches a great deal more. We discovered some dynamics of the ezine market, ranging from basic interest in the ezines (not much, by anyone), and what types of mind-sets exist (there are four of them, corresponding to our four segments), and, finally, a competitive analysis of who is saying the right thing and who is not. A single RDE project gave information almost overnight, and with the material that the competitor ezines were kind enough to provide in their publicly accessible Web sites!

By knowing the full range of what the competitors feature in their communications, both specifics and in terms of language, RDE can put companies on the verge of competitive intelligence that goes beyond information gathering to pattern recognition, and even to "prescription." We now know what the ezines are saying, but if we wanted to, we would also be able *to synthesize the contents* of a new ezine to appeal to each of the segments. RDE allows you *to create with the knowledge rather than just to know with the knowledge.*

Let's now go back to our Allison-the-Entrepreneur and see whether she is an iota closer to her business objectives, having studied diligently the content of this chapter.

It is a truism to say that it is not enough to invent a great product—you have to *sell* it. Allison-the-Entrepreneur does not project (yet) an image of a seasoned marketing guru. She is about to face competition from a plethora of eBay-generation street- and Web-smart entrepreneurs who have probably already *established* themselves in the marketplace, even if it is with some potentially inferior products. They might even have managed to proliferate across cyberspace through an ever-growing number of ezines and other means of communication. Allison can see their Web sites and newsletters, their messages and graphics, but she does not know which ones work and which ones do not. She simply does not know where to start, and she does not have the time and resources to repeat all the steps her competitors followed and learn from mistakes that they made.

What does she do? Allison does not shy away from the challenge. Armed with the guidance from this chapter, she *deconstructs* the messages, ideas, and graphics from the competitors' sites and adds a couple of her own. Indeed, she is quite inventive, as we know. Then she puts them into a ready-to-use *experimental design* through a commercially available Web-based tool. Virtually anybody can easily use the tool without consulting a statistics book (which, by the way, she does not have in her possession since that less than pleasurable test back in the university). After that,

Allison invites her target respondents for a *short survey* on the Web via an e-mail invitation, Web-intercept, or recruiting from a panel. In just a few hours, or perhaps a day, she gets enough respondents to complete the survey, and the system *automatically* generates actionable results by showing what works and what does not, who did it right, and what are the customers' mind-sets and attitudinal segments for the most efficient targeting and the highest returns.

The beauty of RDE for competitive intelligence is *simplicity, affordability, speed of knowledge-building, and immediate actionability of results.* Allison does not even need focus groups; she just has to deconstruct the competitors' sites. She does not have to worry about Web servers and IT departments; all she needs is a PC with an Internet connection. The highly sophisticated servers of the tool provider handle the rest, including the experimental design, data collection, regressions, analysis, segmentation, and more. In general, the cost compares quite favorably to the popular focus group, which she does not need after all. RDE might take just a few hours or a day to complete. The business benefit: Allison gets to discover the different mind-sets of her potential customers, which she might never ascertain by other methods.

Not bad for a funds-strapped entrepreneur with just a laptop! So for all the people who feel intimidated and overwhelmed by aggressive competitive advertisement, for those who do not know where to start, who keep asking themselves while tossing and turning in the middle of sleepless nights:

Would I? ... Could I? ....

here is an answer:

Try them! Try them![9]
And you may.

ENDNOTES

[1] Sources: Michael Green, "From 'Fanzine' to 'Ezine': A Brief History of Ezines." How To Corporation, 2005. www.easyezinetoolkit.com/articles/briefhistoryofezines.html.

[2] Mani Sivasubramanian, "How to Publish the Perfect Ezine," In *The Ezine Masters*, Ed. Dr. Mani Sivasubramanian (MediKnow Publishing Company: Madras, India, 2002).

[3]   For example, IdeaMap.NET, a completely hosted do-it-yourself tool for message optimization online. We describe it later in the book. In fact, all the screen shots in this chapter were made using a variation of the IdeaMap.NET tool. Also, as a registered reader of Prentice Hall, you will have an opportunity to "test-drive" the tool yourself.

[4]   As we have mentioned already, all the math and complexity of the step is hidden inside tools such as IdeaMap.NET.

[5]   The total number of concepts that our teens tested is: (48 concepts per respondent) × (386 respondents) = 18,528 concepts. Some of the concepts might repeat; it depends on the size and structure of the design and the number of respondents.

[6]   P. E. Green and V. A. Srinivasan, "A General Approach to Product Design Optimization via Conjoint Analysis," *Journal of Marketing* 45 (1981: 17–37).

[7]   The utility values in Table 5.4 are relevant when interest ratings are converted to the 0–100 scale. For example, if the respondents used numbers between 1 and 9 to rate their interest, they have to be converted as the following: Ratings 1–6 are converted to 0, and ratings 7–9 are converted to 100. In the case of a 1–5 rating scale, ratings 1–3 are converted to 0, ratings 4–5 are converted to 100, etc. See the previous sidebar.

[8]   P. E. Green and A. M. Krieger, "Segmenting Markets with Conjoint Analysis," *Journal of Marketing* 55 (1991: 20–31).

[9]   Dr. Seuss, *Green Eggs and Ham* (Random House: New York, 1976).

PART II

Making the Future

The Genie was out of the bottle. With RDE's proven record of making fortunes for many astute companies, it's no wonder there's an ongoing development to push the limits and expand the use of this approach to new areas. Read here how RDE drives innovation and creates better packages and magazine covers, pushing opportunity at every corner.

6

Rubik's Cube of Consumer Electronics Innovation

On a recent trip along the New York–Miami route, while skimming through *AmericanWay* magazine, one of the authors (AG) discovered a couple of short but interesting articles that revealed once again that stream of continuing innovation that creates that hypercompetition so dreaded by companies and countries alike.[1]

First article:

"Listening Power"

At last count, there were 2,345 types of miniheadphones and ear buds for movable music players, but Sennheiser's three iPod companions really sing out in a crowd. The PX100 ($60) offers eerily good sound reproduction with deep bass tones that were, well, unheard of a few years back. Ditto the PX200 ($70, shown), with a closed-back design that cuts down on music bleed. The lower-end MX500 ($20) doesn't bring quite the same thumping depth, but you gotta love its striking metallic-blue finish and in-line volume control. www.sennheiserusa.com

—Chris Tucker

Second article:

"Big Return on Small Investment"

The Nokia 770 Internet Tablet occupies the middle ground—smaller than a laptop, bigger than a cell phone—in the increasingly crowded web-on-the-go space. Based on the open-source software Linux, the Wi-Fi-enabled 770 sports a dazzling high-res screen for viewing photos and websites, and delivers Internet radio and RSS feeds, so you can get frequent updates from your favorite blogs. $350. www.nokiausa.com/770

—C. T.

If the avid music lover wants to test every available mini-headphone for just a minute each, it would take him more than 40 hours, or 1 workweek, to do so. And this is for the mini-headphones category alone! The sheer volume of competitor offerings astounds us more and more. How can a corporation create new products that really stand out in this overcrowded market? Is there help around?

An enormous amount of research goes into the area of new product development. Whole volumes and comprehensive issues of magazines are dedicated to this topic. And the opportunities are still endless. Beyond the products and services themselves, there has sprung an entire academic discipline focusing on innovation—what it is, how to foster it, how to tame it, how to benefit from it, and the list goes on and on.

What does one need to succeed in developing and selling, for example, consumer electronics? Is it a designer who *feels* the pulse of the crowd (as in the case of iPod), an aggressive marketer (as in Microsoft), a no-nonsense advertising guru, or all of the above? Perhaps the real business lies in inventing new products by combining features from others, as in the Nokia device described earlier? Of course, if invention is really recombination, the features ought to be complementary so that the mix makes sense. That's a lot of questions to answer, but the answer can be more positive, more available, and more achievable than one might think.

Let's look more closely at the RDE-based *combinatorial approach* to R&D and see the opportunity for Allison-the-Entrepreneur—and, indeed, for the rest of us. The results of this systematic exercise could well be new product ideas in shorter time. At this point, the Doubting Thomas, jumping ahead to where this approach to invention might be going, might well exclaim in distress that this notion of innovation by combination by itself is simply too mechanical, too soulless, too automatic, and, therefore, is certainly not related to the magic of creativity. Such complaints are not really founded. Michael Vance, a well-known American creativity expert, lecturer, and Dean of Disney University, once said, "Innovation is the creation of the new or the rearranging of the old in a new way."[2]

We share General Manager of IDEO Tom Kelley's belief in the "cheaper, faster, simpler approach."[3] If you have the luxury to spend months and months on research to observe your customers and at the end come up with a "perfect" product, you are lucky, but you occupy a rather unusual position in today's market. Your competition might not be willing to wait that long and might grab the market share before you. Remember the runaway success of Microsoft Windows 3.0 (followed by 3.1) released shortly before OS/2 2.0? The latter system, OS/2 2.0, was superior to Gate's creation in many aspects, but at the end it sadly failed. One can argue that there were many reasons for this failure.[4] Let's see the role of one of the aspects—*the timing*—in the success and failure.

In the mid-1980s, IDEO was working on a Dynabook laptop—one of its sleekest portable designs, a black cast-magnesium computer with a look well ahead of its time. Some of the most successful visionary people of the time believed that the design would be a winner. Among them was Tom Kelley himself, along with major venture capitalists known for a stellar record of sensing "what is right." One thing that neither Dynabook planned for nor supporters could anticipate was that Intel was soon to offer the market its new processor chip, Intel 386. So when Dynabook finally introduced its gem of design built around an old Intel 286 processor, they realized that *all the good looks and well-integrated features in the world couldn't make an old technology successful.*[5] Timing was everything.

As we saw in previous chapters, the RDE process embraces and nurtures speed. Can the whole approach be made even more democratic, faster, and easier so that anyone, anywhere in the world can use RDE to understand the mind of the consumer virtually overnight or, say, within 24 hours?

With today's increasingly sophisticated (and more simple for users at the same time) technologies available, and with the extraordinary penetration of the Internet worldwide, the answer to streamlining RDE is a resounding "Yes."[6] Let's see how—and, just as important, let's see why.

RDE AT THE HEART OF A STREAMLINED, COMBINATORIAL APPROACH TO R&D

An easy way to understand streamlined development is to imagine a scenario and then work back to what is needed for that scenario to happen. Our scenario focuses on a new start-up company in Asia. The company, Abacus (real name as well as the product name, Gamester, are disguised), is in the business of creating, commercializing, and selling off new consumer electronics products. Abacus's management, all under 30 years old, each one filled with the enthusiasm of visionary youthfulness, has very little money—indeed, almost none. However, all four Abacus professionals are so-called Internet geeks, people who have grown up with computers and who find the Internet more a way of life than a technology. Before coming together to form Abacus, the management group had worked in different companies, programming, creating Web sites, selling computer software, and playing an almost uncountable number of computer games.

To understand *what* to create, it was important for Abacus to measure how consumers would respond to new ideas about consumer electronics. After some initial market research into their own business world, these young entrepreneurs soon discovered that the majority of inventive efforts they discovered followed a more or less consistent pattern: scan the environment for ideas, bring new ideas to consumers in focus groups around the world, and then create prototypes. Engineers were in charge here, so the approach was *develop, measure, launch.*

Perhaps there was a better way. The ingoing vision was that perhaps through the Internet and through a technique such as RDE, they could synthesize new ideas for consumer electronics. But how? What was the secret?

It first became clear that the *conventional ways to create ideas were too slow.* Tracking competition worked, and the market research professionals around the world certainly provided large reports that detailed what people were doing. There were rooms filled with reports in company after company—or at least cabinets, for companies that were less retentive. Focus groups could be easily arranged for a new product idea, but it was very expensive to run them, and, quite often, the groups did not lead to much more than confirmation of known ideas.[7]

Yet scanning the Internet revealed repeatedly that people were indeed inventing new products and services for consumer electronics at an alarming pace. It was clear from browsing sites such as CNET that the pace was accelerating, that one new product might appear and, just when that product was accepted, a host of competitor products then appeared, proclaiming one improvement after another. Figure 6.1, for example, shows just one of several e-mail letters sent out weekly by CNET. Multiply this by 10 or 20, and you get a sense of the intense, almost Darwinian struggle for survival in consumer electronics. Virtually all the hit products on the list are multifunctional. Just a few years (or maybe even months) ago this type of combination would belong to a science fiction world or be downright unimaginable.

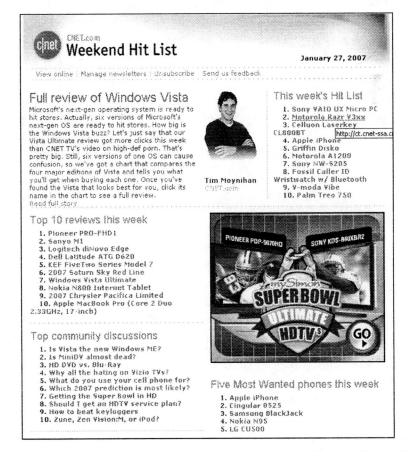

Figure 6.1 Example of an Internet e-mail from CNET presenting the week's latest offerings in consumer electronics

STREAMLINING ABACUS'S INVENTION PROCESS THROUGH RDE TO MEET THE CHALLENGES

Following the Abacus story, let's look at how they restructured the invention process to make it simpler, faster, and inexpensive. The adaptation can be summarized in the following three principles:

- **Principal 1: Democratize**—The RDE method has to be based on an Internet tool that can be used anywhere, anytime, by anyone—even by someone with minimal experience.

- **Principal 2: Think *genomically***—Let RDE identify winning ideas from many different consumer electronics products and, by so doing, create a "database of the consumer mind" for electronics. At the same time, let the RDE experience generate other ideas so that the consumer participant becomes an *active co-creator*, not just a passive judge.

- **Principal 3: Think innovation as recombination**—After identifying the winning ideas in separate, small, and easily run RDE studies, combine these winning ideas into a set of new-to-the-world product concepts, and test them in a final RDE study.

FROM STRATEGY TO SPECIFICS: HOW ABACUS DID IT

Before we go into the nitty-gritty of the process, is this RDE tool appropriate and relevant for *designers and engineers*? Maybe it is designed only for the marketers? Here is a short answer (although we go into more details in Chapter 7, "Bridging Cool Design with Hot Science," when we deal with graphical design and RDE) describing an experience of a design firm:

> Ford & Earl is a design company based in Troy, Michigan, specializing in brand building. Consumer Insight Manager Renee Cameron has put hundreds of surveys through IdeaMap.Net. "The appealing thing about this method is that, for the price of one focus group and in less time, you can have quantitative data. That's appealing from the cost and time standpoint. But even more appealing is the integrity of the methodology."[8]

And what about engineers? We saw the process in Chapter 1, "Hewlett-Packard Shifts Gears," describing the experiences of Hewlett-Packard. So the process appeals to both the technical and the artistic, to the engineer and the designer, as well as to the marketer. Indeed, as Jeff Ewald, Renee Cameron's colleague and president of the Optimization Group, Inc., has so aptly put it when describing RDE and the Hewlett-Packard experience, "We now do six months' work in two weeks—and we know specifically what to recommend to our Hewlett-Packard customers."

Now we can follow the next steps to "invent" a new product. In essence, think of development in terms of combining components, and then create those components yourself. The computer technology will do all the heavy work, from mixing and matching ideas to acquiring data, to automatically analyzing and reporting. These steps are a variation of the general RDE process we described in the Introduction.

STEP 1: CREATE (CHOOSE) A GENERAL STRUCTURE OF SILOS THAT APPLIES TO THE DIFFERENT PRODUCT AREAS

This structure lets Abacus mix and match ideas of similar types on the computer. For product development in consumer electronics, the structure appears very much like what we see in Table 6.1.

Table 6.1

Basic structure in which to embed ideas for consumer electronics

Silo (Category)	Content
Silo A	What is it? What does it do?
Silo B	Who or what is it for?
Silo C	Ease of use
Silo D	Features
Silo E	Accessories
Silo F	Where do you find it? How do you shop for it?

STEP 2: SELECT COMPONENT IDEAS TO "MASH TOGETHER" IN THE GENOMICS-INSPIRED SYSTEM

Abacus took elements from three different consumer electronic products and "mashed them together" to create their new-to-the-world idea. Table 6.2 shows some of these different ideas.[9] Of course, they did some preliminary work to identify which ideas seemed to make sense, but only after mashing them together did Abacus discover how correct their guesses were. But the truth of the matter is that being right on the first iteration was not really important because the RDE approach allowed them to return with other, newer, and different ideas as well, very quickly after discovering what ideas worked.

Table 6.2

List of ideas for Silo 1 ("What does it do") from three consumer product categories. Abacus selected the shaded ideas to appear in the mashed concepts.

Tablet PC	Portable DVD	Portable Games	New Features—Tablet DVD Gamester
A successful combination of notebook performance and tablet functionality	A 7-inch-wide-screen portable DVD player lets you take the show on the road	Elevates portable gaming to the next level with its multimedia functionality	**A successful combination of tablet PC with DVD player performance and portable game functionality**
PDA-sized PC with laptop-caliber power	A portable DVD player with a 10-inch LCD screen turns tiresome travel time into fun time	A slick multimedia portable gaming device that includes Palm, video, and MP3 capabilities all in one	**A portable "Tablet DVD Gamester" with a 10-inch LCD screen...turns tiresome travel time into fun time**
A fully equipped PC that can fit right in your pocket	A multiformat portable DVD player with 3D Virtual Surround Sound	An all-in-one portable entertainment unit... games, music, and so much more	**An all-in-one portable entertainment unit games, music, and so much more**

STEP 3: INVITE POTENTIAL CUSTOMERS TO LOG INTO A WEB SITE TO PARTICIPATE

This is essentially the same process as in previous examples—done by e-mail invitation to a panel of respondents.

STEP 4: CREATE (AUTOMATICALLY) AND TEST NEW PRODUCT IDEAS WITH CONSUMERS (FIELDING)

The participants rate one concept after another, pretty rapidly, probably without paying much attention, giving their "gut feeling" about the ideas. Participants do not know and certainly would not care that the ideas in these concepts are mashed together from three different products in a genomics-inspired way. In fact, if participants were to know this, they would probably forget that piece of information in a moment, if they ever thought of it at all after reading. Many participants in any of these Internet surveys are not particularly attentive, do not read every word, and, in fact, simply respond like anyone else responds—at an intuitive or "gut" level, as most of us do when we see an ad or an offer. We are lucky when the participant pays a modest amount of attention. We cannot hope for much more. *The strength of RDE is that it works because the experimental design reveals what is important to the participant, whether the participant is even aware of the reasons for his choices.*

The *incompleteness* of the test concepts for Gamester is worth a note here because it lies at the root of why RDE is so powerful in designing new products and messages. The Abacus project created an "idealet reservoir" comprising six silos and six elements each.[10] The intuitive but ultimately *incorrect* approach would require Abacus to test *complete concepts* for the Gamester. These complete concepts would contain one element from each of the six silos. The *incorrect and ultimately failure-producing belief* would be that only in this way with complete concepts would study participants get the correct idea of any product. Indeed, many traditional methods of concept development use this logic of complete test concepts.[11]

RDE does not follow this paradigm, and for a very good reason. RDE measures the absolute value or contribution of each of the items for each of the participants, on a person-to-person basis. The only way to get these absolute values, to database them for learning, rules, and trends, uses what statisticians call an "incomplete design." Some of the test concepts must, by design, lack silos. The specific arrangement of these concepts in the incomplete design is not relevant here; textbooks and computer programs can create those for you.[12] Just keep in mind that, with an incomplete design, the data can be analyzed by statistical methods such as regression, to discover these absolute impact values. Hence, RDE's strategy to create small concepts produces three clear benefits: It makes the concepts easy to read for a pleasant interview, provides solid data that can be readily interpreted, and finally stores the results in databases to reveal trends across products and across time.

STEPS 5–7: LEARN THE RESULTS AND GENERATE RULES FOR ACTIONS

One of the guiding principles of RDE is that it should reveal the answer directly, without too much effort. S. S. (Smitty) Stevens of Harvard University, the senior author's doctoral advisor, put it succinctly in 1967 when he said, *"It ought to be clear by ocular trauma."* Ocular trauma, in Smitty's usage, was that "pain you get in the middle of your head when you look at a plot of data and the line simply doesn't fit the points...that sense that what you are seeing is forced, too complicated, and simply not real."

So, following Smitty's dictum, let's look at what RDE reveals to us about this new genomically devised product, with features that come from DVDs, portable electronic games, and tablet PCs.

All the information we need for some basic direction about Gamester can be found in Table 6.3, which shows the average utilities or impact factors. However, as we have seen again and again, dividing people by their mindsets generates more powerful products and messages. Gamester was no different.

There appeared to be at least three distinct segments. Abacus could have tuned into any of the three, probably quite profitably, as you will see. These three segments emerged from dividing Abacus's 236 participants by the pattern of what drives their responses in terms of the Gamester features.

Before we begin to look at the data in detail in the way Abacus did, let us first try to *name the segments* by examining what particular ideas scored best for each segment. Remember that the segmentation is a statistical procedure, easily done by the computer, but the computer is neither a developer nor a marketer. The computer program that does the clustering or grouping of people into these segments cannot name the segments; it can just assign people to groups. No problem—we look at the *best ideas* *and try to name the segments as we see them.*

- Segment 1 appears to be people who are interested in power and convenience:

  "An optional CD-RW or DVD/CD-RW drive can be purchased to back up data, install software, or even watch movies"

  "Customize your device to fit your needs..."

- Segment 2 appears to be people who want versatility and might be techies:

  A "Tablet DVD Gamester" that includes all the features and functionality of Windows XP Professional

  A multifunctional device...in addition to DVDs, you can enjoy CDs and MP3s, play games, and use as a tablet PC

- Segment 3 wants portability for entertainment and convenience:

  One of the lightest multimedia devices on the market...take it with you wherever you go

  Watch movies anywhere in the house...not just in one room

From Abacus's view, the mashing exercise produced many interesting findings and opportunities to create a new product. It is easy to enumerate these findings because this is how the developers grasped the meaning behind the information:

1. **Basic interest in Gamester is moderate for Total as well as for segments**—The additive constant for Total, 34, means that about one out of three participants would be generally interested in the idea of the Gamester product. There is no lurking segment that really wants the product. We'd see that by a segment with a high

additive constant. There are none. However, none of the three segments has dismissed the notion of a Gamester as irrelevant, as people often do with credit cards.

2. **Abacus can and should create different products, targeted to the segments**—One size does not fit all. Each of the three segments has ideas that it finds interesting (shaded in Table 6.3). These strong-performing elements become the basis of a new product.

3. **Abacus has used its customer's mind to create a product**—Because Abacus mashed together properties genomically in a simple system, the participants' "mind" is the real tool that creates the product, albeit through the help of the Web program. *Participants might not even be able to articulate what they want,* but Abacus does not have to worry about the creation of idea blends. Rather, Abacus needs only a database of ideas with which to work. We deal with such databases in Chapter 8, "Mind Genomics: Consumer Mind 'on the Shelf.'"

Table 6.3

Performance of some elements (abbreviated) for Gamester by total panel and the three segments (S1, S2, S3). The most important elements are highlighted.

	Elements	Total	S1: Power and Convenience	S2: Versatility and Techies	S3: Entertainment and Convenience
	Base Size	*236*	*53*	*116*	*67*
	Additive Constant	*34*	*42*	*34*	*28*
A1	A successful combination of tablet PC with DVD player performance and portable game functionality	6	0	7	10
A3	A multifunctional device...in addition to DVDs, you can enjoy CDs and MP3s, play games, and use as a tablet PC	9	0	13	8
B1	Convertible...can be used as a tablet PC or a laptop	6	0	7	8
B4	Watch movies anywhere in the house...	6	−1	4	15

	Elements	Total	S1: Power and Convenience	S2: Versatility and Techies	S3: Entertainment and Convenience
C2	One of the lightest multimedia devices on the market...take it with you wherever you go	3	1	0	10
C4	The lightest multifunction device on the market...	1	–2	–1	8
D1	Three fully programmable shortcut buttons...	3	7	–3	10
D4	Includes a slim-size remote control, AC adapter, audio/video cables, and a rechargeable battery pack	3	10	–3	8
E2	Customize your device to fit your needs...	6	13	5	0
E4	Comes with a travel kit...	4	13	4	–3
F1	Available at large department stores like Target...	6	9	1	10
F2	Available at your favorite electronics store	4	1	1	11

HOW DID ABACUS CREATE ITS GAMESTER MACHINE USING THIS DATABASE?

At the end of the day, how exactly does the RDE approach come up with these new combinations? New product-development mashes together these elements into a new whole, following some working rules to make sure the results are meaningful:

- **Criterion #1 (subjective):** The elements must make intuitive sense together and complement each other so that they really seem to "fit."
- **Criterion #2 (RDE-driven):** The elements must score well in a segment so the appeal is targeted to a coherent group.
- **Criterion #3 (business):** The ideas must be affordable.

When the three criteria are combined, the result is a possible new product—or, better, a possible stream of new products. Following this strategy of combining elements, let us look at just two product concepts that Abacus created by mixing and matching the elements (see Table 6.4).

Table 6.4

Two product concepts for Gamester

Techie Segment Product	Convenience Segment Product
A multifunctional device...in addition to DVDs, you can enjoy CDs and MP3s, play games, and use as a tablet PC	A successful combination of tablet PC with DVD player performance and portable game functionality
Convertible...can be used as a tablet PC or a laptop	Watch movies anywhere in the house... not just in one room
Cinema mode adjusts picture contrast in dark situations	Three fully programmable shortcut buttons...so you won't waste time carrying out frequent function tasks
An optional audio splitter divides the single stereo output into two for shared audio when viewing movies, listening to music, or playing games	Available at your favorite electronics store

The outcome of this system for Abacus—or, indeed, for any company following this approach—is a *system to create new ideas*. These ideas have to be tested. Later the ideas will have to be fine tuned, polished, and modified a bit for economic considerations and for judgment about what combinations really work together. Those latter judgments are subjective—or are they? The next section gives a different spin on these considerations of "working together."

HOW ABACUS SHARPENED ITS DEVELOPMENT BY DISCOVERING WHAT IDEAS AMPLIFY EACH OTHER

Up to now, we have been talking about the creation of products and communications as the act of finding those elements that perform well, either among the total group of participants or among a segment. But what about interactions among pairs of concept elements? Sometimes there might be two elements that perform quite well separately, but when we put them together, they make the product a dud because they contradict each other—or, more typically, they simply don't exhibit any chemistry with each other. Other times we might find combinations of elements that simply delight us. Perhaps each of the elements does well, but the combination seems to ring out loudly and clearly.

Let's move forward with some advances in RDE that might help Abacus and other developers identify (actually, *discover*) particular combinations of features or ideas that do very well together (this "amplification" of elements performance is called *synergism*) and pairs that do really poorly when used jointly (*suppression*).

The analytical foundations for this process need not be covered in this book (again, a tool can automatically do the whole discovery process for you). Let's concentrate on the results, in Table 6.5. For example, the combination $C_3 \times E_6$ is expected to show a neutral sum, almost 0 (+2), if we just add their utilities (+1 and +1). However, the system has discovered that there is a very significant synergy between the elements (+16), which brings the Real Sum of them to +18.

Based on the extensive analysis of many projects, the authors noticed that only a very few (if any) of the elements in each given project interact appreciably. And, as before, the RDE tool (IdeaMap.NET) discovers them automatically.[13] The Abacus developers then took these synergisms into account when designing Gamester.

Table 6.5

The combinations of features in Gamester that really make a difference (partial list)

Combination	Element	Text	Utility	Interaction	Simple Sum	Real Sum
True Synergism (Real Sum > Simple Sum)						
C_3*E_6	C_3	Cinema mode adjusts picture contrast in dark situations.	1			
	E_6	An optional audio splitter divides the single stereo output into two for shared audio when viewing movies, listening to music, or playing games.	1	16	2	18
A_5*F_3	A_5	An all-in-one portable entertainment unit games, music, and so much more.	2	16	2	18
	F_3	Find it at specialty electronics stores such as Best Buy or Circuit City.	0			

Table 6.5 continued

Combination	Element	Text	Utility	Interaction	Simple Sum	Real Sum
True Supression (Real Sum < Simple Sum)						
C_5*F_4	C_5	Designed to endure accidental falls.	4			
	F_4	Buy it directly from the manufacturer's Web site and get a $30 rebate while supplies last.	2	−15	6	−9
B_2*F_5	B_2	Personalize messages to friends, family, and co-workers…even send handwritten notes, drawings, and add your handwritten signature to your e-mails.	5	−15	9	−6
	F_5	Available online for convenient, faster, and more efficient shopping.	4			

SUMMING UP: CREATING NEW PRODUCT CONCEPTS WITH RDE

Will these combinatorial ideas be successful? Will Abacus sell a lot of products? RDE can only partially answer these questions. Ideas that come out of the genomics recombination of elements from different products and that perform well in these types of studies tend to do well in subsequent tests and in the market itself. The reason is pretty simple. With all the mixing and matching, and the rapid-fire presentation of test concepts to participants, it is unlikely that the project is a so-called "beauty contest" whose goal is to pick one winner from a set of contestants. It is more like a torture test. Any element that does well in this type of interview stands out against many thousands of backgrounds in which it appears. Betting on that element is like betting on a horse with a great track record, of many races, in many climates, on many different tracks, with many jockeys. The odds are that winning elements, like winning horses, have something good going on that's worth incorporating into a product.

So, where is Allison-the-Entrepreneur? Can she benefit from the experience described in this chapter? Her business is growing quite nicely, offering an increasing line of products. However, it happens, Allison ran out of new revolutionary ideas for her products at this specific point. That is why she was very excited when a national wholesale club chain called her with a suggestion to create a family-sized frozen SKU that combines several varieties of her products in one large package. Does Allison have an opportunity here to get access to the "supersized" market, including the chain whose name is especially dear to her? It reminds her about her childhood hero.

No new products need be developed—just combinations. But what are the *best combinations* of her multiple varieties? Random choice alone will not work—if she happens to put "incompatible" combinations on the shelf, most of them will be rejected by customers who were otherwise ready to buy. To make things even more complicated, Allison has very little time before the holiday season. She needs her RDE tool *now*! This simple recombination experiment of the available products might be her best shot at the moment.

One of her fans recently sent her a book on innovation. Allison found there a rather amusing thought that compares experimenting with a dance:

> "Sometimes the music doesn't move you or your steps fail. But that's no reason to stop. Just as writer's block happens when writers stop writing, so, too, does innovation grind to a halt when prototypes stop being built. When the muse fails you, don't mope at your desk. Make something."[14]

Sound familiar? Yes, it's the same dear-to-her-heart phrase, "Try it, try it! And you may!" all over again! Just a few years later—and in more sophisticated language.

ENDNOTES

[1] *AmericanWay*, 1 November 2005 issue; AA Publishing, Fort Worth, TX.

[2] As quoted in Kerri Salls, "Of Butterflies and Bumblebees," *Breakthrough Success Newsletter, BBS* 4(26) (2 August 2005).

[3] Tom Kelley, *The Art of Innovation: Lessons in Creativity from IDEO, America's Leading Design Firm* (Currency: New York, 2001).

[4] Some believe that the "blame" cannot fall on Microsoft alone. Its success wasn't always because MS was so smart or so ruthless; it was often because its competitors were so "slow, inept, incompetent, and short-sighted" (Brad Wardell, "Celebrating OS/2 2.0's 10th Birthday," www.stardock.com/stardock/articles/os2_birthday.html, 31 March 2002.

[5] Tom Kelley, *The Art of Innovation*, referenced earlier.

[6] Alex Gofman and Howard Moskowitz, "Consumer-Driven 'Concept Innovation Machine': A Dream or Reality?" In *Proceedings of the XVI ISPIM Annual Conference*, "The Role of Knowledge in Innovation Management," Porto, Portugal, 2005.

[7] See Chapter 1.

[8] Tim Macer, "DIY MR ASAP OK?," *Research Magazine* 432 (May 2002: 42–43).

[9] Products in high-tech sectors such as consumer electronics frequently are outdated before they are even commercially available. Keep this in mind when reviewing the elements in Table 6.2 because they might look somewhat outdated even though they were ahead of their time when Abacus assessed them for Gamester.

[10] For some reason, many users found this particular design very useful. The authors tend to like it as well. It does not mean that you should not use other designs—e.g., other popular ones like five silos with four elements in each, 10 silos with three elements, etc.

[11] Dan Lockhart and Matt Knain, "An Overview of Alternative Conjoint Approaches," *The Research Report* 11(1), Maritz Marketing Research, Inc. (Winter 1998).

[12] For example, SYSTAT, SPSS, and many other programs—if you do not use hosted tools such as IdeaMap.NET, which does it for you automatically.

[13] This patent-pending technology is unique to IdeaMap.NET.

[14] Tom Kelley, *The Art of Innovation*, referenced earlier.

7

Bridging Cool Design with Hot Science

A world-renowned, award-winning fashion and goods designer, Cynthia Rowley, who with her two ponytails looks much like a schoolgirl, frequently gets inspiration and novel ideas just by looking at some everyday objects. Rowley gets excited talking about designing unusual, unconventional, sometimes even counterintuitive things such as toilet paper, but with a twist: a *designer* toilet paper, for example, with a Louis Vuitton pattern. Or a designer binky (pacifier). Who else should rely mostly on inspiration in her job if not a fashion designer like Cynthia? Isn't it the inspiration that makes a designer? Asked to choose whether she feels inspiration or experimentation to be more critical for her job when looking for the next hit product, she answered, "Hmm, this is a chicken-and-egg problem.... Actually, both—I'd say 50/50."

Experimentation can propel a good designer beyond simply "okay" to a successful, often outstanding creation. One proven approach for designers and business people uses *inspiration* to conceive a new product and then *experimentation* with it to make it successful. Another lets experimentation narrow the options and uses inspiration to make those options go from good to great. This "I&E" (inspiration and experimentation) should go together, hand in hand. They enhance each other rather than being the mutually exclusive enemies often proclaimed by fearful creatives.

Unfortunately, and all too frequently, design moves separately with the product features but fails to focus on users, or perhaps even occasionally downright ignores them for the sake of "art." Some creators try to outdo each other by crafting cumbersome, unattractive (from customer point of view) designs. Such self-indulgent design in the so-called search for art might initially attract some customer attention because it is so different, so novel.[1] However, the attention given to the design might not guarantee the conversion and could possibly alienate the very people it was meant to entice. Is there a way to prevent this unhappy turn of events? Can RDE evolve from working with *ideas* to working with *designs* so that the discipline it imposes on the process enhances creativity in the direction most desired by consumers?

A very dear friend of the authors, Marco Bevolo, is one of those rare and lucky people who sees clearly beyond the clutter of post-modern designs. Actually, it is a large part of his job description to do so. As Director of Foresight and Trends, Marco leads the CultureScan trend research program at Philips Design. Along with some other visionaries in the world of design, Marco believes that companies must move toward *ambient intelligence*.[2] Intimidating as it sounds, the Ambient Design paradigm advocates a people-centered design that is friendly to the user, with technology that allows the design to *self-adjust* to the user's needs and preferences. Ambient intelligence may be a way of the near future, with sensing, changing, and getting feedback built into the machines. What about now? How does the designer sense, change, and get feedback?

This type of consumer-driven approach is a job for a trained professional with consumer insight knowledge and a designer background—someone like Marco and maybe a handful of other visionaries. No algorithm or software can replace them—at least, not in the next few years. Fortunate companies do everything possible to retain good designers. Can we make their job a bit easier and more productive?

Today's technology has real benefits for designers. For instance, technology helps designers use a disciplined approach to sift through the intimidating plethora of possible design features and their combinations, to find what works. The output is a narrower set of design options, comprising the most feasible and acceptable ones, created out of the designer's talent, but created to be more productive at the outset by using hard data from consumer insights on a timely basis.

Timing in the design process is critical. A pattern of productive guidance ought to occur *before* designers start spending lots of valuable time exploring options that consumers could have told them "would not fly." Productive guidance to artists ensures that they can concentrate on the more profitable direction, such as the next iPod. Even the less fortunate companies that don't enjoy having such visionary people on board or just cannot afford them might close in on the next blockbuster by following the clear guidance of RDE in design.[3] You'll see this later.

So how should a designer use the RDE tool without feeling threatened? The Luddite movement of 1811–1817, that negative and sometimes violent reaction of the working class to the introduction of mechanized production, was fuelled by the fear of workers that the machines would replace them. However, the future was quite different; machines would just make their work less strenuous and more productive. Personal computers and AutoCAD have not replaced engineers and architects they merely made their life a bit easier and more fruitful. Indeed, the professionals are not threatened by them anymore, nor, in fact, by most design-aiding technologies. A similar situation exists with RDE to help designers. Fortunately, today there are no fears that the machine can replace the designer's touch—at least, not in the foreseeable future. RDE makes the designer's job easier and more efficient by calculating and analyzing the algebra of consumer minds, albeit with visual designs as the test stimuli instead of verbally expressed ideas.[4] Think of an intelligent 24/7 assistant, but one who does not complain, does not have mood swings, does not talk back, and does not ever forget.

In Chapter 6, "Rubik's Cube of Consumer Electronics Innovation," you saw what happens when a highly reputable design company, Ford & Earl, successfully applied the RDE approach to a range of problems at the conceptual level. As products become increasingly commoditized and new goods are introduced at a dizzying pace, designers are being invited—indeed, drafted or conscripted—to create the visual surround for a product. The quest is to differentiate the specific offering from everything else against which it competes. It is likely that good design will increase the odds of a consumer picking a product off the shelf, a recipient opening a mail offering instead of discarding it, a visitor remaining on a "sticky" Web site to explore rather than exiting hastily and somewhat confused, or a shopper pulling a magazine off the rack.

Our next example about magazine cover development using RDE goes beyond the conventional "beauty contest" of cover research that measures which cover wins and which loses. The RDE objective is more profound: How does the buyer's mind work when the designer creates covers with different physical features in certain ways? What visuals work; what visuals do not work? What types of colors work? And, if you measure *how long* the person gazes at the cover before reacting, a measure of *engagement* with the cover, RDE reveals what features "hold the eye" and what features get processed so fast that they are hardly brought into conscious focus. This knowledge allows a designer to expand his or her creativity, learn what works, and then design a much better magazine cover.

RDE IN ACTION: MAGAZINE COVERS FOR THE FIXER-UPPER

Eye-catching magazine covers are a key driver of newsstands sales. Magazine covers are designed for at least two purposes: to establish an image about the magazine by conveying a look/feel, and to drive purchase and readership. A magazine cover that attracts the buyer's attention in the critical moment when the buyer looks at the selection, increases the chances that the buyer will reach for the specific issue. But, as always, what specific visuals invite the reader in, and what specific messages get the reader curious enough to want to look further? Magazines struggle with an increasingly competitive environment, as the available options continue to multiply, such as printed vs. Web-based, paid for versus free, general topic versus one's private syndicated feed, with ever-decreasing time. It's vital to design magazine covers that pull in the reader so at least the magazine is purchased and scanned, even if only for a minute.

Our example (simplified and disguised for the purposes of this book) deals with a magazine for the do-it-yourself homeowner. The RDE challenge was to discover what aspects of the cover invited the reader to consider buying the magazine on the newsstand. Were there any rules to be learned with RDE that could make the editorial staff smarter, at least in terms of knowing what features of the covers drive responses? The RDE project was both strategic (get rules to make the group smarter) and tactical (what's up for the issue three months from now).

FILLING IN VISUAL BLANKS

As we mentioned in the previous chapters, RDE uses experimental designs that require the absence of silos in some concepts (prototypes). The first question crucial to graphics work is "Does the mind fill in the visual 'blanks,' and what does this mean to RDE and cover design?" We know that we fill in the blanks when we read, and we don't need to read every word to get the gist of the text. However, what about graphics, where we look at a picture that's missing parts? Say, magazine covers. Do we simply glance at the incomplete picture and somehow form our judgment in the same way that we fill in text blanks?

The extensive previous experimental work by the authors is summarized below. Figure 7.1 shows the effect of reducing the amount of information in text concepts. When it comes to verbal ideas, the respondent often fills in the missing information. Concepts can be incomplete, and the respondent will still react to the concept with little discomfort.[5]

5 Elements concept	A heavy red wine with a warm plumy fruit flavor and a little bit of dryness Made in the tradition of the greatest wine producers all over the world You can imagine the taste even before you drink it A great way to celebrate special occasions From Northern California
4 Elem.	A heavy red wine with a warm plumy fruit flavor and a little bit of dryness Made in the tradition of the greatest wine producers all over the world A great way to celebrate special occasions From Northern California
3 Elem.	A heavy red wine with a warm plumy fruit flavor and a little bit of dryness Made in the tradition of the greatest wine producers all over the world A great way to celebrate special occasions
2 Elem.	A heavy red wine with a warm plumy fruit flavor and a little bit of dryness A great way to celebrate special occasions

Figure 7.1 Example of a wine concept showing the impact of reducing the amount of information (text only)

Now let's move to the comparable case, but work with graphics only. We use a package design for a meat product to illustrate the point (see Figure 7.2). You see the complete package design and then a "degraded" design with fewer features. Each picture has less information, making a decision harder. Although the design looks incomplete, *only when a lot of the information is removed* do we begin to feel uncomfortable trying to judge the design. When we stay with the complete design or perhaps remove only one element of the design, participants probably will not feel confused when they rate it.

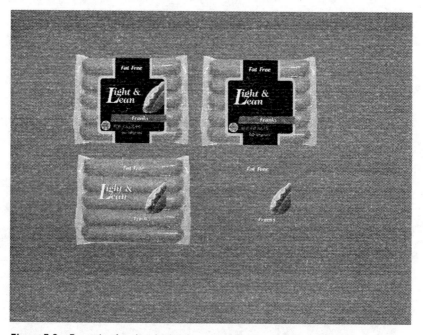

Figure 7.2 Example of a visual stimulus with progressively reduced information. At what point does the mind stop filling in the blank space?

Fortunately, there is a way to limit the number of missing categories in the design to no more than just one.[6] Therefore, based on our experiments, the *first rule that we learned about using RDE for graphics design is that the test stimuli should contain most, if not all, of the information.* This learning has some process implications; for design work, the number of magazine covers needs to be increased. This additional effort is not a big problem for the Web-based RDE tools that handle the heavy work of combining visual elements. And from what we found, consumers don't mind, either. They're just looking at magazine covers, so it's not a big problem.

The most disturbing point for the respondents seems to be the cases when the package itself is absent. They seemed to be okay with occasionally missing pieces, as long as the package still looks like a package. The *second rule for graphical RDE is that a "bare" package or its outline should always be present.* Figure 7.3 shows that the concepts look reasonable, and not disturbing, if they are created with always-present outlines of the package and the label and if we use the first rule above—no more than one option should be absent from any magazine cover (from any test stimulus).

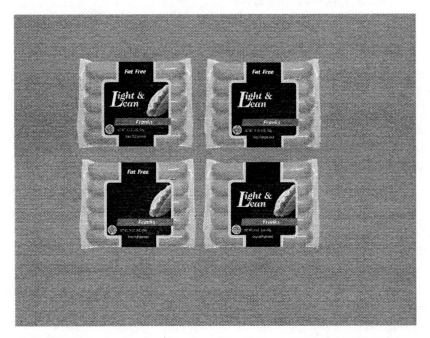

Figure 7.3 Example of a visual stimulus with modest reduction in information. Only one option is missing at a time, and the general shape of the package is always placed in the background.

The results of actual work with graphical RDE are encouraging: Participants evaluating different visual designs in multiple projects reported no problems when some—albeit, a relatively small part—of the information was missing from the test stimuli.[7]

THINKING THROUGH THE ISSUES

RDE applied to design is very similar to RDE with just words or with text and pictures. To illustrate the thinking underlying graphical RDE, let's dig into a simplified example of a magazine cover constructed of just three layers (see Figure 7.4). An example with only three basic cover features is certainly a lot simpler than what happens in real life, but it's easy to understand. Each feature of the magazine cover (or package) can be thought of as a transparency (or a cake layer). Adobe Photoshop users find this analogy very easy to understand. Think about layers in a Photoshop project, which are transparent everywhere except for the key object of the layer. The computer (browser) superimposes these transparencies according to the recipe dictated by the RDE design, which thus creates different packages or magazine covers. It's as straightforward as that. Each new combination defined by the RDE design corresponds to a new package or magazine cover. Over the course of the interview, the participants get to see different magazine covers (combination of options). The browser has been instructed how to choose a specific set of transparencies and shows them in combination. The participant never sees the individual transparencies; the participant sees complete magazine covers.

The actual evaluation of magazine covers is easy to do. The computer does all the work because RDE gives it the design (the "recipe" for each cover), and the computer needs only to combine these components. The individual transparencies are already in place at the participant's computer because the server uploaded them at the start of the interview.

When participants are exposed to these synthesized magazine covers, they do not really know that the experimental design lies underneath the combinations, nor could they. The transparencies are combined so quickly that, to the participant, it looks like a single magazine cover. The participants evaluate cover after cover, one at a time. If the evaluations last about 12–18 minutes, most respondents have no problem and actually say that they enjoy the experience. The trick is that people assess visual stimuli much faster than it takes to read text. This speed of the response, almost a "gut-feel response" compensates for the increased number of concepts that graphical RDE uses.

Despite designer worries that somehow participants will not be able to respond to anything but a complete magazine cover, reality is just the opposite. Participants have no problem evaluating both the complete magazine covers, an example of which appears in Figure 7.5, and the partial magazine covers, an example of which appears in Figure 7.6. When asked after the interview through a so-called exit survey whether they felt uncomfortable, almost no participant reported feeling uncomfortable with the partial, incomplete magazine covers.[8]

Figure 7.4 The analogy of RDE in design to layers in a cake (or project layers in PhotoShop). The shading and semitransparency are for illustration purposes only.

Figure 7.5 Example of a simplified complete magazine cover, of the type one might see on a magazine rack in a newsstand

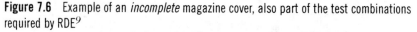

Figure 7.6 Example of an *incomplete* magazine cover, also part of the test combinations required by RDE[9]

SO WHAT DOES THE MAGAZINE EDITOR GET OUT OF A GRAPHICS RDE?

We started the project with the objective to learn how strongly each element of test covers drove interest in the magazine. If we were the editors, we would be sitting on the edge of our seats waiting for both specific findings to answer immediate problems and also general rules to make us smarter. Much as they dislike having their creative efforts measured ("You cannot measure creativity," they claim), many editors now accept consumer ratings of covers as a precondition for a go-forward decision for the magazines.

Three different silos were used, each with three different options. Figure 7.7 shows utilities for each of the elements in the project.[10] The RDE project tried to identify just how crucial each was, and which particular content and executions really worked. The graphics feature must also drive consumer interest in a positive direction. The potential gain from such information is enormous. If editors learn what specific elements drive interest up front for a particular cover, they can optimize that specific magazine cover, but also extract some operating rules to become smarter.

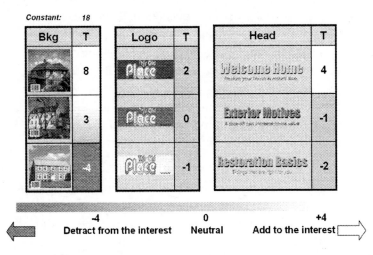

Figure 7.7   RDE applied to the components of magazine covers. Utilities (column 'T') above (+4) add to the interest; below (−4) detract from the interest. Those between (−4) and (+4) are generally neutral.

RDE still generates mixed feelings among design creatives because it adds a level of discipline that one might not perceive as coming from the designer's art. The first issues raised by the editors were "Isn't this survey just too long? How can anyone be certain of his answers? How can we learn from all these test magazine covers on the computer screen?" RDE certainly requires that there be many different alternatives to identify which features of the magazine cover drive acceptance. When we dealt with food products at the start of this book, we didn't see too many problems related to producing prototypes. For the most part, product developers who make pasta sauce or other consumer products are by now accustomed to producing prototypes. Testing many alternative magazine covers is, however, fairly new to magazine editors, so they respond with the same initial skepticism as did product developers 30 years ago when RDE made its inroads into developments. Happily, participants are not editors and have no problems, despite what the editors averred. After a short orientation, participants completed the interview in the comfortable time of 12–15 minutes.

The first results emerged very quickly after the RDE servers automatically analyzed the response patterns from 657 participants, each of whom was either a current reader of the magazine or a potential reader interested in the topics and thus accessing the magazine Web site. Which elements would win? The story was primarily cover photos, which did not surprise anyone. The numbers in Figure 7.7 in the column marked "T" (for "inTerest") are the percentage of participants who said that they would buy the magazine from the newsstand rack, *as contributed by the individual design elements*. The numbers are additive. Begin with the additive constant (18) and start adding elements. The sum tells us how well the combination will perform.

Let's just stay within the category of cover pictures. You can get about 26% of the participants to be interested by putting in the first house picture (18 points baseline (constant) plus 8 utility of the first picture). You get only about half of that, or 14%, by using the last picture (18 – 4 = 14). Following this way of thinking, you get about 20% of the participants interested when you talk about "Welcome Home: Restore Your House in Record Time," but only about 14% of the participants when you tell about "Restoration Basics: Sidings That Are Right for You."

Another thing that editors want to know is what grabs and holds the customer's eye. You can have good covers and bad covers, but how exactly can RDE engineer a cover that "engages"—that is, a cover that looks good and a cover that keeps the buyer staring? RDE uses a very simple method: Measure the time elapsed between the start of the exposure, when a participant sees the magazine cover, and response when the participant rates the cover for interest. A special software feature in the system starts timing only after the visuals are completely shown on the screen. Download/upload time is not counted. Some of these response times are longer, some are shorter. The task for RDE is to trace the response time to the different magazine elements. This response time is important information for the editor because, for the first time, the editor objectively identifies what elements hold attention. These elements might or might not be consciously interesting to the buyer, but they rivet him or her.

Figure 7.8 shows the values of stare time in milliseconds ('ms'). Some of these values are positive, meaning that when the cover feature is present, the stare time is longer. We and the editors interpret this to mean that the feature engages—that is, the feature adds to the stare time. For example, when the cover has the words "Exterior Motives: A Face-Lift Can Increase Home Value," we can expect the average participant to spend an *additional* [3/10] of a second looking at the cover beyond the time to look at a plain cover without text. What happens? The participant must be doing something! It's likely that the participant is reading the message. And from the level of interest, we know that this is a good message, driving the participant to say he will buy. We have the best of both worlds: a good message that people spend time reading. RDE has measured both their interest and their attention.

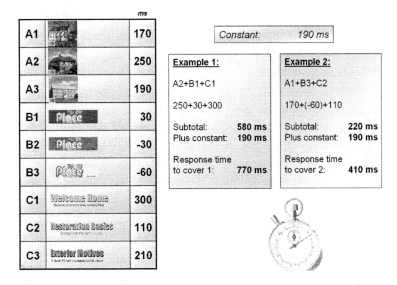

Figure 7.8 How some features of a magazine cover increase (decrease) stare time[11] (milliseconds)

There are some negative numbers here as well; they decrease staring time from the baseline. For example, two of the three executions of the magazine title have negative utilities for staring time. Of course, it does not mean that people look at them less than 0 seconds. It means that adding this element to the cover makes people look at the latter less raptly than the average (baseline) staring time.

Are all good ideas riveting—or, better said, does our customer ever look at anything for a long period of time, but at the end actually dislike what he or she took so long to look at? This is a typical question from the editor. A set of data like that shown in Figure 7.8 is very useful in answering this question. For instance, the more interesting cover lines look like they take up more time. If a buyer is interested in what we are going to tell him or her (higher interest values in cover lines), it is likely that he or she will spend more time staring and reading. That makes sense. Let's look at other questions:

1. **Are there aspects of the magazine that capture attention but are basically turn-offs?** These are the elements that have *negative interest* (decrease the number of interested readers) but have *positive stare time* (they capture attention). Let's look for elements that have low or negative interest but high stare time. We do not find many; if people do not like what they see, they do not spend time looking at it.

2. **Are there aspects of the magazine that people look at for short periods of time (not engaging), but yet are turn-ons?** These may be elements that people use to make snap decisions, but positive decisions nonetheless. We see this in the cover photos. They are mostly positive, but the reader processes the information quickly. People just do not stare a lot at the photos. They look at them quickly and then make their decision.

PUTTING IT ALL TOGETHER: RDE TO ENGINEER A BETTER MAGAZINE COVER

We have just seen how RDE provides the editor the type of information it gives the marketer and product developer. And the bottom line is the same: an idea of how the reader's mind works, and concrete, specific direction about putting together features that drive acceptance and, hopefully, magazine purchase. How does an editor put this cover together? The answer is by selecting ideas from among the winning elements and merging them. Of course, the objective is not to replace the editor's judgment by a computer program, but just to give the editor a sense of the mind of the participant, about what works and what does not. You see one cover that works in Figure 7.9 and one cover that does not work in Figure 7.10. The rest is up to the editor, but now the editor is armed with a specific direction about how the different colors, pictures, contents, and tag lines ought to do among readers.

Figure 7.9 The highest-scoring cover synthesized by RDE by combining winning elements from the total group of participants

Figure 7.10 An expected poor-performing cover synthesized from the poorer-performing elements of the RDE study

FROM FLAT GRAPHICAL DESIGN TO 3-D PACKAGES

RDE seems to be quite easy in the "flat" world of 2-D objects such as printed materials and flat packages. What about three-dimensional objects? Some of our experiments in the 1990s with a custom-made futuristic device to re-create a "real" 3-D experience did not prove very usable. Other providers do occasional experiments with virtual reality devices, such as the one shown in Figure 7.11. Skeptics feel that putting this type of device on the head of an average respondent to evaluate a new packaging for canned soup does not re-create anything like the reality of shopping.

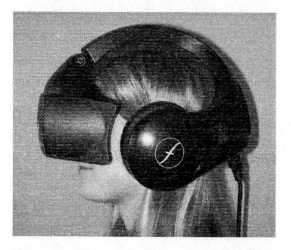

Figure 7.11   An example of a virtual reality helmet used in some experiments to simulate a 3-D environment for consumer testing (courtesy of Swinburne University of Technology, Australia). Skeptics believe this approach with the current level of technology is much too invasive and cumbersome to the consumers.

The majority of people become accustomed to perceiving three-dimensional images through a flat medium, such as pictures in books or magazines, in photos, and on TV. So evaluating 3-D packages on a flat PC screen is not the biggest problem. The issue is, how easy is it to dissect an object such as a package into pieces that can be mixed and matched? Let's see a partial solution that fits with today's technology using the example of a bag for the ever-popular pretzels.

PRETZELS PACKAGE EXAMPLE

A major pretzel producer was interested in new packaging ideas for these salt-encrusted snacks with a distinctive, twisted shape that would appeal to its consumers around the world. The question that RDE had to answer was which type of features work for the different countries? Now, how can one engineer a sensible package for a product so popular that it has two U.S. National Months dedicated to it?[12] Here are some fun facts to "prime" you for the task.

Did you know that pretzels have been around for almost fourteen hundred years? As the story goes, an Italian monk decided to reward his students with baked scraps of leftover dough. He rolled and twisted the dough to resemble arms folded in prayer. He called this new golden-brown product "pretiolas," which in Latin means "little rewards."

In the Middle Ages, the wedding phrase "tying the knot" got its start when a pretzel was used to tie the knot between two prominent families. The pretzel's loops stood for everlasting love.

And how did hard pretzels come into existence? In fact, hard pretzels were discovered by mistake, when a bakers' apprentice fell asleep by the furnace and let the treats bake too long. At first, the master baker was mad at his apprentice for his carelessness, but upon tasting these pretzels, quickly realized he had a big opportunity.

Some believe pretzels arrived in America on the Mayflower. The Pilgrims used them to trade with Indians for just about anything they needed. Today, annual consumption of pretzels in the U.S. is two pounds per person. In the Mid-Atlantic states, it's 4 pounds—and in Philadelphia, it is more than 20 pounds!

This invention of one of America's modern favorite snack foods is quite peculiar, although it was not the result of a disciplined experimentation. Can we utilize RDE to design the packages for this enticing product? Unlike a box of cereal, a pretzels package is completely "unflat." The obvious question was how to work on a two-dimensional screen with a three-dimensional problem. Surprisingly, the solution was straightforward.

The designers first created several executions of each of the six features of the pretzels package, shown in Figure 7.12. Each option was created on a transparent "layer" with the feature positioned properly to allow correct matching during overlaying. All the surface bending was consistently captured inside each option. The designer can do that quite easily based on a single template, shown in the middle of Figure 7.12. The result is a set of more graphically realistic pictures, assembled by the principle of RDE.

Figure 7.12 Pretzels packages (3-D) have six features (silos) with four options (elements) each and a "bare" package image as a background.

Looking further, we see from Figure 7.13 how RDE assembles these design options or components so that the combination looks more like a package.

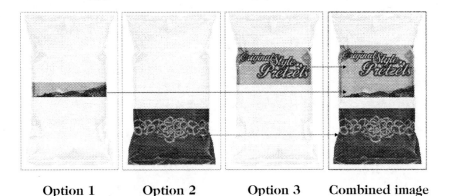

Option 1   Option 2   Option 3   Combined image

Figure 7.13 Assembling the options or design components to create a combined image, the package (the outlines of the package on the left three layers are for demonstration purposes only)

A very important difference from our previous text-based RDE is the need for a "filler" background image for the situations when the package on the screen occasionally must be without an option, as required by the experimental design. The best solution places a bare package in the back of each screen, behind all the layers. This way, a "zero condition" (the absence of an option in the design) does not create a disturbing image with "holes" in it. The background image of the bare package makes the test stimulus on the computer screen look like an acceptable package, meaningful to consumers even if it has an element missing (e.g., the last package in Figure 7.14).

The outcome of this exercise brings the designer a long way toward merging art, science, RDE, and consumer knowledge. The packages look real, as we see in Figure 7.14. The most important people, the consumer participants, report feeling that they are evaluating realistic packages. Everyone wins.

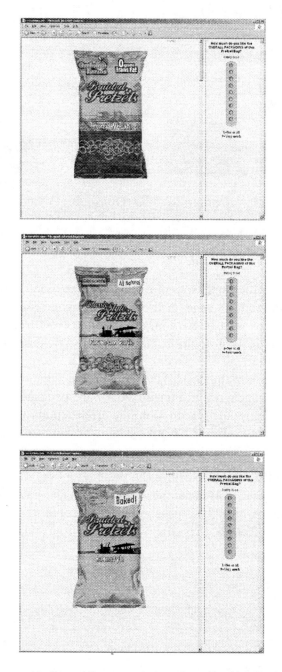

Figure 7.14 Three combinations of the new pretzels package. The third screen has a missing option as dictated by the experimental design, but the design strategy reduces any discomfort with that incompleteness.

The data from this RDE project, run internationally, showed exactly what features drive responses in each country. This is the objective of RDE. In a nutshell, RDE made the job easier for the package designer, who could create these components and then combine them on the computer, rather than having to fabricate many different prototypes, always a long, arduous, and nonconclusive task that also makes testing with consumers much more difficult.[13]

SHAMPOO PACKAGING EXAMPLE

Let's finish with another project, again with design. This project is similar to the pretzels one, but in a different product category: health and beauty. The principles are the same and the results were even more promising, but the story of why RDE was selected this time changes. Designers had a task to choose the best combination of packaging options before doing the final rendering. Focus groups did not produce a definite winner, but identified many options that the customers liked. The problem was that these options were separate components, evaluated by the focus group participants and further evaluated in a survey. What, however, was the best combination of them? This was the question for RDE to answer.

Figure 7.15 shows the six features of the shampoo bottle, with four options each (the similarity of the design to the pretzels study is just a coincidence; RDE projects can have a different number of features and options). The designers had already identified the general appearance of the package but did not know the best options for pictures, descriptions, and other elements.

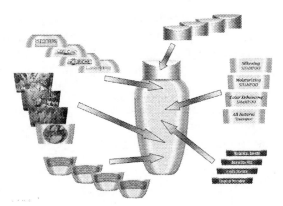

Figure 7.15   Shampoo package with six features, four options in each

It took the designer just 30 minutes to put the RDE project together *after the visuals were created.* Then the designer mailed the Web project link to the panel. In this project and in many others, the stakeholders then sat around, drank coffee, and watched the data accumulate in real time in front of their eyes. As in previous graphical RDE projects, the computer superimposed individual options (layers) on top of each other in real time, virtually unnoticeable to the respondents. You get a sense of that process in Figure 7.16.

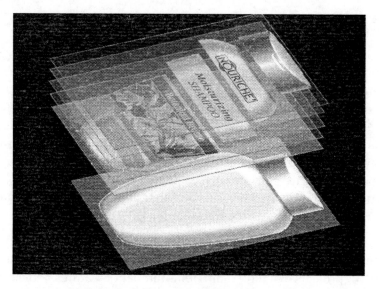

Figure 7.16 Conceptual representation of the shampoo package as a set of overlaying transparencies, including a bare package at the bottom of the stack

The next morning, the designers knew exactly what worked and what did not. We will spare you from going though a set of tables again—essentially, they are the same type as for magazine covers or any other RDE project. Suffice it to say, there were substantially different reactions from respondents located in the South and West of the U.S. The segments and interactions allowed the designers to create even more targeted executions of the packages. Another happy ending for the RDE exercise that was neither difficult nor broke the bank.

"DOES THIS REALLY WORK IN THE ARTISTIC REALM?"

One other question that continues to be important to the designers is the issue of *validity of the additive model for graphical elements.* This validity issue was often raised for text-based concepts in the early research days as well, when RDE was first applied to ideas. The goal those days was to identify how ideas combine to generate concepts. The question has surfaced again for packages due to the belief that package design is an art form.

The authors have done extensive research to address and answer validity questions.[14] One way to show validity of the RDE model for package features is called the hold-out method. Hold-outs require that RDE use only some of the different combinations to build a model showing what elements drive the ratings. After the model is developed, RDE can use the model to estimate the likely response to combinations of elements that were tested but had not been used to create the RDE model (hence the word *hold-out*). According to our experience, usually the predictions are quite high; RDE can estimate the likely rating of the hold-out designs to within +/–7%. Most critics are comfortable with such a closeness of predicted vs. actual performance and have little problem accepting the RDE method afterward. This simple method of showing validity by predicting responses to new combinations goes a long way to dispel the designer's and marketer's fears.

SUMMING UP: CREATING BETTER DESIGNS WITH RDE

This chapter on graphics design and RDE might seem more controversial than the previous chapters, and for a simple reason. Graphics, whether package design, cover design, or shelf design, are almost always considered to reside in the domain art. Artists do not like to be judged. The notion of "art for art's sake," not a hallmark of the business community, pervades graphic design. Even though packaging is considered to be one of the new hot areas for marketing, a typical designer request for consumer insights was routinely couched in terms of discovering what the consumer *says* he or she wants, not *how he reacts* to systematically varied stimuli, and certainly not to the technology-driven results of RDE. Happily, today's designers are changing their views, adopting RDE thinking, and welcoming the marriage of art and technology.

While we were doing our exercises with graphics, many things happened in Allison-the-Entrepreneur's company. She became a really "big shot" businessperson. Allison has decided to expand her booming business of multicolored products to the ready-to-serve frozen food sections of supermarkets around the land. An obvious problem is how to choose a good package design to make her product stand out from the crowd. She was also encouraged by her fan-club president (who also happened to be her lead VC) to create a mail-catalog of her products. From Chapter 5, "Discover More About Your Competitors Than They Themselves Know—Legally!," Allison already knows what features she should showcase in the catalog. She has been using the messages since then—and quite successfully. Now she needs a striking and attractive catalog cover to ensure that the catalog will be opened and will add to her business's bottom line, not to the recycle bin.

Allison-the-Entrepreneur had spent all her available capital on extending the product line, and the holiday season is awfully close. She needs to complete the task in no time. Now, the chances seemed remote of retaining a top-notch designer for the time needed to design, from scratch, attractive packages and the catalog cover. Allison also discovered that it is not that easy to find a creative person who shares her unconventional views. In her previous experiences with a design house, she was not convinced that their "masterpieces" were the best matches for her specific products and her particular customers. So, back to homework. Allison should hire a good freelance designer who can spare an evening or two to do final touches on the proposed renderings.

What might Allison prepare as materials for her designer? Here is where RDE can help, especially if she can get familiar with one of the graphical design packages (such as Adobe Photoshop) that she can install on her laptop. Let's follow Allison-the-Entrepreneur a bit, after she installs the design package, and looks around for ideas that could fit her new product.

In addition to quite a few visuals that Allison used (or considered) for her supermarket size products, there are probably some stock pictures that she might think are appropriate for her package. Which ones are the best?

What is the most appropriate background color? She can think of several. Which one of the few proposed logos should she use? Similar questions are on her mind for the catalog cover as well. Some of these she can create herself; others she can grab from stock photographs and artwork for her home-grown design efforts.

As in her previous RDE tasks, Allison decides to use the proven, externally hosted do-it-yourself Web tool. She chooses the design that has enough variables to render the packages; she uploads the visuals of backgrounds, inserts pictures and logos, and so on. She may even use some competitors' graphics to test and compare to her own. Then Allison spends an hour or so creating the template for the package. She can immediately preview the sample rendering so the job makes her feel like an artist and designer at the same time, even though she is neither.

Inviting her target respondents for a *short survey* on the Web is not a big task for Allison. She did it before and found it easy and affordable. Her participants who log on to the survey over the Web see and rate a series of different packages (project 1) or catalog covers (project 2), depending on which of Allison's projects they were directed to. Allison's participants do not even realize that each different rendering is done dynamically on their screens according to an RDE design. The next day, the system *automatically* generates the rules for her package (what wins, what loses). As before, Allison discovers what works.

It is amazing what can be achieved in just two days of work using a laptop and some stock pictures that are readily available. Now Allison's freelance designer can finish the job in no time (meaning, not a lot of *billable* time) with quite impressive results because he already knows what the customers like and what Allison approved. Together with Allison's catalog sales, this will bring her a new fortune.

Again, not bad at all for someone with an aptitude for experimenting and today's inexpensive but powerful laptop computer!

ENDNOTES

1 Some argue that "the ugliness itself [lends] legitimacy...in a marketplace otherwise dominated by slick corporate products" (Steve Bryant, "MySpace Is
Successful Because It's Ugly," *Intermedia*, 21 February 2006;
http://blog.eweek.com/blogs/intermedia/archive/2006/02/21/6156.aspx). Although
that's occasionally true for some segments of the population (such as teens), it
usually fails in the long run with the majority of consumers.

2 Reon Brand and Marco Bevolo, "The Long-Term View: Using Emerging Socio-
Cultural Trends to Build Sustainable Brands," In *Proceedings of Interactions
2002, The 6th European International Design Management Conference*, Dublin,
Ireland, March 11–13, 2002.

3 For more information, see Alex Gofman and Howard Moskowitz, "Consumer-
Driven 'Concept Innovation Machine': A Dream or Reality?" In *Proceedings of the
XVI ISPIM Annual Conference*, "The Role of Knowledge in Innovation
Management," Porto, Portugal, 2005.

4 Alex Gofman and Howard Moskowitz, "State-of-the-Art Research and Development
Tools to Put Innovation in the Hands of the Many," The XV ISPIM Annual
Conference, "Successfully Creating Innovative Products and Services: Integrating
Academia, Business, and Consulting," Oslo, Norway, 2004.

5 Howard R. Moskowitz, Sebastiano Porretta, and Matthias Silcher, *Food Product
Design and Development, 2005* (Blackwell Publishing: Ames, IO, 2005).

6 As usual, you do not need to worry about it—the RDE tool does the work for you.
All the designs for graphical RDE are specifically optimized to address this issue.
The RDE tool uses sets of designs exclusively created to deal with the need to
have complete or almost-complete graphics.

7 Johannes Hartmann, Howard Moskowitz, Alex Gofman, and Madhu Manchaiah,
"Understanding and Optimizing Communications and the 'Look': Sustainable Co-
Creativity Using Internet-Enabled, Visual Conjoint Analysis," In *Proceedings of
2004 ESOMAR Asia Pacific Conference*, Shanghai, 2004.

8 Howard R. Moskowitz, Sebastiano Porretta, and Matthias Silcher, *Food Product
Design and Development, 2005* (Blackwell Publishing: Ames, IO, 2005).

[9] Despite the "incompleteness" (the headline is absent), participants appear to have no problem evaluating this magazine cover, either based on their data or based on their comments about the test experience. Also keep in mind that in real-life applications, there are usually more than three features, and the absence of one of them is less noticeable.

[10] As we mentioned earlier, this case has been simplified and disguised from the original project that had more features and options.

[11] A positive number means that this element adds to the staring time; a negative number means that it subtracts from the staring time. To obtain an additive value of staring time, the number has to be added to the constant.

[12] According to the Kansas State University web site, March is National Soft Pretzel Month and October is National Pretzel month. "Just for Fun." http://housing.k-state.edu/dining/FitCourse/justforfun.html.

Other sources for this section:

"The History of the Pretzel," www.kitchenproject.com/history/Pretzel.htm.

Wikipedia contributors, "Pretzel," *Wikipedia, The Free Encyclopedia*, http://en.wikipedia.org/w/index.php?title=Pretzel&oldid=102772743.

"The history of pretzels," http://msms.essortment.com/thehistoryofp_rrka.htm.

"Bush makes light of pretzel scare," http://news.bbc.co.uk/1/hi/world/americas/1758848.stm, BBC News Online, http://en.wikipedia.org/wiki/BBC_News_Online, 2002, http://en.wikipedia.org/wiki/2002, -01-14, http://en.wikipedia.org/wiki/January_14, http://news.bbc.co.uk/1/hi/world/americas/1758848.stm.

[13] Alex Gofman and Howard Moskowitz, "Rule Developing Experiments (RDE) in Package Co-Creation." In Proceedings of 2006 IIR FUSE Brand Identity and Package Design Conference, New York, 2006.

[14] Howard R. Moskowitz, Sebastiano Porretta, and Matthias Silcher, *Food Product Design and Development, 2005*, and Alex Gofman and Howard Moskowitz, "State-of-the-Art Research and Development Tools to Put Innovation in the Hands of the Many," both referenced earlier.

PART III

Flying to Venus

Now buckle your seatbelt and prepare for take-off! We take you to the destinations that have been out of limits for disciplined experimentation before. As with space exploration, it is difficult to predict what one can see during the journey. We might discover new horizons. Or we might find that our anticipated goals are unreachable. Who knows? Let's start our countdown....

8

Mind Genomics: Consumer Mind "on the Shelf"

Think Americans crave ice cream and chocolate candy more than anything else? According to the Crave It! study,[1] ice cream and chocolate are joined by BBQ ribs and steak on the list of foods consumers crave. Differences also exist between men and women, along with ever-present variations by geography. Of the foods studied, right behind BBQ ribs and steak, we find potato chips, coffee, and chicken. The data reveals that men crave steak and ribs, whereas women long for chocolate candy and ice cream. Geography gets into the act as well. Northeasterners crave pretzels and pizza, whereas Southeasterners crave cheese and BBQ ribs. It doesn't stop there. Continuing on this crave-across-the-nation trip, we find that Midwesterners and Northwesterners crave steak, whereas Southwesterners crave tortilla chips and hamburgers.[2]

To get that deep understanding of consumers, the astute marketer could, of course, peer into a crystal ball or hire a trends consultant to scope out what's coming up. Of course, the business objective is to intercept the trend, ride it with offerings, and, hopefully, succeed by being there "firstest (sic) and smartest."

Okay, what about the reality of business, where there isn't time, there isn't money, and knowledge needs to be available in "Google time" at the press of a button, predigested and ready to be used, in nice, neat buckets? Today's marketers and developers need off-the-shelf, almost shrink-wrapped, systematized knowledge—organized insights about the customers' mind in specific topic areas, to guide development on one hand and messaging on the other. We came a bit closer to this encyclopedia of the customer mind while working with Abacus's Gamester, when our entrepreneurs searched three different databases for ideas—a portable DVD, electronic games, and a tablet PC. By incorporating multiple sources of ideas into a single new product, following the genomics approach, the Abacus folks "mashed together" a new product idea.

The overwhelming message from that three-component study is that there is a need for *databased* information of the type RDE provides, *but not limited to one topic area nor constrained by one product*. When we talk about food, for example, we should be talking about many *parallel* databases of foods. These databases might be of different products (steaks, cakes, coffees, colas, fruit juices). The database creates a common structure around the knowledge that RDE provides. The user of this database might merely need to look up both the ideas and how well they really do. Both types of information are readily available from RDE exercises. But let's go a bit further and be more daring. The database becomes even more useful to the developer or marketer when the structure of the information, the silos and the elements, is consistent from product to product within a single database. Understanding deeply how to use information from one product empowers the developer or marketer to scan the database across all products, to get a bird's-eye view. So what happens then? Quite simply, the developer and marketer learn what works, what doesn't, what segments exist, and what segments transcend specific products to apply all over. At the end of the day is the payoff—what opportunities make themselves known from the bigger picture that simply would have been consigned to noise or irrelevance if the database were small and myopically limited to only one product. That myopia often masquerades somehow as disciplined focus, a none-to-pleasant variety of perfectionism whose mantra is, distressingly, "Crawl before you walk, walk before you run." Let's use our database to begin at running and maybe move up to sprinting, or perhaps to the long, slow miles that give such delight to runners.

Why such effort? What is so special about a database that comprises different types of elements (product feature, brand name, emotion, availability, and so on), a database that goes beyond one product to encompass many, and a database whose elements are already quantified by RDE before anyone thought to ask? Is there a need for the encyclopedia of the customer mind that transcends simple information (what exists) by adding a relevance metric to that information? One metric in the spirit of RDE is how much utility that element in the database *really* contributes to driving the interest for the total panel and key subgroups. We believe that this database could become the logical expansion of our organizing principle for RDE—namely, the "algebra of the consumer mind" that we have been discussing up to now. (Note that some people have called what we're doing the *arithmetic of the consumer mind*, but we've been using the word *algebra* for so long that for now we'll stick with it.)

This encyclopedia of the consumer mind is the foundation of the emerging new science Mind Genomics, modeled on the science of genomics and the technology of informatics. The goal of this new science is to better understand how people react to ideas by using a formalized, structured, fact-based approach.

THREE REASONS FOR A MIND GENOMICS DATABASE OF THE CUSTOMER MIND

The approach uses today's tools, but in a new way. Mind Genomics begins with the principles of stimulus-response from experimental psychology, continues with experimental design and conjoint analysis from consumer research and statistics, and roars forward with Internet-based testing from marketing intelligence and multiple tests to identify patterns of mind-sets. We model the approach after today's very powerful biology application of genomics.[3]

1. A CENTRAL, ARCHIVED SOURCE FOR ACTIONABLE INFORMATION ABOUT THE CONSUMER/CUSTOMER

A countless spate of publications assaults the business community on the issues of consumers. These publications range from economics to psychology, from popular magazines to scientific tomes, from disciplines as varied as economics, psychology, marketing, and a host of technologies. These publications present different facets of the consumer, from understanding needs/wants, to studying the choice behavior in a store, and further to advertising/communication.

A recurrent, key problem with this information is the sheer mass of material. Sit in an office in a job any way related to consumer research, and you're likely to be bombarded with offers for one journal after another, for book after book, for conferences, and for a never-ending stream of short courses promising instant expertise. The amount of information simply overwhelms. The efforts to systematize this information continue to suffocate under the plethora of material. There is just too much "stuff," in the words of comedian George Carlin. It might be good stuff, but it defies access.

Despite the richness of raw material, most marketing and development professionals have less time than ever to learn about consumers or customers. They can read executive reviews of the latest business books, listen to abbreviated books on tape, or get briefed in-depth during a one- or two-day short course. The onus is on the business practitioner to absorb this material. And at the end of the day, the practitioner has to turn this material into action.

Therefore, *the first reason* to create a database of the customer mind is to centralize and organize the information about the consumer mind so the business can act on the knowledge in a timely manner.

2. A SOURCE OF TREND INFORMATION

By now, most companies of reasonable size have instituted so-called tracking studies in which they ask participants about their attitudes and habits. For example, in the computer industry, a tracking study might ask participants which particular brands of computers they plan to buy. The consumers have no problem telling the interviewer what they perceive or what they prefer. It is a lot more useful, however, for the corporation to know what the consumers really want, not just at a superficial, knee-jerk level such as "Make it good."

The *second reason* for the database is to monitor and analyze the trends in the market on a broad scale, to foresee the new needs before the customers can even articulate them directly. Paraphrasing Yogi Berra, prediction is hard, especially about the future.

3. A SOURCE FOR NEW PRODUCT IDEAS

Most professionals in marketing-related businesses have heard the platitude "Innovate or die." Whether this alarming statement appears on the cover of *Business Week* magazine or a forward-looking executive emblazons it on corporate communications, today the notion that innovation is a key competitive strength reigns supreme. But just how does the company develop new ideas on a systematic basis? In Chapter 6, "Rubik's Cube of Consumer Electronics Innovation," which deals with innovation, we presented a method inspired by genomics in which the developer mashes together elements from different product categories and generates new product ideas such as the Gamester. For such methods as mixing ideas to reach their fullest potential, the marketer and the developer must be able to reach into an *already-created database* and emerge with ideas that are ready for mashing together using RDE.

The *third reason* for the consumer minds database is to energize and inform an "innovation machine" for new ideas on a sustained basis by mixing and analyzing diverse ideas from multiple areas.

CREATING A DATABASE USING RDE: HOW IT HAPPENED

A great deal of today's so-called innovation thinking revolves around two poles, neither of which is systematic creation. One pole is the activity of coming up with new ideas, the so-called ideation phase. The second pole is metrics.

The ideation phase is typically executed via brainstorming, focus groups, or individual ideation. We have already discussed the intrinsic problems with focus groups (see Chapter 1, "Hewlett-Packard Shifts Gears"). Let's take a quick look at the brainstorming. Whole generations of American business professionals were raised to trust in teamwork and persuaded by that wonderful inventor of brainstorming, advertising executive Alex Osborn, to storm corporate problems "in commando fashion."

In a recent *Wall Street Journal* article,[4] Jared Sandberg analyzes traditional brainstorming, which, in his opinion, is doomed to fail. The article cites John Clark, a former university dean of engineering, saying that usually during the brainstorming, someone hijacks the topic, tries to prove everyone else wrong, works hard to impress the superiors who are present, or just converts the exercise into Comedy Central for his own enjoyment. "I can't remember a single instance where a group produced a really creative idea," Clark says.

Instead of trying to find an ultimate solution for the problem, RDE promotes a very democratic "equal opportunity" approach, with a significant amount of respect for the participant and privacy as well. The participants should generate the ideas—the more, the merrier—and let RDE do the "heavy lifting" of judging what works and what does not. Otherwise, warns David Perkins, a professor at the Harvard Graduate School of Education, group sessions can result in one person's bad idea tainting and restraining the range of others' ideas. "The best way to get good ideas is to get people to write them down privately," he says. Therefore, in many situations, the best results can be achieved even without herding people into one room. Banker Joe Polidoro cites self-consciousness as another problem of group exercises: "We sit there looking embarrassed, like we're all new to a nudist colony." To make it even less effective, it is very difficult to "schedule" someone's mind to be innovative at the specific meeting time.

In either case, whether with group ideation by brainstorming or individual contribution, RDE substantially enhances the process. How? Simply by *separating the idea generation from the idea evaluation* and by providing objective, hard metrics for each individual item on the list. Business loves metrics about processes and output. Endless papers exist about the numbers of ideas that are generated in meetings, such as the Stage Gate process and its ability to funnel ideas.[5] *What is missing, however, is a formalized system that actually creates the ideas.* RDE provides that system. Let's see the RDE "boot camp" that puts creative ideas to their test, finds out what works, and then databases these hot buttons for further use.

Let's move it one step further. Because RDE mixes and matches ideas in the test phase, why not mix and match disparate ideas *systematically from different product categories*, to create an invention machine in the service of innovation?[6]

Shortly after the new millennium began in 2000, we found ourselves unexpectedly involved in a series of discussions on the topic of creating a database about the consumer mind for understanding trends in the service of product innovation. The initial conversations involved food, perhaps because things move relatively slowly in the food industry. The topic was, what makes food delicious and craveable? The subtopic was whether we could create a database of the human mind with respect to ideas about food, such as descriptions of the food itself, brand names, emotional satisfaction, and so on.

These initial conversations with McCormick & Company, Inc., led to one of the first systematic databases of the consumer mind using RDE, called the Crave It! Studies. When these studies were planned, the notion was to create this database and rerun the RDE studies every few years to track how consumers were thinking about food and issues surrounding food. Four things made the Crave It! Studies very different from what had come before[7]:

1. **Depth of results**—The database would use experimental design to understand the algebra of the consumer mind and would use classification questionnaires to understand how the consumers described themselves.

2. **Range of topics**—The database would cover a variety of topics, ranging from descriptions of foods to emotions, consumption situations, brands, and health/wellness reinforcement.

3. **Range of products**—The first Crave It! database was run with 30 different products, each constituting a full, large-scale study. In a sense, it was a *mega RDE study.*

4. **Comparability**—As much as possible, the individual studies were set up to be parallel with each other. Parallelism adds power because it shows how customers react to the same type of messaging, depending upon the product.

The Crave It! database was only the first. As you will see, once we got the hang of creating a mega database using RDE, the rest was easy. We partnered with the U&I Group in New Jersey to create the It! Ventures, Ltd., and together rolled out the database for beverages (Drink It!), fast food (Grab It!), healthful foods/beverages (Healthy You!), insurance (Protect It!), charitable donations and nonprofits (Give It!), and even anxiety-provoking situations and public policy (Deal With It!). Quite a range, but all nicely handled and easy to use, embodying the principles of RDE.

For demonstration, we deal with the shopping experience. For obvious reasons, we have called this shopping-oriented database Buy It!. The database was developed with the support and guidance of the Kelley School of Business at Indiana University.

A word about developing these databases might be of interest. One's limitations always make themselves known most clearly when writing. We might fool ourselves that we know a lot, but when it comes time to write down our knowledge on paper, we often realize how little we know—or, at least, how disorganized and unstructured our knowledge turns out to be. We experienced that shock of recognition when we began applying the discipline of RDE to the shopping experience and to the eating experience. It became clear that we might easily create one RDE study on shopping—say, shopping for televisions—but it was quite daunting to create 30 parallel databases on 30 topics, all with the same structure. We had to think, what were the real silos? What was common in shopping? Just trying to satisfy the RDE demands of parallel design for the database sharpened our thinking. The same experience had occurred a year earlier with the Crave It! database. What were the basic silos? Fitting these basic silos to 30 different food and beverage products made us think more deeply about how to communicate to consumer participants in these studies. What could we say about olives, cola, and French fries that would allow us to compare these different products, make sense out of a mountain of data, and lead to real development and marketing actions?

The first thing we discovered is that, when developing these databases, it is vital to involve experts in the respective fields. So much specialized knowledge is involved in setting up the studies that a generalist probably cannot do justice to the task.

The second thing is that it might seem hard at first to create elements for 30 different studies, but a good trick makes things very easy. At the start of the database project, create a template that states what the element is supposed to communicate. Use that template as a guide, fitting in the appropriate element for that template. You will see this later when we talk about element rationale.

The third, and probably most important, lesson was to just do it. It was not going to be perfect—knowledge building through consumers and databases just never is. During the up-front work, we were excited. During the execution of the project, when we collected the data, we were apprehensive. Finally, during the analysis of the results, we were delighted. The data uncovered patterns that developers, marketers, and merchandisers alike said was helping them in a new way to understand their customer's minds, identify trends, and find new opportunities. The database also satisfied a lot of curiosity about what ideas and brand names really work and, just as important, what do not. Never underestimate the value of curiosity about "How is my brand or my messaging doing?."

THE BUY IT! DATABASE

Because in today's choice economy there are often many more options than can be handled, marketing professors at the Kelley School, along with those at Moskowitz Jacobs Inc., and It! Ventures, Ltd. (which specializes in these databases), joined together to create this revolutionary-in-scope database aimed at merchandisers, marketers, and developers. The goal was straightforward: to create a searchable database of the customer's mind using RDE to explore ideas.

We designed the database and the data-acquisition method to be simple and efficient, based on the following criteria:

1. **Range and type of products**—We chose 30 different products (see Table 8.1) for this database. We wanted to explore a large range of products that one might find in department and specialty stores. We also wanted coverage—household items, personal items, and big-ticket items.

Table 8.1

Range and type of products for the Buy It! database

Household Items	Personal Items	Big-Ticket Items
Toaster	Bathing suit	Car
Blender	Sandals	Television
Dishes	Boots	Refrigerator
Towels	Business suit	Couch
Bed sheets	Ties	Lawnmower
Drinking glasses	Socks	Tires
Tablecloths and napkins	Sunglasses	Washer/dryer
Candles	Pens	
Electric drill	Exercise equipment	
Decorative pillows	Writing paper	
Drapes and curtains	New baby gift	
Lamps		

2. **Range and type of elements**—Looking at Table 8.2, you can see the different silos and examples for one product, a toaster. A database of elements becomes useful when we use language that people ordinarily use in conversation to describe how they shop for the products or when they search for information about the product. In addition, when we begin to talk about the customers' feelings, we expand the focus beyond the product or situation, into emotions. The database developer need not stop here: The database becomes a jumping-off point for further probing with qualitative and observational research, the bread and butter of consumer insights.

Table 8.2

Examples of silos, element rationales, and actual elements for one of 30 products: the electric toaster, in the Buy It! database (partial list)

Element Rationale	Element Text—Toaster
Silo 1: Store Design/Physical Location	
Features areas for…everything you need for…	We have catalogs that feature toasters, food processors, juice extractors, and professional equipment… page after page of toasters
Lots of choices in the kind of…you use today…	Online or in the store…lots of choices in today's most popular styles or models
Silo 2: Merchandise Selection/Pricing Scheme	
Lots of…in your style…it's easy to find what you want, then try it right away…it makes you feel good	The price is JUST RIGHT… ALL OF THE TIME
One-stop shopping…lots of choices and options…brands, colors, sizes	Start anxious, leave happy… spending that is well worth it
Silo 3: Target Customer, Shopper/Emotional	
Lets you get your shopping done quickly	Lets you get your shopping done quickly
Come in anxious…leave happy, even though you might have spent a lot of money	One-stop shopping…lots of choices, options, brands, colors, and sizes

Silo 4: Hierarchy of Brands/Level of Service/Benefit	
Hierarchy of store names	At a store such as Lowe's, Home Depot, or Menard's
	At a store such as Wal-Mart, Kmart, or Target

3. **Collecting data from a diverse set of consumers**—It is inefficient to invite participants separately to 30 different studies. What if we send a willing participant the wrong invitation—for a product that he does not use at all, for example?

Let's turn the process around and allow the participant to select the particular study that most interests him. This strategy quickly builds our database, using participants who are interested in the product. The participant clicks on a link in the e-mail invitation, goes to a "wall" that presents the different topic areas, and chooses the study topic that most interests him. Afterward, the participant goes through a standard RDE interview, first evaluating systematically varied vignettes and then completing a self-profiling questionnaire.

LEARNING FROM THE DATABASE, AND WHAT WE CAN DO WITH THAT LEARNING

The key to using the data for meaningful business decisions is to know what to look for. Most businesses today have access to a lot more data than they know what to do with. In fact, the best description is that they are "flooded with information." The problem is how to organize the information, progressing from data to knowledge, from knowledge to insight, from insight to action.

We could spend this entire book presenting results just from the Buy It! database, but that would defeat the purpose of our quick overview "from 20,000 feet." Let's just look at a few highlights, introducing each of them with a question that a marketer might ask and then seeing what the Buy It! Database returns.[8]

QUESTION 1: WHAT'S REALLY IMPORTANT AS A "DRIVER" OF SHOPPING?

What do customers look for, and, just as important, are the patterns similar across different products? Or do the rules change so that some factors are important for certain products but fade into irrelevance for others? Let's look at what people say is important for three substantially different products—exercise equipment, drapes, and bathing suits—appealing to different types of people (see Figure 8.1).

Cutting right to the chase, we see that *price* is the most frequently mentioned. But something else starts to emerge. Price is almost always mentioned as key for exercise equipment, but only two-thirds of the participants feel that price is important for bathing suits. The practical implication: The customer might look at price more closely when shopping for exercise equipment and probably comes to the store armed with a lot of information ahead of the purchase. The salesperson had better be prepared. Such price knowledge is probably less important for clothing. So far, this is something that could be expected.

Product quality is another interesting driver. As with price, product quality is important for some items, such as the more expensive exercise equipment, but virtually irrelevant for bathing suits. It could be that, for clothing, perceived quality is simply not very important and should not be emphasized, whereas it would be a smart policy to talk about quality for exercise equipment. And drapes—well, they're in the middle, but quality doesn't seem to be very important for them, either. We are already on our way; we are learning what is important and what is not important—at least when the participant has to think about importance in general. However, as the infomercials tell us, "Wait, there's more."

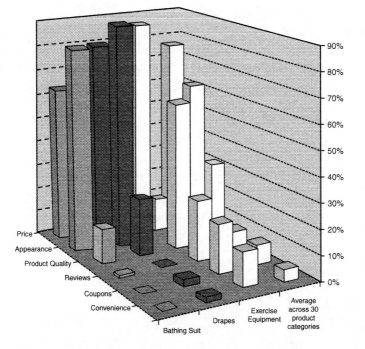

Figure 8.1 What percent of the participants choose the topic as relevant for their decision making when buying a product? A huge variance exists across different product categories (partial data).

QUESTION 2: IF I SAY SOMETHING ABOUT "SELF-SERVICE," DOES THE SAME LANGUAGE PLAY SIMILARLY ACROSS DIFFERENT PRODUCTS?

Today self-service is all the rage. Even some major sources of market and business intelligence information are self-serviced.[9] As service establishments control costs, one of the key ways to do so has the customers do the work, whether this means picking up the food in a restaurant instead of having a waiter/waitress, or checking themselves out at the supermarket instead of having a cashier do so.

The element for self-service (see Figure 8.2) was expressed as "Self-service—no one to get in your way or slow you down." The reason for this neutral-sounding expression is that it goes well with all of the 30 different product categories. *Keep in mind that, for the database to be really useful, the same idea ought to be applicable to the different products.*

You will see where this phrase works and where it does not, and whether it works equally with men and women. You are beginning to see how the mind genomics approach uses RDE to create a *database of marketing and merchandising language.* Figure 8.2 shows the retailer that self-service plays well for some product categories—for example, those that are low cost and low involvement, such as socks, pens, and sunglasses. We also learn that self-service does not do well for tires, but that is about it. Just as importantly, for high-involvement items, such as tires and lawnmowers, women want the attention and service.

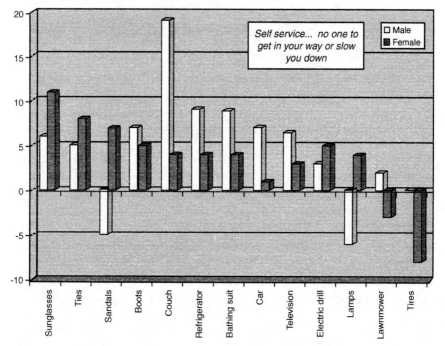

Figure 8.2 How the idea of self-service works across different products and among both males and females. The values are the utilities, showing the incremental percentage of participants who would be interested in buying if the element were placed in the message (partial data; list of the product sorted by the total panel).

We can do the same type of marketing and merchandising analysis with another phrase: "Offering a GREAT DEAL on the suggested retail price." Again, we see differences across products, but the pattern is not as clear. Price sensitivity is high for some unrelated products, such as sunglasses, refrigerators, and dishes. The real differences, however, occur across gender (see Figure 8.3).

What is the bottom line here for the business? Quite simply, RDE makes it possible to create a database that any marketer and merchandiser can use to discover what works and what does not. Does our particular set of elements cover everything? No. But until we actually see the results of such a database, we (and, indeed, most marketers and merchandisers) really don't know at a deep level what will work and what will not. RDE provides the tool to create that database for most general areas whose topics, product categories, or major issues can be enumerated and structured.

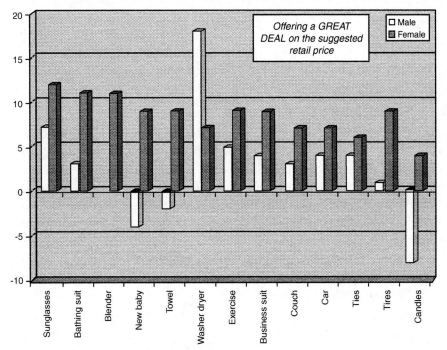

Figure 8.3   How the phrase about a great deal on the manufacturer's suggested retail price works across different products and among both males and females. The values are the utilities, showing the incremental percentage of participants who would be interested in buying if the element were placed in the message (partial data; list of the product sorted by the total panel).

QUESTION 3: WE KNOW THAT PEOPLE SHOP DIFFERENTLY; ARE THERE DIFFERENT MIND-SETS? IF SO, ARE THEY THE SAME ACROSS PRODUCTS?

One of the ongoing motifs of this book in general and of RDE in particular is that there exist in the consumer population people of different mind-sets.

These groups look at the world differently, react to the test concepts with radically different patterns, and thus provide the opportunity for a product or a message to go from good to great. We find these segments by analyzing the pattern of responses to the different concept elements, people who react similarly to the same messages—that is, who show similar patterns of what RDE messages they like and dislike.

But what about 30 studies in which the elements differ somewhat across the products? The first question is whether we find segments at all. Do people differ in the way they think about shopping? Based upon everything we have seen up to now, the answer is a strongly probable "yes." But if we stop there, we're simply using RDE the way we used it before: to discover what to do for specific products or communications.

Let's stretch a bit and look for the "really big idea": *Do we find the same general segments across the different products?* If we do, the database more than pays for itself because now the database becomes a Rosetta stone for understanding consumer responses to shopping messages. When we find the same groups repeatedly, across different products, marketers and merchandisers will have new guides to what generally to say and do when they advertise and when they display a product. Finding the same segments in product after product means that we can feel comfortable adopting a general organizing approach to develop, market, and merchandise an array of related and possibly not-so-related products Instead of getting lost in minutiae, the developer, the marketer, and the merchandiser can begin to apply *general rules* to solve specific problems. *Rules,* not abstractions from innumerable examples, are easier to work with.

Let's see what our data show us. By looking at patterns of the responses, study after study, for each of the 30 products, and following the segmentation procedure, we find that the Buy It! database suggests three *general patterns.* You should keep in mind that the participants in the shopper database study might have no idea that from their responses, we can put them into different segments. But we can. And when we do, we see the three overarching groups of shoppers in Table 8.3. We characterize the shopper by the specific elements or messages in the test concepts that excite them. We know what they respond to, allowing us to define them (left side) and to form some hypotheses about them (right side).

Table 8.3

The three shopper segments across all 30 products in Buy It! projects, and some hypotheses about them

Segment	Hypothesis
Easy Shopping—Love to shop and want *service, availability, ease of use, and price.* They are not interested in the overall store environment.	This group is actively looking for help to entertain their kids and spouses.
Product Involved—Love to shop and want *style and variety.* They are *influenced by the store environment* and want it to reflect their interest in style. Some of them are willing to pay a little more for a better store environment and shopping experience.	This group is so involved with the product, they are unaware of their kids and spouses until disaster hits.
Price/Service Sensitive—Love to shop and get a *thrill from finding a great price or bargain.* They are not interested in the overall store environment.	This group is interested in finding the bargain; they will include others to help them find it.

Figure 8.4 shows the distributions of the respondents by segments in some of the Buy It! projects. It's clear the segments exist in the different populations, but also that the segments distribute in different ways, depending on the product.

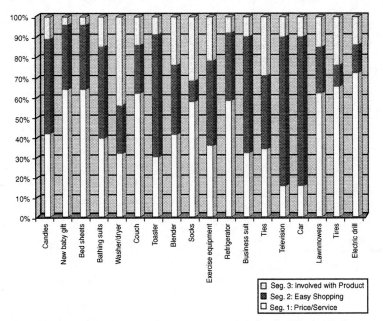

Figure 8.4 How the segments distribute for each product (partial data)

Knowing *what to say, how to say it, and to whom to say it* can be extremely important. If we do that, we are likely to find the right message for the consumer in any category, as we see in Table 8.4 for electric drills. For the price/service segment, it's probably best to talk about the right price and hit home with that message all the time. For the easy shopping segment, in contrast, it is probably best to talk about store service at purchase (wrapping, shipping, and so on). Finally, for the product-involved segment, it is good to talk about designer tools and stores that appeal to do-it-yourselfers. Knowing what to say to the customer can create powerful messages. These messages can take us from a good sales environment to a great one.

A very important related issue is knowing which segment any prospective customer belongs to. This in itself is a big topic—the topic of assignment. When the marketer meets someone, how does the marketer discover the segment to which the person belongs? In the simplest scenario, one may combine the optimal messages for each of the segments (for example, place them in different places around the store, catalog, etc.) instead of using a single offer optimized for the total panel. Clearly, if the marketer can sense the proper segment, then the breakthrough messaging and even the product that will delight are simple to choose. This is a topic for a book by itself. Additional information is readily available on this assignment problem.[10]

Table 8.4

Hot buttons for electric drills. Each segment is attuned to different messaging.

	Total	S1	S2	S3
Base Size	126	91	15	19
Constant	33	33	26	38
Segment 1: Price/Service Sensitive				
At a store such as Lowe's, Home Depot, or Menard's	11	**12**	2	13
The price is JUST RIGHT...ALL OF THE TIME	8	**12**	3	–8
Electric drills chosen to fit your work or "do it yourself" style, lifestyle, and personality...to try out at your leisure	6	**10**	–10	4
Simple, easy shopping...no hassles	6	**9**	7	–11
Helpful staff, not patronizing...the service is personalized, but you don't feel like you're being taken advantage of!	6	**8**	2	–4

	Total	S1	S2	S3
Segment 2: Easy Shopping				
Offering affordable packaging and gift wrapping for your electric drill	–9	–11	**13**	–13
With a chain of stores all over…buy your electric drill anywhere	2	1	**13**	1
Shop at our online store for every kind of electric drill you can imagine…plus all the accessories you could want	2	4	**12**	–12
Shopping with salespeople just like you…who take the time to appreciate your needs!	2	4	**10**	–12
Online or in the store…lots of choices in today's most popular models	0	0	**9**	–9
Segment 3: Product Involved				
At Sears Brand Central	4	1	5	**16**
At a store such as Lowe's, Home Depot, or Menard's	11	12	2	**13**
At a local building supply store	4	5	–15	**12**
At a store such as Wal-Mart, Kmart, or Target	8	8	4	**11**
Designer tools with a range of matching complementary items	1	–2	5	**8**

WHAT MAKES CHEESECAKE CRAVEABLE? HOW CRAVE IT! DEFINES OUR TONGUES

Let's move away from the department and specialty store into the dining room. We talk now about one of nature's most delectable items (at least, to some): cheesecake. Anyone who loves cheesecake knows that this delicacy can be found in many tempting varieties—indeed, the Cheesecake Factory, a casual family restaurant, boasts more than two dozen. You can have Oreos in your cheesecake, if you want, and for those who can't make up their mind, there is the cheesecake of the month, delivered right to the door and available only by ordering online. Just the descriptions of some of the Cheesecake Factory's offerings, shown here, may make your mouth water:

> Our Original Cheesecake, with delicious spiced pumpkin filling all baked in a graham cracker crust and finished with whipped cream rosettes. Better than the best pumpkin pie!

Flourless Godiva Chocolate Cheesecake: Flourless Godiva chocolate cake topped with a layer of Godiva chocolate cheesecake loaded with chunks of Godiva milk chocolate and topped with a layer of Godiva chocolate mousse.

While running Crave It! projects, we realized pretty quickly that some foods were simply more popular than others. It is no surprise that chocolate was by far the most popular study, with almost 500 people participating. People like chocolate. Pizza and ice cream were about two-thirds as popular, followed by the caffeine twins, coffee and cola. Cheesecake and steak were tied for third place. Beyond cheesecake, however, there were many popular foods. You would think that products such as cinnamon rolls, potato chips, and chicken would all be craved. Not as much as cheesecake. Another interesting finding was that men and women differed (surprise!), but the way they differed made a lot of sense. Women craved chocolate candy—more than four-fifths of the participants in the chocolate candy database were women. Men stuck with steak—almost half of the participants were men. And cheesecake? No surprise here, either. Women crave cheesecake. The numbers are in Figure 8.5.

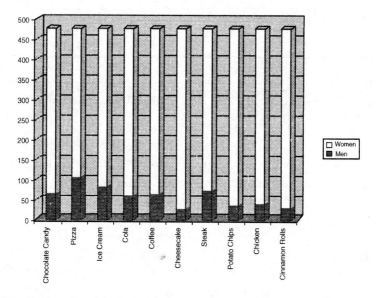

Figure 8.5 Number of participants in 10 of the 30 Crave It! databases. More participants mean that the food is more intrinsically interesting and more frequently craved.

The real "meat" (or the real cheesecake, if you will) comes from the performance of the individual elements (see Table 8.5). We saw the same thing with our Buy It! database for shopping. The big ideas are descriptions of food. *It's not brand, it's not reassurance of health or quality; it is the food itself!* Just look at the ideas that excite our 172 participants (first column, labeled "Total"). The big hits come from the words that picture the product itself. You do not get a lot of pull from a phrase such as "When it's cold outside, cheesecake is cozy and inviting." This phrase gets a paltry utility (+3), meaning that 3% of the participants would change their vote from "okay" to "crave it" when you use that phrase. You're likely to get a lot more hits when you describe the cheesecake the way a restaurant menu might describe it when trying to entice the customer. This is the kind of language that pulls the customer: "Cheesecake with swirls of raspberry, chunks of white chocolate, baked in a crunchy crust, and garnished with pecans." You go from a measly (+3) to a strong (+19), meaning that almost one in five participants would change his (or her) vote from "okay" to "crave." Now that is strong.

Table 8.5

Hot buttons for cheesecake for the three segments from the Crave It! database. The real action is in the three segments.

	Total	S1	S2	S3
Base Size	172	36	88	48
Additive Constant	41	55	32	45
Hot Button for Segment 1: Imaginer				
When it's cold outside, cheesecake is cozy and inviting	3	**11**	6	–8
Hot Buttons for Segment 2: Elaborate				
Cheesecake with swirls of raspberry, chunks of white chocolate, baked in a crunchy crust and garnished with pecans	19	–38	**42**	20
Cheesecake wedges with thick filling, gooey sauce, chopped nuts, and slices of fresh fruit	14	–27	**35**	5
Dense cheesecake swirled together with ribbons of chocolate chips in a chocolate crust...served with a raspberry sauce drizzled across your plate	18	–20	**35**	17

Table 8.5 continued

	Total	S1	S2	S3
Hot Buttons for Segment 3: Classic				
Cheesecake with a smooth appearance; light flavor; fluffy, creamy texture; and a graham cracker crust	16	−3	15	**32**
Cheesecake so rich it melts slowly to release a delicate, intense flavor	17	8	17	**25**
Real cheesecake made with ingredients like eggs, cream cheese, sugar, vanilla, and lemon juice	11	4	7	**23**
Cheesecake with swirls of raspberry, chunks of white chocolate, baked in a crunchy crust, and garnished with pecans	19	−38	42	**20**

An interesting recent development with Kentucky Fried Chicken confirms these findings. Trying to ride the health food wave, Kentucky Fried Chicken changed not only the menu (albeit quite minimally), but even the company name. Apparently, they thought that by removing the word *fried* from their establishments, they could attract healthy eaters. They used a heavy marketing campaign to promote their more "healthful" food under the KFC brand. Unfortunately for KFC, the customers did not buy KFC's pretense. In addition to losing their loyal patrons, who used to devour their deep-fried delicacies, electing taste over healthiness, they missed would-be customers they could have won from the competition. Recently, the company has announced that it is changing the name back to Kentucky Fried Chicken.[11]

So the food itself and its description make people crave. No message, such as healthiness, can replace them. These "off-the-real-topic" messages probably ought to be used as an addition to, not a replacement of, the main food descriptions. Quite an interesting finding!

But that's not all. The It! databases were designed as a consumer encyclopedia, to show how the product category—and, indeed, the supercategory of food—works. We return to our old strategy of segmenting to find that there are three segments. There could be more, but from food to food (and beverage), we find these three types of mind-sets:

1. **The Imaginer**—"Describe the situation, the ambience to me, and paint me a romantic picture. I am not so interested in the food." It is hard to picture a product for the Imaginer segment. And it's not so easy to find this segment. There are not too many of them out there—only 36 out of the 172 participants could be called Imaginers.

2. **The Elaborate**—Describe the product by painting a word picture, and these people will love the product. They are about half the participants. They start out low—do not use just the single word *cheesecake* with them. They have a low additive constant, (+32), meaning that only one of three of them will even be interested. But just use the right words, and you can go from 32% to 74%, or three out of four (32 + 42). These people are really into the food (Figure 8.6 shows a sample rendition of what cheesecake would delight the Elaborate).

3. **The Classic**—Just give them the traditional product. They are about a quarter of the participants. They are okay with the basic idea of cheesecake. About half of them will say they crave cheesecake, even without any enticing words. Add the right words describing the way a traditional, not over-the-top cheesecake ought to be ("Cheesecake with a smooth appearance; light flavor; fluffy, creamy texture; and a graham cracker crust"), and 32% more of them will turn on. Figure 8.7 shows a rendition of a cheesecake to delight the Classic segment.

Figure 8.6   Cheesecake for the Elaborate segment

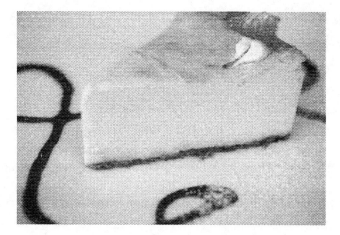

Figure 8.7 Cheesecake for the Classic segment

SUMMING UP: A VISION OF THE FUTURE

Business information in databases is not a new idea. Whether the databases comprise unstructured information that can be accessed (as with Lexis/Nexis or Web search engines) or structured tables of data, it is now standard practice to access the information as an aid to decisions, or even simply to do background research.

What the It! databases have begun to demonstrate—specifically, in shopping, but now with many others—is the now-practical application of RDE to create a *unique, new type of database,* focusing more deeply on the customer mind. Instead of having a database of activities summarizing what information we know from who buys what, economic trends, and so on, we show here how to create a ready-to-use, simple-to-interpret, affordable, and immediately available database about mind-sets, using communications that the marketer might use for advertising, product development, and merchandising.

What is the future of such a database? With RDE, one can begin creating many of these databases fairly simply to ultimately develop a marketer's library. For relatively low cost, we envision such a library being created using many different databases, updated on a regular basis, comprising the collections of the RDE results cited here. Each database might pertain to one topic, such as shopping, insurance, the fast food experience, or the automobile experience. Each study in the database would deal with one specific aspect. For example, in the case of automobiles, we would have separate studies concerning comparison shopping on the Web, layouts of the automobile showroom, test drives, financial payments, car design, car advertising on television, and so on. Each of these separate studies would, in turn, comprise experimentally designed vignettes to understand the algebra of the customer's mind, as well as extensive self-profiling classification. The material for the vignettes would be taken from everyday experience (what is out there), deconstruction of current communications (*a la* the ezines exercise in Chapter 5, "Discover More about Your Competitors Than They Themselves Know—Legally!"), and future visions of the topic.

With these databases available, the authors envision a simple[12] pay-as-you-go digital, searchable library that, with the proper technology, can quickly reveal what consumers think about ideas, what to say, and how to say it. We even envision online tools to invent new ideas in that area by recombining old ideas and one's own thoughts into new mixtures using the recombinant, genomics approach described in this chapter.

The next step is extending the use of such broad libraries into one-to-one marketing (or any other type of real-time content optimization).

During her visit to China to explore possibilities of global cooperation (that is, in search of affordable production facilities and possibly new markets), Allison-the-Entrepreneur got fascinated with Chinese music and its history. Two instruments she liked the most were the *dizi* and *pipa* (pronounced "deets" "pi-pah"). They are quite different. The first is a *simple* bamboo flute with eight holes. The second is a *sophisticated* four-string lute. Both instruments sound heavenly, despite their substantial differences. You need to have several different *dizis* to play various music pieces because each *dizi* supports only one music key. But a *dizi* is very simple to make and inexpensive. It is quite easy to learn to play the *dizi,* and it can be carried and used anywhere, anytime! On the other hand, a *pipa* can play the most complicated music and can do it magnificently. The trade-offs are that it takes a very, very long time to learn to play, it is expensive, and it is fragile. So Allison was not surprised to learn that when the Yellow Emperor decided to standardize the music pitch many years ago, in an attempt to bring music to masses, his choice was, of course, a *dizi*. Simplicity won out.

Allison found this story enlightening. She was captivated by some completely novel business ideas that looked very promising for her business. The problem was that she might need to market it to a totally new segment of consumers that she has no knowledge about. She hesitated about which type of RDE to use. Should Allison use the classical, in-depth exercise with lots of material, but also a lot of effort and resources? Or should she limit the number of options and use the simpler, faster, but more limited yet more expedient do-it-yourself (DIY) version of RDE she used many times before?

Allison's problem was the absence of any knowledge about these new customers and the new area of products she was thinking about. Allison had neither the luxury of extra time nor the money needed to explore the area, but she was nonetheless shrewd enough to understand the importance of knowing her customers before taking an important step.

The solution for her business problem was quite easy for Allison. As in the case with the Yellow Emperor, simplicity won out: She decided to use precompiled databases of the customer's mind, similar to the It! databases described in this chapter, to jump-start the process. She saved time and money skipping several iterations of her trusted *ad hoc* studies in the area completely new to her—the task was too daunting, given the time limitations and variation in the customer's mind, and the fact that she does not know where to start. Allison learned a lot just by going through the database, as we did for the shopping study. Of course, with Allison being the go-getter that she is, we're sure she'll mine her It! database thoroughly, gleaning a lot of insights from this marketer's bookshelf.

Now she has a pretty good idea about the customers' mind in that new for-her product category. If Allison needs it, she can easily execute a few simple follow-up RDE studies to fine-tune her ideas. The most important thing: *Allison need not start from zero.* Afterward, we would not be surprised to read about her using the off-the-shelf database to springboard her own efforts. Allison will undoubtedly succeed here as well—to a great degree because she now understands how *most effectively and rapidly* to mine her customer's mind.

ENDNOTES

1   A series of RDE studies sponsored by McCormick & Company, Inc. and conducted by Moskowitz Jacobs Inc., with The Understanding and Insight Group, LLC.

2   "Americans Crave Meats and Sweets: McCormick Sponsored Ground-Breaking Study Reveals the Nation's Food Cravings," McCormick & Company, Inc., press release (Hunt Valley, MD, 2001); "McCormick & Company, Inc., Releases More Findings from Sponsored Crave It! Study," McCormick & Company, Inc., press release (Hunt Valley, MD, January 2002).

3   For more information, read Howard R. Moskowitz, Alex Gofman, Jacqueline Beckley, and Hollis Ashman, "Founding a New Science: Mind Genomics," *Journal of Sensory Studies* 21(3): 266–307.

4   "Brainstorming Works Best If People Scramble for Ideas on Their Own," *Wall Street Journal*, 13 June 2006.

5   R. G. Cooper, *Winning at New Products: Accelerating the Process from Idea to Launch.*, 3rd ed. (Cambridge, MA: Perseus Books, 2001).

6   The notion of such formalized mixing and matching of disparate ideas from different realms was presented in the mid-1990s by HRM in his book *Consumer Testing and Evaluation of Personal Care Products* (New York, Marcel Dekker, page 430, in the section "Creating a truly new product or new category"). The topic was oral care. At that time the development of RDE was not sufficient to make the process a very simple one. That time has now arrived for a formal, easy-to-implement system. See also Chapter 6 of this book.

7   J. Beckley, H. R. Moskowitz, "Databasing the Consumer Mind: The Crave It!, Drink It!, Buy It!, and Healthy You! Databases." In Proceedings of Annual Meeting of Institute of Food Technologists, Anaheim, CA, 2002.

8   H. Ashman, S. Rabino, D. Minkus-McKenna, and H. R. Moskowitz, "The Shopper's Mind: What Communications Are Needed to Create a 'Destination Shopping' Experience? In *Proceedings of the ESOMAR Conference,* "Retailing/Category Management: Linking Consumer Insights to In-Store Implementation." Dublin, Ireland, 2.

9   For example, www.marketresearch.com, an aggregator of global business intelligence.

[10] W. R. Klecka, "Discriminant Analysis," In *Quantitative Applications in the Social Sciences Series* (19) (1980): 7–19; Howard R. Moskowitz, Sebastiano Porretta, and Matthias Silcher, "Concept Research," In *Food Product Design and Development* (Ames, IO: Blackwell Publishing, 2005).

[11] Robert Gordman and Armin Brott, *The Must-Have Customer: 7 Steps to Winning the Customer You Haven't Got* (New York: Truman Talley Books, 2006).

[12] As opposed to *ad hoc,* more involved projects that might follow the database analysis stage and might be more relevant for larger-scale objectives.

9

Making the President and Public Communications into "Products"

Many political consultants agree that owning a dog is a virtual prerequisite for the future president. Americans love "First Dogs," sometimes more than the dog's owners. From Washington's Foxhounds to Bush's Barney, dogs are as traditional as baseball. Twenty-two U.S. presidents have owned purebred dogs, and most shared the White House with them. Some First Dogs even had jobs—the pet Springer Spaniel of Barbara and George H. W. Bush, Millie, authored a book;[1] Lyndon Johnson's Beagles, Him and Her, modeled for *Life* magazine; and an Airedale Terrier Laddie Boy, owned by U.S. President Warren G. Harding, oversaw presidential meetings from his hand-carved cabinet chair.[2]

This short history of dogs and presidents brings us to an even more mystifying area than artistic design: social and political life, ruled by high-profile, high-power political gurus who inexplicably try to "make" the new public figures by avoiding such obvious mistakes as politically incorrect dogs' names and much more. But what about the role of RDE in that byzantine, sometimes illogical world of politics? Up to now, we have been talking about applying RDE to make profits, whether the profit comes from products, communications, or inventions. Can our future senators and presidents be *engineered* in the same systematic fashion that we saw with foods, electronics, or packaged goods?

Let's go a little further. What about social and political issues? *Can*—and, even more important—*should* RDE find a proper and productive place in public policy? In a few known cases, adaptive experimentation has been used to evolve public policy.[3] To underscore the difference between political science and the rest of the world, there are even different names for known terms. For example, instead of using the word *segmentation*, political scientists use the terms *preference structuration* or *single-peakedness.*[4] Can the disciplined and somewhat idealistic RDE find a home inside this fortress? Can RDE create its own niche in this field—say, a science of prescriptive public policy?

For a public person to be elected, he needs to present himself in a way that convinces the voters to "buy" this candidate. *What* to say to the people and *how* to communicate the proper messages are simply critical. Essentially, the public person faces a task similar to what the marketers face with credit cards and jewelry (message construction) and ezines (message deconstruction), but rather than profit, it involves public policy. The astute candidate needs to keep adjusting messages depending on the geopolitical situation and specific locale of the campaign. Seems like a job for our trusted RDE-based segmentation under the politically correct name of "preference structuration," if needed (see the previous paragraph).

Let's shift focus, keeping an eye on the public, but back into the company once again—our area of comfort now. What about a corporate PR manager working on a difficult and surely unpopular announcement? Can we find ways to communicate the upcoming hard changes that the corporation will implement without triggering too much anxiety among the employees? Can RDE give government officials the necessary science-based tools to make the documents they create get more of the citizen's positive feelings, even when the documents are not tinged with the rose-colored glasses of a Pollyanna?

Without any further ado, we look at two examples here using RDE and the *vox populi*, the voice of the people. First, we deal with the president as a consumer product. Then we look into the government's attempt to communicate in times of high anxiety—specifically, during terrorism. Even in these situations, disciplined RDE works—and gives us some rather remarkable direction.

THE PRESIDENT AS A PRODUCT

If a presidential candidate were a food, what would he be, and what kind of shoppers would be putting him in their carts?

The subtitle of this section (in the context of the 2004 elections) might sound a bit politically incorrect, but it is actually a modified quote from an article in *The New York Times* written by the well-known columnist John Tierney. Tierney describes the authors' RDE experiments in politics.[5] Tierney named these political experiments "Dr. Moskowitz's supermarket," to underscore the surprising similarity between product optimization and political messaging. The original Tierney quote we used in the subtitle was meant for George W. Bush, but the RDE approach applies well regardless of one's political affiliation.

Voters don't usually think of political candidates as consumer products. The democratic heritage instills within citizenry a sense of civic pride and responsibility. We are taught from grade school on that the right to elect public officials by voting is a fundamental benefit of becoming a citizen. But reality must intrude, of course. It always does. At some level, we recognize that, for an official to get elected, it is important to know what the citizens want, how to express these wishes, and how to create the appropriate political machinery to drive the vote. When you think of it that way, politics is not much different from product and service marketing.

So what about thinking of the president or any other official as a consumer product? The idea is not really far-fetched when you think about it. Certainly, the president is promoted as a product in the media. Today's presidential candidates hold focus groups, try to understand public opinion, and, in general, do all the things that we might expect from the astute marketer. The candidate is searching for *volume*—not volume of purchases, but volume of votes. The U.S. president is more or less similar to a big-ticket item purchased once every four years.

Then why not treat the president as a product to be sold to do a job? The next logical step is to have RDE pinpoint messages that the candidate ought to broadcast to the public—that is, the advertising appropriate for this "president as a product." If, in fact, we treat the candidate as a product, the job of electing a president becomes a bit easier. Simply monitor the environment, identify what issues come to the fore, let RDE discover hot buttons that drive the consumer (voter interest), and present those new ideas to candidates. Why not? And why not do so on a micro scale—say, in neighborhood after neighborhood? The Internet makes it easy, rapid, and affordable. Maybe even fun.

Earlier work of the authors around 2000, when RDE was really being integrated into the Internet, suggested that a candidate's political platform is not really much different than the RDE work done in the commercial sector.[6] But to be specific, let's look at the 2004 presidential campaign and focus on messages chosen by John Kerry and George Bush. What did they say? More important, can RDE tell us unambiguously what they *should* have emphasized and whether the candidates' messages hit the best hot buttons throughout the campaign?

Let's begin by deconstructing Kerry's messaging at the start of his campaign. Figure 9.1 shows the types of snippets from Kerry's speeches. Deconstructing a mass of communication is not particularly difficult. It just means doing homework: collecting the speeches at a certain time and identifying the themes and simple quotes. Content analysis works here, as long as we make every effort to keep the candidate's words and, of course, the tonality of the message.

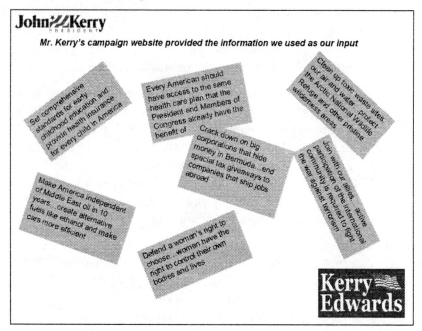

Figure 9.1 Some of the snippets of language used by RDE. These are Kerry's words, albeit in somewhat stripped-down form to become simple declarative statements.

The veritable abundance of Kerry-relevant messages was then collapsed to four silos of 9 elements, each in order, to generate a representative set of 36 such elements. As you saw in previous chapters, the elements were automatically combined by experimental design into 60 different combinations for each participant, with a specific combination or test concept comprising either one or no elements from each of the four categories.

> **Note**
>
> Because of the experimental nature of this project, U.S. participants were selected simply at random from the list compiled by a panel provider. The participants were required to be over 21 and residents of the U.S. Of course, for conclusive and actionable results, the respondents have to be chosen the same way as is done for traditional political polls, from a representative sample. The data in this section should be viewed as "proof of concept" only.

Each participant evaluated a unique set of 60 concepts (see an example in Figure 9.2) so that across all the participants, none of the individuals evaluated the same stimuli, although all of them are constructed by experimental design from the same set of 36 elements. So far, it's hard to tell whether we're dealing with communications about pickles or presidents. In the end, it might not matter. Both might wind up being different sides of the same coin.

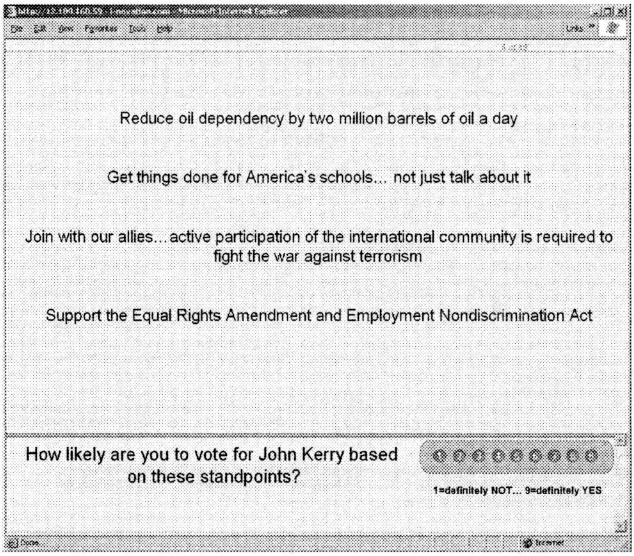

Figure 9.2 Example of a test concept for Kerry, comprising four elements, one element from each of the four silos

WHAT KERRY SHOULD HAVE EMPHASIZED TO HAVE BEEN ELECTED AS THE NEXT U.S. PRESIDENT

The bottom line of RDE applied to political candidates is the ability to make midcourse corrections. Today's candidates live in a complex world, with shifting relevance of different messages depending upon who a candidate talks to, but also what else is happening in the world. It makes sense, therefore, that RDE could provide a way for the candidate to choose what's most important at the moment.

Let's see the results from executing the *exact same RDE project once a month,* on the third Wednesday, for the eight months prior to the 2004 election. Conducting the RDE study in this disciplined fashion is quite easy; all one needs to do is have the study ready on the computer and launch the study once per month, with a new group of participants invited each month.

We get a good idea of what Kerry should have said by seeing the utility or impact values of the individual ideas. Our participants had no idea that the elements were systematically varied, nor did they know that Kerry had actually made these statements. The participants were shown the vignettes and asked whether they would vote for candidate Kerry based on what they read.

As we saw in previous chapters, the method of regression analysis relates the 36 messages that we used in the RDE interview to the participant's response of "I'll vote for Kerry." If the participant rated the vignette 7, 8, or 9, we conclude that the participant would most likely vote for Kerry based on what the vignette presented; if the participant rated the vignette 1–6, we conclude that there would be a most likely "No" or undecided vote for Kerry. The nice thing about RDE is that it uses the response ratings to *specific vignettes* so that a participant need not be stuck in a yes or no vote—it is possible to change the vote, depending on what Kerry said.

The regression analysis provides us with a baseline (how many people out of 100 would vote for Kerry if he did not say anything) and the number of people out of 100 who would say they'd vote for Kerry if he used a certain message when campaigning. The utility can sometimes be negative if the candidate were to say the wrong thing! So now you will see what *RDE can do to show us the inside of the voter's mind and the power of the message to change the mind.* This is not much different from ezines, even though we are dealing with a presidential candidate. We're still looking inside the customer mind, but this time the customer is a voter and the product is the president.

Let's look at the candidates' baseline interest each month, from March 2004 to October 2004. In Figure 9.3, both candidates' data are plotted on the same graph.

Kerry's baseline starts at 54 in March, which means that of the people who chose to participate (the 544 individuals), 54% were predisposed to vote for Kerry, even if he did not say anything else. Looking further, we see that by September and October 2004, our new participants (different sets of individuals each month) are becoming more pro-Kerry. In fact, RDE applied to political candidates is telling us that the voter participant is getting more hardened in his basic position.

Switching candidates for a second, let's look at the same type of results for Bush. We ran a parallel study using George Bush's own statements, constructed in the same way, with the same types of silos, also with 36 elements. When a participant got an email, the participant could choose the Bush or Kerry study. Bush's data doesn't look quite so strong. The predilection to vote for candidate Bush fluctuates quite a bit, almost as if the voter were actually undecided about voting for him.[7]

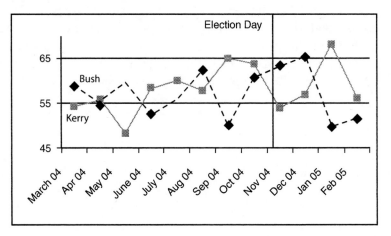

Figure 9.3 Graph showing how the propensity to vote for Kerry and Bush changes over months

RDE should tell us much more than simply propensity to vote for a candidate—that is pretty simple and can be done by asking the voter "Who will you vote for?" We should use RDE for the really tough job: *recommending to the candidate what specifically to say*. We get these recommendations by looking at the utility or impact values of the different messages. Keep in mind that we did the same exact study, month after month, prior to the election and analyzed the results for each month.

The amount and richness of RDE data can become overwhelming when we think of 36 elements, each of which is tracked over the eight months prior to the 2004 election. We see this in Table 9.1. Let's see what came out.

- Kerry's strongest messages focused on health care, such as "Every American should have access to the same health care plan that the President and Members of Congress already have the benefit of." This element consistently scores well (between +8 and +11) and really hits home to the voter. In fact, three of the health care messages score well, as we see in Table 9.1. We might imagine Kerry's war room taking these results from RDE and crafting even stronger, more compelling messages. Certainly, health care is important and can add up to 10% more votes. Kerry should have continued to hit home on this topic.

- Kerry's weak messages vary all over. Even health care can be weak, if tied to AIDS. What we see from the weak messages is that participants in the Kerry RDE study are interested in themselves, not in great social problems. Kerry's voters become interested when they see themselves as fitting into a group that could directly benefit from what he says. No bleeding hearts for him.

Table 9.1

How elements performed for candidate Kerry prior to the 2004 election. Strong messages have light shading. Weak messages are shown in italics. The rest are mostly neutral.

		Mar	Apr	May	Jun	Jul	Aug	Sep	Oct
	Base	*544*	*248*	*175*	*150*	*241*	*107*	*75*	*366*
Topic	*Constant*	*54*	*56*	*48*	*58*	*60*	*58*	*65*	*64*
Economy/ Jobs	Bring back the 3 million jobs that were lost under the current administration	4	4	4	9	3	–2	0	5
Health Care	Restore Medicare and provide real prescription drug relief for all Americans	6	10	7	3	7	3	5	5
Health Care	Every American should have access to the same health care plan that the President and Members of Congress already have the benefit of	8	8	11	5	8	8	1	5
Health Care	Make health care affordable for every American	7	8	8	6	9	4	7	4
Environment	Clean up toxic waste sites, our air and water...protect the Arctic National Wildlife Refuge and other pristine wilderness areas	2	–2	6	0	1	1	1	4
Women	Stand up for the rights of women...fairness and dignity	–1	–1	1	4	–1	*–8*	–1	–2
Foreign Policy/Iraq	Involve NATO, international troops, and the United Nations to create a stable and democratic Iraq	–1	0	*–5*	0	–1	*–5*	*–8*	–2
Minority/ Equal Rights	Support the Equal Rights Amendment and Employment Nondiscrimination Act	1	*–5*	–4	0	–1	*–6*	–3	–3

Table 9.1 continued

		Mar	Apr	May	Jun	Jul	Aug	Sep	Oct
	Base	*544*	*248*	*175*	*150*	*241*	*107*	*75*	*366*
Topic	*Constant*	*54*	*56*	*48*	*58*	*60*	*58*	*65*	*64*
Women/ Business	*Expand the number of women-owned businesses...eliminate the glass ceiling that keeps talented women out of top positions*	*–2*	*–6*	*–4*	*–4*	*–1*	*–1*	*–5*	*–3*
Terrorism/ Iraq	*Win the peace in Iraq...it will have a profound impact on the war on terrorism*	*–2*	*–4*	*–3*	*–6*	*–4*	*–6*	*–3*	*–3*
Health Care/AIDS	*Increase funding for programs that assist people living with HIV/AIDS*	*–5*	*–4*	*0*	*–6*	*–7*	*–6*	*–3*	*–4*
Health Care/AIDS	*Combat the AIDS epidemic at home... increase research funding, fund the search for an AIDS vaccine*	*–1*	*–2*	*0*	*–5*	*–5*	*–6*	*–7*	*–4*
Women/ Abortion	*Defend a woman's right to choose... women have the right to control their own bodies and lives*	*–2*	*–3*	*–1*	*–1*	*–5*	*–11*	*–3*	*–5*
Education	*Mandatory funding for schools...no questions asked*	*–2*	*–6*	*–3*	*–8*	*–4*	*–12*	*–1*	*–5*

The advantage of the RDE way of thinking is that people do not have to and cannot be politically correct in their responses, which they do in direct polls or focus groups. Participants in the RDE exercise cannot figure out exactly which issue they are supposed to be responding to because each vignette comprises a combination of messages. RDE's computerized interview tool throws a lot of information at voter participants and does so quickly, forcing participants to respond at a gut level. Then RDE picks up the pieces simply by sorting through the data to figure out which issues sway them. The picture is there, emerging rapidly from the data.

RDE discovers patterns at the individual level and essentially gets into the mind of the individual voter. Knowing this, let's search for different mind-sets of voters. After all, if the president is a product, then all we have seen up to now tells us that products are liked for different reasons, with these reasons corresponding to mind-set segments.

Switching to George W. Bush, we find three mind-sets of voters who would be swayed to vote for him if given the appropriate messaging. The Self-Centereds, as we called the first group, mainly wanted tax relief. The Safety Seekers cared primarily about protection from terrorism. The Better Living Standard Seekers liked hearing promises to revitalize cities, create jobs, and reduce dependence on foreign oil. *What is nice about these segments is that at the same time the segments emerge, the candidate knows exactly what messages resonate with the segment.* That is, by using actual messaging, RDE guides the candidate, first providing knowledge and then suggesting the specific messages. Not bad for business thinking applied to the social sector.

A few issues were tricky, even for Bush voters:

- Promises to hang tough in Iraq appealed to the Safety Seekers but turned off the other groups.

- Talk of environmental protection won over the Better Living Standard Seekers *but yet* made the rest less likely to vote for Mr. Bush.

- The Self-Centereds did not like hearing about health care benefits, but the other two groups did.

- *On the whole, though, the three groups agreed more than they disagreed.* The Bush voters were generally middle-class, upwardly mobile people who responded to promises of more money and security. There were not that many polarizing issues among the Bush voters (relative to Kerry's). Bush reminded one of pizza: variations on a theme. Someone who would eat one kind of pizza would eat most other kinds as well, unless that person disliked the toppings.

To locate Kerry in our "supermarket," and using Tierney's language, we have to leave the pizza in the frozen-foods aisle. When we analyzed the Kerry voters, we saw something like the flavor polarization one found in pickle consumers.

- Some people like high-impact sour and garlic pickles; others hate them and like a pickle with a mild crunch. You absolutely cannot please people by giving everyone a middle-of-the-road pickle. It's impossible when flavor segmentation shows up.

- Kerry's overall support was about equal to Bush's, but the voters who could be swayed to vote Democratic fall into three radically contrasting groups, sort of Kerry's own personal flavor segments, his "political pickles."

- Some are Improvement Seekers, whose priorities were education reform and new energy policies.

- Others are Idealists, who could be wooed with promises to fight discrimination against women and minorities, improve health care, protect abortion rights, and defend workers against corporations.

- And then there are the Issue Aversives, who were so strongly predisposed to vote for Mr. Kerry that none of his campaign promises could further strengthen their loyalty. In fact, specifics were liable to drive them away because they were turned off by some promises, such as protecting abortion rights, fighting discrimination, and reforming education. The Issue Aversives weren't so much pro-Kerry as they were anti-Bush. The more Kerry promised the other groups, the more chance he had of offending the Issue Averse voters. It was a tough challenge for Kerry to figure out a coherent strategy that straddled the needs of very different people.

In the end, it was not that easy for each of the candidates to keep the voters in their camps. "Bush had to harness a group of dogs basically pulling in the same direction. Kerry got to harness a group of cats"[8] that had different agendas.[9]

A DATABASE FOR THE SOCIAL ANGST: THE "MIND" OF THE PUBLIC SECTOR

The public sector is not known for its quick embrace of new technologies. Although social science together with ecology research and management are familiar with the occasional experiments on a large scale and with relatively long timelines, some of the experiments are extremely slow and can last for years.[10]

Knowing that, it should come as no surprise that we were excited and a bit nervous when a few years ago, we decided to try RDE for social policy as a newer, perhaps better way to understand the *vox populi*. As we stated up front, we had a sense that we might be on to something, sort of like a new *knowledge plus engineering* science, tentatively named prescriptive public opinion. Let's see how far we got.

These first few years of what we had hoped to be a promising new millennium, from 2001 through 2006, have been fraught with anxiety-provoking events, especially for Americans, but now for Europeans, Australasians, Latin Americans, and indeed virtually everyone. These years have been deluged with a litany of problems ranging from war to health to ecology to economics. The list of anxiety-provoking issues begins to numb the mind. The declaration of two wars (Afghanistan and Iraq), with the ensuing backlash worldwide; continued focus on worldwide terrorism; SARS and the Avian Flu impacting consumers globally (Asia especially); North Korea nuclear missiles; Iran threatening the world stability; suicide bombers becoming routine in country after country.... If this is not enough, we see global climate changes, devastating hurricanes, melting ice in the Arctic.... And economics is not perfect, either: Wall Street and corporate troubles, such as pensions that are gone, futures that are destroyed, and a lack of trust in corporate governance; huge deficits by the U.S. government; job layoffs and outsourcing of both white-collar and blue-collar U.S. jobs to other countries with lower labor cost.... It all defines the birth of a new economy that does not always seem to follow the rules of Adam Smith. All of these produce anxiety and social upheaval, grist for the mill of consumer research methods.

People experience anxiety as a normal reaction to threatening, dangerous, uncertain, or important situations. Normal anxiety can enhance some people's functions, increasing motivation and productivity. Some people work better under pressure, with anxiety focusing their thoughts, enabling them to achieve what needs to be done. Pathological anxiety, however, is a different story; it is excessive and chronic, and typically interferes with the ability to function in normal daily activities. Our general level of distress determines how well we feel able to deal with the impact of change in our lives.

The cost of mental distress is high. The American Institute of Stress reports that job stress costs U.S. businesses $300 billion annually in lost productivity; absenteeism; accidents; employee turnover; medical, legal, and insurance fees; and worker's compensation awards. It is not much better in other countries, either. Stress causes a loss of more than $16 billion a year in Canada, and as much as £7.3 billion in the United Kingdom.[11]

If someone wants to find solutions for stress-related losses or other related issues (or at least a way to control them), it's necessary to understand the algebra of the citizen's mind. Can these topics be meaningfully treated by RDE, an approach that seems to have its greatest applications in the mundane world of commerce? The answer, again, is yes, as you will see, provided that the investigator treats the social issues in the way that RDE dictates: as vignettes describing anxiety-provoking situations in the world of social policy. It was possible with the president. Now let's see whether it's possible with the communication of social policy.

RDE + TERRORISM = DATABASE FOR SOCIAL POLICY AND COMMUNICATION

Let's return to the notion of a database of the customer's mind, which we presented in Chapter 8, "Mind Genomics: Consumer Mind 'on the Shelf,'" but extend that application to social policy. When we first introduced the topic, we dealt with different shopping situations, studying each one with an RDE experiment. The design of the 30 different experiments, 1 per shopping topic (shoes, tires, candles, and so on) was deliberately structured to be identical, allowing us to compare the same idea across different topics. Following the same strategy to create a database, consider now what would happen when we apply RDE thinking to social policy, dealing this time with situations that are anxiety provoking.

A properly phrased rating question plays a crucial role in RDE related to such sensitive issues as anxiety. We used the question "How well can you cope with the situation described? (1 = Easily ... 9 = Not at all)." The wording of this question took a lot of effort. Our experience in applying the principles of RDE showed very few people wanting to take part in the study when we asked the question "How anxious do you feel when you read this situation?" People simply shied away from participating in the survey; that one rating about "anxiety" was simply too much. But changing the focus to "coping" made all the difference in the world. Many more participants completed the interview.

Some statements drive anxiety (high utility values—cannot cope with it), and some statements drive relief or an ability to cope (low utility values—can easily cope with the situation). The way the question is phrased allows the participant to concentrate on a less anxiety-provoking response—dealing with an issue—rather than on the more anxiety-provoking response.

Our results are somewhat as you might expect, but not completely. Look at Table 9.2 to see the actual results. The additive constant, a measure of basic anxiety, is low (around 19), meaning that 19%, or one of five participants, says that they cannot deal with an unspecified terrorism situation. Things that frighten the ordinary person are the usual suspects: bombs under cars, dirty bombs going off, bombs blowing up under buildings, and so on. It is hard for the government to counter this anxiety; little from the study came out "negative"—that is, that reduces anxiety or increases the ability to cope.[12] Certainly, faith in God, timely information from the media, and contact with friends and family reduce anxiety and allow better coping. Yet, surprisingly, these are minor palliatives against real terror situations. *RDE says to the government that the government's simple reassurances do not work.*

Table 9.2

Strongest performing "anxiety-provoking" communications (left) and "anxiety-reducing" communications (right) for terrorism

Anxiety-Provoking Messages	Util.	Anxiety-Reducing Messages	Util.
		Base Size	121
		Constant (basic predisposition to be anxious and not cope)	19
Total group of participants			
A bomb under your car	21	You trust that God will keep you safe	–3
A dirty nuclear bomb set off	20	It's important for the media to keep you informed	–5
Bombs blowing up in the middle of a building	15	You need to contact your friends and family to make sure they are okay	–6
Segment #1: Traditionalists			
A dirty nuclear bomb set off	39	You need to contact your friends and family to make sure they are okay	–1
A bomb under your car	38	It's important for the media to keep you informed	–2
Bombs blowing up in the middle of a building	31	You believe that Homeland Defense will keep you safe	–3
A deadly disease such as smallpox or anthrax let loose	28		
Segment #2: Isolationists			
You think United Nations forces will keep you safe	34	Family and friends play a big role in your life	–5
You believe that international cooperation in the United Nations will keep you safe	33	It's important for the media to keep you informed	–7
You believe that Homeland Defense will keep you safe	20	You'd drive any distance to get away from it	–7
You believe that the Center for Disease Control will keep you safe	18	You trust that God will keep you safe	–10
You think that your local police will keep you safe	14	You need to contact your friends and family to make sure they are okay	–11

However, there is more. When we divide our participants by the pattern of what bothers them, we find two radically different groups, roughly about the same size. The first group is what we might expect: enormous fear of what has come to be the standard terrorist threats. We called this group Traditionalists.

The second group *is entirely unexpected.* RDE shows this group (or segment #2) to be deathly afraid of *communications* about outside organizations helping in times of crisis. What the government might believe to be helpful in assuaging fear (for example, "You believe that Homeland Defense will keep you safe" and "You believe that the Center for Disease Control will keep you safe") sets off alarms in these people. We were surprised! This segment reacts quite strongly, responding that they simply cannot cope with that type of messaging. The government needs to back away from messaging for these people. These individuals respond a little more strongly to reassurances of God, friends, and family. We called this segment Isolationists.

Certainly, terrorism is not a particularly simple situation. RDE suggests that there are segments or mind-sets when it comes to public policy and anxiety-provoking situations. Perhaps more important, RDE identifies some of the workings of people's minds, shows what types of threats these people respond to, suggests what not to communicate, and calculates the likelihood that communication will assuage anxiety.

Segment 1, our Traditionalists, fear the standard terrorist tactics, and very little works with them to assuage their fears. The government just has to keep reassuring them.

Segment 2, Isolationists, react very strongly when the government takes control and attempts to reassure them. Isolationists are even more strongly assuaged than are Traditionalists by the same reassuring communications about God and family. It is best to tread softly with these people and de-emphasize government. Perhaps an emphasis on family, coping, and the historical national character would do well among the Isolationists.

PRESCRIPTIVE PUBLIC POLICY AND CITIZENS ANXIETY INDEX

We are quite accustomed to a wide range of indices that characterize the different aspects of our life: inflation, prime rate, Dow Jones Industrial Average, and so on. By nature, people love metrics. "How am I doing?" is a favorite phrase spoken from everyone from Ed Koch, former mayor of New York City, to a corporation asking its customers, to a child trying to find out how he is doing in school.

Most major indices of interest to any large swathe of citizens are compiled by a government, educational, or private entity and are used by other people. For example, the Michigan Consumer Sentiment Index (MCSI), which is published monthly by the Institute for Social Research (ISR) and widely used by professional and private investors for their everyday decisions, gives a snapshot of whether consumers feel like spending money. There's a simple and compelling idea behind this index, as well as many others: compile once (regularly) by professional staff and make available to many people for their many uses. The strategy works, of course.

Is it possible to create an index in conjunction with databases of consumer sentiment regarding social policy? Depending on how we look at the issue, we might call this the anxiety index if we want to accentuate the negative, or the charity proclivity index if we want to accentuate the positive. As we hinted earlier, perhaps it will be possible to create a new science of prescriptive public policy (PPP) using RDE-type thinking. In this scenario, entities such as the ISR, government agencies, and research institutions would regularly compile databases of communications or messages for different areas of social policies. These databases would comprise the elements and the utility values of the elements for the total panel and the segments (the so-called preference structuration). Other governmental agencies or private institutions could subscribe to receive this information and use it in their work. Now any communication can be created with the confidence that it has been engineered to achieve the desired results among the target audience. So whether you are in the PR department of a multinational corporation writing a letter explaining the decision to close some plants, or an IRS document writer, you will have some help in more profoundly knowing the mind of your customers—what messages are better understood or even can reduce anxiety, for example.

Looking at the vision more grandly, perhaps RDE and social policy can be extended to education—how to explain different topics to different groups of students, what examples are more easy for them to relate to, what words to use, and so on. Or, if you are in the non-for-profit world, what is the most impactful way to communicate your message? It does not matter whether we call the approach RDE, mind genomics, or PPP. The more people who use these databases, the more affordable, wide-ranging, and valuable these databases will become to the advancement of the social well-being.

With her business healthy and growing under the supervision of competent loyal managers and employees, suddenly Allison-the-Entrepreneur has free time. After years of passive donations to charities, Allison realizes that she enjoys being involved in the community and in charity work. She decides to apply her extensive knowledge of RDE to fund-raising campaigns. And to some people's surprise (but not to Allison's—she was confident it would work), the results are spectacular. Now, encouraged by her fan club members, she considers running for a seat in government. With Allison's natural business acumen, persistence, and popularity, she definitely has a chance. She just needs to know how to talk to people. Isn't this the same problem Allison faced at the beginning of this book? Just in a different area and context.

So Allison is ready for the challenge and is working on her platform, subject to fine-tuning, based on the results of her RDE studies with her electorate.

The next step is to design the posters using a graphical RDE tool and create a very convincing mailing piece for fund-raising. Allison can do that! She did it before for her business, and quite successfully. Allison's supporters are very optimistic about the upcoming elections. They know that if Allison finds the right message, the voters will strongly support her. She has some great ideas on how to improve the life of her electorate and beyond, and she has the integrity and energy to implement them. Her supporters know she has substance. All Allison needs to do is apply the knowledge and tools she has. She can now fine-tune and adjust her messages for different voters based on demographics and mind-sets to create an offering that the voters will buy.

ENDNOTES

1 Millie Bush, *Millie's Book: As Dictated to Barbara Bush* (New York: William Morrow & Co., August 1990).

2 American Kennel Club press release, 2 August 2004.

3 For example, see J. S. Fishkin, *The Voice of the People: Public Opinion and Democracy* (New Haven, CT: Yale University Press, 1997).

4 Operationally, the proportion of individuals whose preferences are aligned along the same shared dimension. See Cynthia Farrar, James S. Fishkin, Donald P. Green, Christian List, Robert C. Luskin, and Elizabeth Levy Paluck, "Experimenting with Deliberative Democracy: Effects on Policy Preferences and Social Choice," *In Proceedings of ECPR Conference*, Marburg, Germany, 18–21 September 2003.

5 John Tierney, "A Trial Balloon Made of Lead?" *The New York Times*, 30 May 2004. According to Wikipedia, Tierney has been working for *The New York Times* since 1990. Curiously, Tierney writes from a conservative point of view and identifies himself as a libertarian. Over the years, Tierney has written columns critical of the war on drugs, Amtrak, and compulsory recycling. His article "Recycling Is Garbage" has the dubious distinction of breaking *The New York Times Magazine's* hate mail record (source: http://en.wikipedia.org/wiki/John_Tierney_(journalist)).

6 Howard Moskowitz, Alex Gofman, Prasad Tungaturthy, Madhu Manchaiah, and Dorit Cohen, "Research, Politics, and the Web Can Mix. Considerations, Experiences, Trials, Tribulations in Adapting Conjoint Measurement to Optimizing a Political Platform as If It Were a Consumer Product," *In Marketing Research in a .com Environment,* Ed. Richard Brookes (Amsterdam: ESOMAR, 2000): 223–243.

7 This reconfirms the fact that no poll, political guru, or research can make a perfect prediction. The purpose of the RDE exercise in this chapter was not to check voters' preferences, but to see what messages worked for the candidates.

8 John Tierney, "A Trial Balloon Made of Lead?," referenced earlier.

9 The particular results described in this chapter were not utilized by either candidate's campaign (to the best of the authors' knowledge).

[10] K. N. Lee, "Appraising Adaptive Management," *Conservation Ecology* 3(2) (1999): 3.

[11] Ravi Tangri, *StressCosts: Stress Cures* (Halifax, Nova Scotia, Canada: Chrysalis, 2003); and Marianne McGee Kolbasuk, Diane Rezendes Khirallah, and Michelle Lodge. "IT Lifestyles Backlash." *InformationWeek* (25 September 2000): p. 58.

[12] This, in turn, calls for more in-depth research using a wider range of the messages.

10

RDE Defeats Murphy's Law and "Bares" the Stock Markets

According to Edwards Air Force Base's History Office, Capt. Edward A. Murphy was an engineer working on Air Force Project MX981 to see how much sudden deceleration a person can endure in a crash. The work was done at Edwards Air Base in 1949, where Murphy created the harness for a rocket-powered sled designed to move faster than a speeding bullet. The test failed, and the sled's passenger, Dr. John Paul Stapp, was temporarily blinded because, as Murphy later discovered, a transducer had been installed backward. Murphy cursed the technician responsible and said, "If there is any way to do it wrong, he'll find it."

His colleagues overheard him and began repeating the adage. Before long, "Murphy's Law" caught on and became widely quoted. Shortly after the accident, Dr. Stapp gave a press conference. He said that their good safety record on the project was due to a firm belief in Murphy's Law and the necessity of trying with all one's ability to circumvent this ever-present perversion of nature. Aerospace manufacturers picked it up and used it widely in their ads during the next few months, and soon it was being quoted in many news and magazine articles. Murphy's Law was born.[1]

As proof of the common nature of the law, in September 2004, Genesis, a NASA space probe designed by Lockheed Martin, plummeted to Earth when its parachute failed to open. The problem? The switches designed to trigger its release had been installed backward.[2]

There are not that many universal laws of nature. Unfortunately, Murphy's Law proved to be one of them. No area seems to be immune to it. Let's examine corporate communications, for example. You'll see the opportunity in a moment for RDE. Crises inevitably happen. That's the way the world works. Inept, unwary communications in crises by the corporation or the government can greatly exacerbate the situation rather than ameliorating it. In the following examples, an *unprepared response to a crisis demonstrates how much damage can occur when an organization fails to communicate appropriately.*

The international motoring community greeted the launch of the Mercedes-Benz A-class in 1997 with enthusiasm. Then a major public relations problem for the company emerged when one of the A-class cars overturned during a test drive conducted by journalists in Sweden, triggering a major crisis for the German car manufacturer. The reputation of Mercedes's star was at stake as critics accused the company of producing an unsafe car. Early unprepared public relations activity by Mercedes only succeeded in exacerbating the crisis, as they fumbled around with what they were going to say and then *said the wrong thing at the wrong time.*

Eventually, and fortunately, Mercedes changed, or perhaps was forced to change, from a defensive to an accommodative response strategy during the crisis. A more open, honest, and proactive approach to crisis communication might have saved Mercedes-Benz a great deal of money and embarrassment.[3] *The lesson here is that one always has to be prepared and know what to say and when to say it.*

The story of PR "muffs," the errors of corporations and governments, who ought to know better, don't appear in this chapter simply for general interest. Kathleen Fearn-Banks starts her frequently quoted book, *Crisis Communications,*[4] with Murphy's Law as a description of crisis. Many organizations and individuals go through life trying to think positively, in hope that if they do not have a negative thought, nothing negative will ever happen. "This is absolute balderdash!" writes Fearn-Banks. "The slogan should be 'Think Negatively.'" According to Fearn-Banks, crises *can* and *will* happen. In a crisis, in contrast to a problem, emotions are on the edge and events develop so rapidly that rational thinking is very difficult. Hence, a very important part of crisis management is active, intelligent, and well-prepared crisis communications, the dialog between the organization and its public prior to, during, and after the negative occurrence.

What is the role of RDE in crisis communications? Can RDE minimize the negative impact of crisis on companies and, ideally, make the image of the organization even more positive than it had been before the event occurred? Can RDE literally snatch victory from the jaws of defeat and, by so doing, influence the perception of the company by the public, and perhaps even the value of company shares on the stock market?

So far, coffee, tomato sauce and pickles, magazines, electronic gadgets, and political messages have each given up their secrets to RDE, allowing them to be restructured for higher customer appeal. Now we look at another type of engineering—this time, engineering opinion—specifically, in crisis situations, and perhaps using such engineering rules (or, at least, patterns) to understand how a consumer shareholder thinks about selling or buying stock. That's quite a wide gap between the two topics, one might think, but they're both potentially knowable aspects of the mind. We saw hints of that earlier in the book. The first topic of this chapter is communications about the energy crisis. The second topic is communications about pain-reliever drugs and what those communications imply for buying or selling pharmaceutical stocks. We echo back a little to Chapter 9, "Making the President and Public Communications into 'Products,'" on government communications and presidential elections, but now we move far more toward *engineering communications in the bigger context of public opinion and the world of finance.*

CORPORATE COMMUNICATION AND A FINGER ON THE PUBLIC'S PULSE

Open any newspaper or news magazine today, and you are certain to see something written about energy. A randomly selected issue of *The New York Times* addresses the topic of energy more than 15 times.[5] The prices of oil and natural gas rise and fall, and with those fluctuations enter the pundits predicting everything from imminent crashes of the economy to a sustained, exuberant public gallantly moving forward like Britain in WWII, toughing it out, coping with the energy shortages, and, at the end of the day finding new substitutes that promise a better future. Such visions of the future make wonderful reading for the buyer of magazines who anxiously looks like a spectator, agonizing and pontificating from the sidelines.

Now let's move into the corporate world of energy producers, public relations agencies, and advertising specialists. What information do they crank out to the public? In the face of simply having to understand and then mold public opinion, what do these experts say? How do they say it? Are they always right? How do they deal in a world outside their control, where they are confronted with messy situations and have to craft good copy on Web sites and in news releases? *They simply want to use the right messaging, appropriate for their company, to influence public opinion.* What will RDE do to help?

Let's turn back the clock a few years. During the cold winter of January/February 2001, before 9/11 changed the world, energy issues were just surfacing. California's own unique brew of utilities, burgeoning demand, and unpredictable energy shortages were threatening rolling brownouts that would momentarily solve some of the 2001 brew of problems in California's energy supply and demand. Consumers in the U.S. were concerned about the availability of energy, as they always are in times of crisis. Many eyes turned to California to find out what might happen when their time would come. Public utilities, in turn, wanted to assuage the fears and deal with the looming crisis of consumer confidence. The question was what utilities should say to their customers in the face of the crisis, without exaggerating the seriousness of what happened.

By 2001, the Web was already established as a way to communicate one's wares and as a medium to use for influencing public opinion. Rather than looking at Web sites as media for product descriptions, it was becoming clear that the Web site was also beginning to find use as a PR vehicle. So the question naturally arose, if this is PR, how can we use this communication tool in the way we use other media? That is, in what way can the specific messaging placed on the corporate Web site increase acceptance of—or, at least, modify—bad feelings toward a public utility?

With a public utility, messaging varies, ranging from specific information about available products to the language of reassurance about the utility.

Utilities don't simply want to maintain confidence in their public, however; they want to sell their energy. Their Web sites are constructed for both persuasion and reassurance.

Let's look at what the different utilities were saying around the time that California experienced its rolling brownouts. Table 10.1 lists the energy utilities and their Web sites that provided the raw material for deconstructing PR and customer relations efforts.

Table 10.1

Energy utility Web sites that RDE deconstructed to find PR messages

Carolina Power and Light	www.cplc.com
Con Edison	www.coned.com
Massachusetts Electric Company	www.masselectric.com
New York State Electric and Gas	www.nyseg.com
Orange and Rockland Utilities	www.oru.com
Pennsylvania Power and Light	www.pplweb.com
Reliant Energy Houston Lighting and Power	www.hlp.com
San Diego Gas and Electric	www.sdge.com
Southern Connecticut Gas	www.soconngas.com
Tucson Electric Power	www.tucsonelectric.com

As we have seen before in this book, many messages simply don't have much of an effect. This truism applies to the energy utility industry as well. In the time of crisis, few messages worked for everyone. Let's look at Table 10.2, which shows the winning overall PR-type messages for everybody, for males vs. females, and for three distinct mind-sets of utility customers (based on the data from the 1,000 energy-concerned respondents who participated). Just looking at Table 10.2 gives the company and its PR firm a few pointers on how to manage the messaging in a time of crisis:

- For the total panel, no single PR-type message stands out. The only reasonable messages talk about service and lowering bills. These winning messages should not come as a surprise—they are what everyone wants.

- For males, it's about service and money; for females, it's primarily about money.

- The real pay dirt for PR comes from dividing these 1,000 consumers into three different groups:

Segment 1 wants a dependable service. They need to hear these messages of dependability spelled out in no uncertain terms.

Segment 2 wants to take control, be in the know, and feel that they are optimizing their choices in light of the complex world of energy.

Segment 3 wants to feel that they are choosing an energy utility that goes out of its way to *help the disadvantaged, the older consumer, and others.* Segment 3 is especially responsive to PR-type messages and represents a powerful target worth influencing.

Table 10.2

The most impactful elements about energy for total panel, gender, and the three mind-set segments (partial list)

Element	Source of PR Message	Util.
Messaging for Everybody		
Service by phone, Internet, e-mail, or in person... we're always at your service	Orange Rockland	5
Messaging for Males		
Service by phone, Internet, e-mail, or in person... we're always at your service	Orange Rockland	6
Messaging for Females		
We provide ways to save money on your energy bill	Con Ed	8
Messaging for Segment 1: Searching for "dependable"		
Dependable energy service that our millions of customers around the world already enjoy	Penn P&L	8
Messaging for Segment 2: Freedom of choice, be in the know, optimize		
Help with higher electricity bills	Con Ed	11
We provide ways to save money on your energy bill	Con Ed	11
Decrease air-conditioning bills and increase employee satisfaction	Tucson Electric	9

Element	Source of PR Message	Util.
Messaging for Segment 3: Help for the less advantaged		
Service by phone, Internet, e-mail, or in person... we're always at your service	Orange Rockland	19
We give seniors special treatment	Con Ed	18
Special services for customers age 62 and over	Con Ed	17
Qualify for energy assistance	S. Conn Gas	15
Decrease air-conditioning bills and increase employee satisfaction	Tucson Electric	15
Mark the gas and electric appliances for the visually impaired	SD G&E	14

USING RDE TO ANTICIPATE AND PREPARE A STRONG PR RESPONSE TO A CRISIS

Crises often come when they are least expected. It's good to be prepared. RDE forces that preparation. Indeed, if the PR agency simply comes up with ideas that it thinks might work, the guesses *might* be successful, but perhaps not. The ideas tend to be single-minded, perhaps responding to a single perceived issue in the environment. Sometimes the PR efforts hit the mark; sometimes they don't. RDE forces the PR effort to broaden the scope, usually to the benefit of all concerned.

As in the previous examples in this book, the key to optimizing PR is to say the right thing to the right people, at the right time. But what is the right thing? Our data from the different energy utilities taken at the time of the 2001 California energy crisis suggests that there is no single "right thing to say." However, if the PR agency deconstructs what the different energy utilities are saying, keeping an eye on those elements that deal with the friendliness and social responsibility of the energy utility, it might quickly discover the different mind-set segments (who to say it to) and what specific messages drive each segment (what to say).

RDE projects *need not be done at the time of the crisis.* It might be far more productive to monitor the environment—say, every three months— with a small study, using only the elements that are deemed to be relevant if a crisis occurs. With the discipline of such periodic monitoring, followed by the actual study, the PR firm then would have a database of up-to-date messaging. Not only would the firm have the messaging, but it also would know what messages work and among what types of people. Such fore-knowledge is exceptionally valuable for organizations that deal in high-risk situations, where they must be ready to respond to adverse government or consumer reactions. *The value of immediately knowing what to say (and to whom to say it to) in times of crisis is far greater than the cost of a few RDE studies done on a scheduled basis.*

BARE MARKET: BENEFITING ON WALL STREET FROM KNOWLEDGE

For the stock market to operate, investors must have different opinions about a stock. What communications about a specific company drive investors and analysts to buy, hold, or sell shares? Could RDE help to understand that world of hopes and dreams, in which "billion-dollar deci-sions" are made on-the-spot from messages of all types?

A lot of today's stock market modeling works using rules emerging from the pattern of stock behavior. For example, depending on the shape of the stock price curves over time, some modelers assert that they are able to estimate the likely pattern of stock behavior. Although they might not be able to give a "rule" that can be easily understood, their pattern recognition rules often work.

Sometimes different (not necessarily limited to crises only) situations in the stock market can be modeled, but there is no easy way to know and affect people's reaction to the situations. Or is there?

Although we generally trust experts and distrust the wisdom of the masses, *New Yorker* business columnist James Surowiecki argues that, "under the right circumstances, groups are remarkably intelligent, and are often smarter than the smartest people in them."[6] Surowiecki means the intrinsic knowledge and wisdom of people, not the ways of extracting this intelligence through the controversial method of group brainstorming (see Chapter 8, "Mind Genomics: Consumer Mind 'on the Shelf'"). Although some individuals—even experts—might know a lot, the actual wisdom might exist in little pieces in the minds of different people. By soliciting their reactions to a question and by averaging their ratings, it becomes possible to extract the "signal" from the "noise" and, indeed, be fairly correct. We can see this principle demonstrated by asking a person to draw a circle again and again. This children's demonstration, with a person making circle after circle superimposed on each other, soon generates a fairly nice circle, albeit with a lot of not-so-nice and quite irregular ellipses. The circle emerges, as it were, from the set of crudely drawn ellipses. The trick here is to formulate the problem in a way that lets the wisdom of crowds to emerge.

BEHAVIORAL ECONOMICS AND EXPERIMENTAL ANALYSIS OF ATTITUDES: MAKING SENSE FROM THE VIOXX CASE

In 2004, the news broke that one of the most powerful painkillers on the market, Vioxx, from Merck, might be implicated in heart attacks and that, allegedly, some of the adverse effects of Vioxx had never been openly reported. Vioxx had been a blockbuster for Merck, with sales of $2.5 billion in 2003, and was widely marketed as a safe alternative to drugs such as aspirin, which is known to cause ulcers and gastrointestinal bleeding. The backlash to this story was what one might expect: individual and class-action lawsuits against Merck, adverse publicity, corporate responses by Merck and other drug companies in the pain-killer business, and, of course, the inevitable impact on stocks of Merck and other drug companies in "Big Pharma."

Indeed, it was big news. *The New York Times* covered the Vioxx case more than 400 times on its pages in just 15 months following that fateful announcement in October 2004. As expected, the adverse news was presented in different FDA statements, with specific and general counter statements by the drug companies themselves. Anyone holding pharmaceutical stocks was in for a rough ride as the stocks were battered by such bad news. Merck, of course, suffered the most.

The question for us here is how RDE might apply in such a situation, where the rating is no longer "acceptance," but rather "sell vs. hold vs. buy" the stock. That is, if a shareholder (or a manager of a hedge fund, for instance) reads a vignette about the FDA statement and corporate reaction, and rates it in terms of his propensity to buy, sell, or hold the stock in question, is there any way to predict the likely future shareholder response (buy vs. sell the stock from other investors)? If we can create such an approach, RDE might well find its next home predicting *stated shareholder behavior* with respect to specific stocks. Such an RDE-created model of behavior toward stocks provides a new set of rules about how the shareholder integrates the mosaic of publicly available information into a buy/sell decision.

By now, the sequence of what to do in an RDE study has been presented quite a few times, ranging from foods and credit cards to graphics. We go a bit more slowly this time, however, when presenting the data from this case history, because of some of the worthwhile subtleties involved.

We follow the steps for deconstruction that you saw in Chapter 5, "Discover More About Your Competitors Than They Themselves Know—Legally!," for ezines, with a few changes that we point out.

STEP 1: DEFINE THE PROBLEM AND PREPARE THE MATERIALS

The problem is to understand the relationship between expected future stock purchase and certain types of publicly available information. In our case, this public information consists of the brand, FDA statements about problems with painkillers, direct corporate statements about what is being done to solve the problem, and, finally, other corporate statements relevant to the pain-killer situation. This type of information is *presumed* to influence one's opinion of the company, its future economic performance, and, thus, one's estimate of the future value of the company's stock. For the most part, it's a fair and reasonable assumption, although certainly not the whole story.

We start by *identifying the companies and brands*. We wanted to go beyond simply Merck's Vioxx into a number of other high-potency painkillers, as well as over-the-counter (OTC) medications. Essentially, we are looking at the different companies that market painkillers as being members of an ecosystem in the midst of being disrupted by a crisis.

Next, we *gather the messaging information available from corporate Web sites*. We limited our sourcing of information to the type of information that an investor might find using Google and that might likely be a first choice for a shareholder or professional. The exercise itself generates many hundreds of statements.

Then we *reduce the information to a limited set of phrases*. Make sure that these phrases reflect the information and tonality that would typically be assumed by the government (the FDA) or by the company's investor relations department. The shareholder might be expected to pay attention to these phrases. By selecting elements that appear on corporate and news Web sites, we can be sure to incorporate the type of information to which a shareholder might be exposed when researching a company. We cannot, of course, be certain that the shareholder actually saw these specific messages outside of the actual evaluation. However, the information is "in the air" and constitutes some of the background buzz to which analysts and shareholders commonly attend.

STEP 2: "MIX AND MATCH" THE ELEMENTS ACCORDING TO AN EXPERIMENTAL DESIGN TO CREATE A SET OF VIGNETTES

This step is done automatically by the RDE tool, which we know creates a unique individual design plan for each respondent. Each vignette is accompanied by a rating question, this time asking the respondent whether *(s)he would sell, hold, or buy the stock based on what (s)he read*. The different vignettes have different company names; some of the vignettes have no company name listed. Participants have no problem rating sell vs. buy because selling vs. buying is just another type of evaluation of the concept.

STEP 3: RECRUIT AND COLLECT THE RATINGS FROM THE RESPONDENTS

There are many shareholders with investable assets, so finding appropriate participants in the general population is quite easy. In this study, one of the classification questions dealt with the amount of money to invest so that the data can be analyzed by those with a high net worth vs. a low net worth. For our project here, we concentrate on the general population, with at least $5,000 to invest. These individuals were recruited by an e-mail invitation and told that they would be asked to participate in a study on medical messaging.

The respondents were not told about the specific topic until they were introduced to the actual interview. We introduced the project in this indirect fashion so as not to call attention to the fact that we were really interested in future stock purchase behavior. We positioned the RDE study as dealing with reactions to clinical trial findings as a reasonable way to disguise the real objective of the study.

STEP 4: ANALYZE THE RESULTS OF THE STUDY AND IDENTIFY WHAT MESSAGES IN GENERAL DRIVE INTENT TO BUY OR SELL A STOCK

Up to now, we have been dealing with measures of interest—the proportion of participants who would be interested in a new product idea or communication. When it comes to stock, we are interested in both sides of the scale—the *strength of feeling* for who will buy vs. who will sell. For example, does a specific message or brand name/company name drive a person to say that he will buy or sell? Because each concept had, at most, one company name, we can assume that the buy/sell rating refers to the shares of that company.

You can see this information in Table 10.3, which shows the driving force of each message. FDA messages by themselves do not drive buying or selling. Brands and companies play a much bigger role in expected buy/sell ratings. For example, Advil from Wyeth drives interest up in buying the stock. Conversely, Vioxx from Merck drives the buying interest down. Furthermore, although the FDA statements do not do much, the corporate responses do a lot more. *What the company says it will do can make a difference to the shareholder.* Agreeing with the FDA and putting some type of caution on the drug "quickly enough" can increase expected buying, as in "We are in agreement with the FDA that this medication can be safely used for pain relief. Consumers should not exceed the recommended dose or take the product for longer than directed."

Table 10.3

Examples of the elements for the pain-reliever messaging (partial list). The additive constant is the average level of response to buy (>50) or sell (<50), with 50 being hold. The actual utilities show the strength of the message, pushing the rating toward buy (positive utilities) or toward sell (negative utilities).

	Element	Buy (+)/ Sell (−)
	Additive constant (proclivity to sell or to buy, without additional information)	*35*
Silo #1: Painkiller brand and pharmaceutical manufacturer		
A6	*ADVIL* from Wyeth	7
A5	*ALEVE* from Bayer	6
A2	*CELEBREX* from Pfizer	−2
A3	*VIOXX* from Merck	−7
Silo #2: FDA statements		
B4	The FDA believes that the overall benefit outweighs the risk when used in properly selected patients as directed in the approved labeling.	2
B5	The FDA is recommending that doctors seek alternative therapies for their patients.	−3
Silo #3: The company's stated actions or planned next steps		
C4	The manufacturer will continue to work with the FDA to sponsor a major clinical study to further assess this medication.	3
C2	The medication was pulled off the market after the company found a greater cardiovascular risk among people who took the drug for more than 18 months.	−6
Silo #4: Factual statements about the product, or findings		
D1	We are in agreement with the FDA that this medication can be safely used for pain relief. Consumers should not exceed the recommended dose or take the product for longer than directed.	6

DO STOCKS REACT DIFFERENTLY TO THE SAME MESSAGE, AND WHAT MIGHT THIS ARBITRAGE MEAN?

Up to now, we have been looking at our RDE data as one big data mass, perhaps divided by people with different mind-sets. We find rules that way, but we don't discover what messages work for a specific drug company to drive expected stock purchases. That is, we know what works *in general*. But suppose we are interested in what will happen to ratings for a specific stock, such as Merck. What do messages do to ratings of buy/sell for Merck shares? Are some messages particularly potent in driving sell-offs of Merck stock? Are some messages particularly potent in driving expected purchases of Merck stock? If RDE can discover these specific *interactions* between company name and messaging, we might have a tool to detect likely changes in sentiment toward each specific stock, as a result of messaging associated with that stock.

We use a straightforward approach to find out what works, in particular. We divide the concepts or vignettes by the specific company names. Each analysis looks only at those concepts that contain the name of one specific pharmaceutical company. Using that subset of concepts, RDE creates a model showing what other messages do well or poorly for concepts that all have a single company name.[7] The other messages vary and can be from the government regarding discoveries or policy (the FDA) or from the company itself (how it plans to respond). *When we do this partitioning and modeling, we soon discover that the same external messaging—that is, messages from the FDA, exert different effects on the buy/sell response, depending on the company with which the message appears.* Look at Table 10.4 to see some of the special interaction effects that can mean so much to future stock performance. For example, when the FDA says that it is "evaluating all prevention studies," participants move toward saying that they will sell their Merck stock and buy Wyeth stock. Yet when the FDA says that it is "concerned about the safety of the entire drug class," the opposite happens. Merck does better when the entire class of painkillers is called into question.

Table 10.4

How messages drive ratings of buy or sell shares of specific pharmaceutical companies (columns)

	PFIZER	MERCK	BAYER	WYETH
Type of message: What the FDA announces				
The FDA said it is evaluating all prevention studies that involve this medication to ensure that adequate precautions are implemented.	2	−2	−2	2
The FDA interim chief said the agency is concerned about the safety of the entire drug class.	1	2	−5	−2
Type of message: What the company says it will do				
Although we believe it would have been possible to continue marketing with new labeling incorporating new data, given the availability of alternative therapies, and questions raised by the data, we concluded that a voluntary withdrawal is the responsible...	−4	−9	3	4
The medication was pulled off the market after the company found a greater cardiovascular risk among people who took the drug for more than 18 months.	5	−2	8	9
The manufacturer is continuing to seek approval for another medication in this drug class in many countries, including the United States.	−9	−9	6	6
The manufacturer will continue to work with the FDA to sponsor a major clinical study to further assess this medication.	0	−10	6	7
The company has suspended all advertising after the FDA asked the manufacturer to suspend its consumer advertising while the agency evaluates new and conflicting information on the drug.	1	−3	8	13
The manufacturer announced that their medication will come with a new warning label, including a stronger warning, now highlighted in a black box.	0	−7	5	8

We see a more striking effect on expected buy/sell when we look at how the company might respond to a crisis situation. Depending on the specific company, the same corporate response can drive up expected stock purchase or drive expected stock sale. For example, when the response is "The manufacturer will continue to work with the FDA to sponsor a major clinical study to further assess this medication," attaching this message to Merck drives participants to say they would sell the stock, but drives participants to say that they will buy Bayer and Wyeth stock. Just look at Figure 10.1 to see a striking visualization of this interaction of company/brand and PR message.[8]

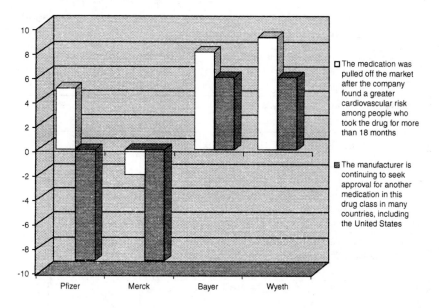

The medication was pulled off the market after the company found a greater cardiovascular risk among people who took the drug for more than 18 months

The manufacturer is continuing to seek approval for another medication in this drug class in many countries, including the United States

Figure 10.1   Example of stock purchase propensity variations in response to different corporate communications for four companies. The same message has a different impact depending on the company/brand combination with which it is paired.

This type of analysis provides an entirely new vista for RDE. Rather than dealing with product or messaging development, RDE now becomes a potential new tool to manage communications. Even more promising, RDE becomes a tool for an investor to guesstimate the likelihood of consumer response to corporate messaging by specific companies in the face of negative situations.

A VISION OF THE FUTURE: THE WELL-PREPARED HEDGE FUND

Is it possible to develop a system that "vacuums" the Web periodically, identifies the messaging for a specific product-oriented topic in the news, and then submits these messages for evaluation by shareholders or by fund managers?

If the answer "yes" seems a bit far-fetched, consider the fact that most of the components of this vision are already in place. An increasing number of companies and technologies are dedicated to "vacuuming" the Web for new ideas. Web spiders, and robots of different breeds are now crawling the Web (and possibly even your computer without your knowledge—but this is illegal). As an example, one Israeli company, Trendum, announced a service that frequently sifts through the Web to determine how ideas are evolving and how the media is presenting stories.

We might now imagine the obvious next step. Specialized Web-mining spiders discover the text for a particular topic, whether that topic is painkillers, iPods, or anything else. The spiders can do really heavy lifting.

When this material is available, the next step organizes the information into silos and elements, following the same approach described throughout this book. Organizing isn't really very hard, although the plethora of information probably requires considerable culling. Eventually, however, in just a day or so, the Web has been vacuumed, the key messaging for the sector or product group selected, and the test messages put into the RDE tool.

The next step is precisely the step we took here: send the RDE interview to shareholders or to analysts, instructing them to read the vignettes and, for each vignette, respond whether they would buy, hold, or sell the stock in question. The task is straightforward, the results come back overnight completely analyzed in the form of a customized model about the sentiment toward a particular sector or a particular set of products.[9]

Beyond the simplicity of the approach, however, is another factor to consider: scalability. Automatic vacuuming of the Web means that the power of the computer can be unleashed to find the raw material and emerging content-analysis tool for some sorting. Easy-to-set-up templates for RDE make the knowledge-gathering approach from shareholders or analysts quick and inexpensive, using people anywhere in the world trained to execute an RDE project. Those who execute need not be experts. Finally, the easy-to-understand results—what wins and loses, interactions between brands and messaging—give the stock analyst and the shareholder a sense of what people say they are likely to do. The *vox populi*, the feelings about each particular stock "in current time," can then be compared against the suggestions of analysts, to determine where there are opportunities, where the analysts say one thing but the common voice of the crowd suggests something quite different.

All in all, an interesting opportunity beckons. RDE might well make that opportunity a knowledge-based reality.

What is Allison-the-Entrepreneur doing now? After long, sleepless nights, she has decided to go public with her company, for the same well-known reasons thousands of other companies have. Good for Allison! But now she has new worries in addition to her normal business problems—how to deal with a possible crisis situation, especially in this sensitive time before IPO. Media and competitors are often forgiving to losers. They are not as kind to the winners, which are usually kept under a microscope for any wrong step. Allison is petrified with ongoing news of litigations, both founded and frivolous, against her colleagues in business. Could she be the next victim? How would it affect her plans of IPO? Can she prepare possible "instant response" scenarios for probable problems in her line of business? If the crisis comes and she has an immediate and powerful (read: correct) response, she might be able to save the day.

Even an idea of such a crisis sends shivers through her. Allison has always tried to avoid even thinking about possible troubles. On the other hand, while putting together her crisis response RDE study (of course, she wants to be prepared), she has realized that she can take a few steps in order to prevent or control the potential crisis. This was a surprise bonus; the disciplined preparations, to which she became accustomed, forced her to think deeply about the problem. And a problem properly identified is a problem half-solved! So Allison decided to do this exercise on a regular basis, both to be prepared in terms of having the knowledge of the right communications and to think through some preventive actions.

She now thinks that she might try to define the right time for the IPO by modeling different scenarios of the market and her company news. Who knows? She just might succeed....

ENDNOTES

[1] AFFTC History Office, Edwards Air Force Base. "Murphy's Law Was Born Here," www.edwards.af.mil/history/docs_html/tidbits/murphy's_law.html.

2   Guy Gugliotta, "Switches Failed in Crash of Genesis: Errors Stymied Craft's Parachutes on Reentry," *Washington Post*, 16 October 2004.

3   H. Puchan, "The Mercedes-Benz A-Class Crisis." *Corporate Communications: An International Journal* 6(1) (February 2001): 42–46.

4   Kathleen Fearn-Banks, *Crisis Communications: A Casebook Approach* (Mahwah, New Jersey: Lawrence Erlbaum Associates, Inc., 2001).

5   *The New York Times*, 8 January 2006.

6   James Surowiecki, *The Wisdom of Crowds: Why the Many Are Smarter Than the Few and How Collective Wisdom Shapes Business, Economies, Societies and Nations* (New York: Doubleday, 2004).

7   Alex Gofman, "Emergent Scenarios, Synergies, and Suppressions Uncovered Within Conjoint Analysis," *Journal of Sensory Studies* 21(4) (2006): 343–414.

8   See also Howard Moskowitz and Alex Gofman, "Bare Market: Uncover Algebra of the Stock Market Mind." *Marketing Research* 18(3) (Fall 2006): 8–14.

9   Alex Gofman, Howard Moskowitz, Samuel Rabino, and Don Lowry, "Stock Market Activity: Market Research Meets Applied Economics," In *Proceedings: 2006 ESOMAR Congress in London*, London, 2006.

11

Asia Calling, Ltd.:
The China Angle

A very loose translation of Russian gang wisdom says that the one with bare hands cannot withstand a direct hit by a large brick. Translating that to today's *realpolitik*, the awakening colossus known as BRIC (Brazil, Russia, India, and China) is hanging over Westerners' heads. It is true that one cannot directly resist the blow of a brick. But some martial arts professionals can challenge that. To do so—at least, as we see it in Jackie Chan movies—these professionals challenged by a nemesis with potentially higher "brute force" realize that they need to be more agile, more trained, smarter, and better prepared than their opponents are. They have to be more adept and perceptive, adapting to the attacker's tactics more quickly and nimbly than their adversary adapts. Just being one step ahead of the opposition frequently makes the difference between survival and oblivion.

From the world's manufacturing backyard, China—as well as the other three members of BRIC—is rapidly emerging as an economic power-player, not content with its current role. By now, China's manufacturers have learned how to produce different products efficiently, constantly improving product quality. The next step for China's businesses will be to design and produce their own products, both for internal market and for export. The China of today, as a nation, is becoming increasingly ambitious. The Chinese are not content any longer to be simply copycats, with better and better knock-offs. As a country, China wants to learn how to design things as the West does—and, to top it off, make the products even better, more stylish, more affordable, and, ultimately, more threatening to the West simply because of consumer appeal. In the words of Michael Dunne, president of the consulting firm Automotive Resources Asia, "The Chinese formed joint ventures for one purpose: to learn how to do it themselves one day. That day is here."[1]

Cheap labor cost puts China into a very advantageous position. Lack of experience pulls them back. Many Western designers now work for Chinese companies. As usual with China, it is not a long-term strategy—it is just a jump-start, a learning experience from the "experienced but slow and sleepy" companies in the West. The "hungry time," when the Chinese consumers were happy to buy just anything appearing in the stores after a generations-long "deficit" of goods, is over. Local customers are facing choices similar to what the Westerns are. To win them over, manufacturers and emerging marketers have to understand their minds. And it has to be done in a nonthreatening way, to prevent the respondents from "shutting up," which frequently happens in countries such as China when people are confronted with direct questions.

Without a culture of open expression needed in qualitative research (such as focus groups), caused by the country's political heritage, the opportunities are great for the RDE approach to grow explosively in China. RDE works quickly and privately, produces concrete results, and, most important, is independent of borders, cultures, and previous market knowledge.

EMERGING OPPORTUNITIES FOR RDE IN CHINA AND THE REASONS IT WILL BE SUCCESSFUL

China is a perfect place for successful RDE deployment on an unprecedented level. Ironically, even the history of limitation on free expression helps RDE to flourish in China, as we will see in the following eight reasons for the success.

- **Reason 1:** Chinese designers want to get innovative ideas about the products. Some of them might be adaptations of Western products for the local markets (which, in turn, are not only huge in size, but also immensely diverse from place to place and require product localization); others are entirely new products. In this uncharted territory, the designers need input from thousands of people in many localities. Moreover, the designers need the information fast—really fast. They are not yet very experienced to make decisive, educated, over-researched guesses, which, in turn, could be just the thing for a rapid-use tool. The answer is RDE because of its fast, scalable, and efficient nature. And unlike direct questioning, as in focus groups, which might not work in countries such as China, RDE is not threatening. Respondents just rate different ideas or products on a scale of liking or purchase intent.

- **Reason 2:** For every locality in China or other countries in Asia, the designers can use RDE with relatively minor incremental cost. Given the population size and growing buying power, RDE is definitely the way to go for China.

- **Reason 3:** Chinese consumers are still apprehensive when asked direct questions. Their instinctive reaction to be politically correct and to please the interviewer, who still could be associated with feared authoritative officials, makes most other market research methods, especially qualitative ones, far weaker than in other countries and, occasionally, virtually useless.

- **Reason 4:** It is much less expensive to create and analyze RDE *in China for China,* compared to the cost American or European companies incur trying to do research in China from their home countries.

- **Reason 5:** China does not have a history of "standardized" approaches to understand the consumer. Hence, the Chinese manufacturer is not hindered with years of process that often holds back new ideas in the interest of "harmonization."

- **Reason 6:** During the past years, Chinese factories made all sorts of new goods for the local markets. But how to market them? People in China are very cost- and value-minded. What are the hot buttons to trigger their interest, beyond the simplistic strategy of lowering price? How do you design the packages to convince consumers to choose the product? There are about 20 million customers in Shanghai alone, another 15 million in Beijing, and so on. How does the manufacturer create packages that might differ in Shanghai vs. Beijing, and might change ten times in two years to catch new trends and defend the territory? RDE provides an easy and fast solution for that.

- **Reason 7:** After conquering China and the rest of Asia with their home-designed brands, the Chinese entrepreneurs will direct their efforts to the West. This also might happen concurrently with the Asian expansion. We see this happening with Korean brands like Samsung and LG that are more and more prominent in the West. These entrepreneurs need actionable insights into these new products for their brands. What should the product be? How should the product be communicated? If China is to design, manufacture, and market to the world independably then how can it identify what to do, what to say, and what to show? More important, how can it do this in real time, changing the products, messaging, and packages to meet local conditions and competitive threats? Although Chinese products can be found everywhere, marketers in China now have very little knowledge about American or European markets. It will be cost-prohibitive for many of them to hire an established U.S.- or EU-based company to do research on the matter. The solution? RDE—an iterative, inexpensive, massive RDE run from China.

- **Reason 8:** By nature, the Chinese are very entrepreneurial. A company that establishes itself as a reputable and efficient provider into insights of the Westerns is poised for enormous success. Other corporations in China will be knocking on their doors around the clock. "What are the most attractive options for this gadget in Germany? I can make it cheap, but I do not know what to make. How to market it? How to package it?" All this work can be done remotely from China very inexpensively and efficiently, virtually overnight.

Rather than continue listing the reasons, let's look at how RDE works in a hypercompetitive world where having early knowledge of the customer's needs and wants can lead to massive advantage.

First, let's look a bit at language issues. You'll see the point in a minute. Have you ever tried to learn a few words in a foreign language before that trip to Europe, the Caribbean, or South America? It is quite simple to learn and use *hola* in Spanish, *bonjour* in French, or *buon giorno* in Italian. Many visitors do it successfully and are rewarded by wide smiles from the locals. Spaniards and Italians are happy to hear your attempts to speak their language, although do not try it in France unless you do it reasonably well. In more remote places, they even *expect you* to speak and understand their tongue. Some of the "single-lingual" readers might recall those awkward and helpless moments somewhere in a foreign land when their humble question as *"Barcelona dirección, ...please?"* is answered in a long and enthusiastic monologue—in Spanish, of course. Most Americans never learn foreign languages because we expect *others* to speak English.

That's not the case in China. Before a trip to China, one of the authors (AG) spent quite a few coffee breaks trying to perfect his *Nǐ hǎo* ("hello" in Chinese) with the help of a native Chinese-speaking employee. In the latter's opinion, it sounded quite convincing and close to the correct pronunciation. And yet, any attempt to greet people in China with *Nǐ hǎo* miserably failed. It was *not* the pronunciation (which was very tough, indeed) that caused the problem. People in China *did not expect foreigners to speak Chinese,* period. They either were fishing for the familiar foreign words (if they knew some) or just ignoring the phrase completely by expecting it to be in a language unknown to them. Is it because only a small number of foreigners ever managed to learn Chinese?

At the same time, millions of Asians moved to Europe and the U.S., and many of them assimilated quite successfully. From Indian entrepreneurs of Silicon Valley to Chinese scientists and accountants, many examples show Asians fast adapting in their new homeland. How many Westerners assimilated in China to the same level?

The bottom line: A well-prepared Chinese company has a better chance of succeeding in a marketing intelligence area than do its competitors in the West. Why hasn't this happened yet? Just wait a year or two. Chinese businessmen are getting ready to understand *both* worlds and speak *many* languages. They do not expect others to learn Chinese. They are eager to learn new languages, even if it is not perfect at the beginning. Foreign-language schools are booming in China, proof enough that China is looking outward.

We illustrate this with a short story of a company that we refer to simply as Asia Calling, Ltd., or ACL. Headquartered in an ultra-modern skyscraper in the Pudong district of Shanghai overlooking busy Huangpu River, ACL is staffed with young, energetic, and ambitious local university graduates. They are not too shy to admit that they need and want to learn.

In fact, the more learning, the better. ACL also employs some of the former executives from top manufacturers, so embedded in ACL's corporate DNA is a profound knowledge about how businesses and the people tick. Initially, ACL worked very closely with a leader in marketing intelligence from the U.S. to acquire knowledge, technology, and methodologies. Now ACL still licenses some of the tools, but very likely not for long—software development in China is not expensive. ACL also has established very good working relationships with several major panel providers around the world. Recruiting the respondents over the Web is virtually transparent, very easy, fast, and, of course, cost-effective.

ACL has a very simple mission: to understand the mind of the prospective customer *anywhere in the world* in terms of product or service features and descriptions, and to send this understanding back to its client factories in China/Southeast Asia or to outsourced service providers in India. Some clients of ACL need to produce new-to-the-world products and want to have a Chinese factory design and manufacture them to the customer's standards. Others need to create an off-shoring service for call centers in a specific product category but do not know the type of language to use that makes the center's offers attractive for the corporate customer and acceptable to the end consumer. These customers (corporate clients) and consumers (users of the products/services) reside in many different countries. Many clients of ACL are from the West, desperate to expand their offerings to the immense emerging markets in Asia.

With this in mind, how can ACL create a dynamite business that can essentially scan the mind of the customer anywhere in the world, process the information using RDE, and then quickly, inexpensively, and powerfully emerge with specifications that a factory can understand or a service center can use?

ACL found the vision of RDE to fit perfectly with its goals. Using its excellent relationship with the *Chinese manufacturing companies, client marketing companies, and consumers,* ACL is perfectly positioned to serve client needs globally. ACL adopted the RDE technology, which it uses to test responses to, say, bedroom furnishing ideas among the target U.S. and Canadian customers. Even though the marketing company is based in Holland and Sweden and the manufacturing plants are located in China and Malaysia, the customers might reside in yet a third location or even many culturally different locations, anywhere in the world.

RDE enables ACL to accomplish at least four different jobs, all of which increase the competitive edge of the company. Consider these examples of ACL's work:

- **Subscription-based competitive intelligence worldwide, as a service to manufacturers**—Companies around the world need to know what the trends are. Instead of simply doing *ad hoc* work, ACL allows various companies to sponsor half-yearly projects, in which ACL "vacuums" the Internet in a specific area to discover what types of products, features, communications, and even graphics are being presented to customers. By rapidly executing the same RDE study in multiple countries, in two weeks, ACL creates a database to show what ideas work and what don't. This standardized set of databases is ACL's Pygmalion[2] database. Pygmalion shows what works in each country and what mind-set segments exist. Because RDE makes such competitive intelligence easy, companies use the Pygmalion database to spot and follow trends and opportunities.

- **Customers' needs translated into product design, worldwide**—Perhaps ACL's most important job is translating marketing goals from client companies into product concepts and feeding these concept specifications back to its Chinese manufacturers. ACL works with a client marketing company to identify the opportunity, structure the architecture of test concepts (what it should look like and what types of features it should have), populate the template with alternative options, test among the target population anywhere in the world, get the results, and feed back the database to the Chinese manufacturer.[3] This sequence of knowledge-developing activities, from the marketplace opportunity to the customer mind, to the factory specifications, might take as little as a day to a week or two, a speed needed to survive and prosper in an increasingly hypercompetitive marketplace.

- **Publicity material created for marketing and sales**—Just as in the case of competitive intelligence, RDE identifies the messages that sell—or, at least, excite the consumers and push them to buy. ACL conducts these projects among the target population, identifying the specific phrases (see Chapter 4, "How to Make People Feel Good Even When They Pay More") and visuals (see Chapter 7, "Bridging Cool Design with Hot Science") that drive customers. Again, RDE

Even When They Pay More") and visuals (see Chapter 7, "Bridging Cool Design with Hot Science") that drive customers. Again, RDE does this work and analysis quickly among the target consumers. ACL need not develop a deep understanding of those target consumers. In most cases, that extensive, high cost, slow-to-do, and hard-won intellectual effort is neither appropriate nor productive for today's short-term world. By the time such arduous work is done, the opportunity likely would be missed and the idea would be outdated. Rather, ACL wants to know precisely what specifically works *now*. The understanding of *why* comes when ACL sees what works, but the real power of RDE is to identify specifics for advertising, in real time.

- **Optimized communication in real time in the world of search-based advertising**—Armed with RDE, ACL works with its clients to optimize their offers using search-based advertising. Current search engines (such as Google) make a lot of their revenue (and in turn even more revenue for their clients) from paid searches, so-called search word advertising. Using the RDE engine and the Google Ad-Words API, ACL systematically varies the composition of the search word ads. The RDE approach now identifies what works in search-based advertising and self-optimizes. Ideas that work in a search, such as those that drive clicks, are identified and kept. The system works with many thousands of combinations in real time—again, a simple application of RDE thinking and the RDE technology tool.

Clearly, ACL, a company of the very near future (say, one to three years), provides many business-relevant applications of RDE to the community. In some cases, the applications of RDE even constitute a true breakthrough, as with RDE-based real-time content optimization, dynamic ad boost, and so on. The bottom line is that technology coupled with people, motivated by economic realities, and unhindered by ossified methods, can create a juggernaut. That juggernaut inhales the consumer mind and exhales superb products, tailored exquisitely to increasingly smaller groups of people around the world.

This road is not a straight, smooth autobahn that guarantees to bring you to your destination. Marco Bevolo, Director of Foresights and Trends at Philips Design, once said, "China may be at the top of the world one day,

Marco's colleague, Murray Camens, Australian-born vice president of Philips Design, warns that the Chinese companies might face disaster *if* they do not understand the complexity of the consumer. He believes that "if Chinese companies want to achieve global success, they will need to learn how to identify consumers' tastes and desires, and then also learn how to meet those demands."

On the contrary, foreign companies looking into expanding their markets to China and other developing markets should "not assume that cheaper is always better." And they should do their homework diligently.[5]

And this is *exactly* what ACL is perfectly set to do: bridge the gap between Chinese production and the customers on both sides of the border. Chinese businesses are ready for brutal competition. "The pace of the market...and the unpredictability—it's not a place for the faint-hearted," says Gavin Heron, managing director of Omnicom Group's TBWA Shanghai.[6]

People usually are scared by something that *might come, something unknown.* And they become more resolute when they actually face the materialized problem. Should we be scared by the emerging BRIC above us? Actually, it does not matter: This is not a threat; this is a reality. We have to live with it. Like the reality of outsourcing IT jobs to India. Frightening? In that case, why do American companies still struggle to recruit domestic, qualified software developers?

What can the West do? The best answer: Just try to stay one step ahead.

ENDNOTES

[1] Gordon Fairclough, "GM's Partner in China Plans Competing Car," *The Wall Street Journal,* 5 April 2006.

[2] Based on the classical myth, Bernard Shaw's *Pygmalion* (also known as the *My Fair Lady* musical) is the story of teaching a Cockney to speak and behave properly, resulting in much more far-reaching consequences.

[3] We have seen this approach in action throughout this book, especially in Chapter 6, on innovation.

[4] "Philips Design Execs Say Chinese Firms Face Challenges," *Plastics News* (12 July 2005): www.plasticsnews.com/china/philipsdesign.

[5] Ibid.

[6] Geoffrey A. Fowler, "Agencies Find China Land of Opportunity and Unhappy Clients," *The Wall Street Journal*, 17 March 2006.

12

RDE's "Brave New World!"

In an old hunters' story, two hunters were preparing to go to the jungle to hunt a tiger. One of them was putting on light and comfortable running shoes, whereas the other had his old heavy boots. "Do you think it will make you run faster than the tiger if it chases us?" asked the latter. "Nope," said the other. "I just need to run faster than *you* do."

RDE frequently allows the "hunters" to "get the tiger" in the first place. In other less glamorous cases, at least it lets the user stay one step ahead of the competition, a distance that is frequently just enough to succeed—or, at least, survive.

This book guided us on a journey from food to magazines, from politics to the stock market, from U.S. factories from the 1950s to Asian factories in the near future. We have seen stories about companies using RDE to understand how to make a product, how to understand the strengths and weaknesses of competitors, and how to innovate on a sustained basis. This final chapter takes stock of what we have in RDE, what we have learned, and where to go from here. Keep in mind that these stories from actual projects were selected from thousands of such successful studies in which the authors have been involved over the years, in dozens of different areas, ranging from foods to hotels, cars to cellphones, jewelry to furniture, publishing to TV commercials, and the like.

QUESTIONS AND ANSWERS ABOUT RDE

After you have read the stories about other people benefiting from RDE, you might be considering trying it for yourself. Of course, there is a difference between reading and doing, but in the case of RDE the gap is not that big and definitely not deep—even if you do not get the best results at the very first attempt, you are more than likely to succeed on the next try. And if you still have questions, read this section—we will try to answer them.

QUESTION 1: IS IT FEASIBLE?

Can these types of problems be solved by the ordinary nonexpert businessperson faced with problems, of which these are a simple random assortment? The answer is a resounding "yes!" Despite the desire to make knowledge acquisition a priesthood, and statistics the collection of magic incantations, the truth of the matter is that the approaches we present for RDE are quite simple. Of course, the *technology* is not trivial, but *executing the technology* is straightforward. Therein simplicity abounds. However, there must be some thinking. In place of the disciplined thinking RDE demands, you cannot substitute simplistic "beauty contests," or choosing the best out of a few possibly less than optimal choices. Yes, RDE *is* exceptionally feasible. Try it—it won't bite!

QUESTION 2: IS RDE WORTH THE EFFORT?

Even if RDE is feasible and, in many cases, downright easy, we are faced with the question of real value. Simply put, is the effort worth it? Will the RDE user in business accomplish more using the discipline, or can one simply guess the way through problems? The answer is as simple as in the feasibility question: Of course, it is worth the effort!

The typical company always faces the tyranny of time. Almost no company today dares to admit having enough time to both do the right things and do things right. Even time to think is precious, fast disappearing. Assaulted by daily threats, it is no wonder that the first thing managers in companies do is search out the easiest way to solve a problem. All too often, that solution is guesswork. The politically correct answer, generally delivered in a plaintive, tired, sincere way, is "Of course, we want to use a disciplined approach...but we just don't have the time!"

From the authors' perspective, however, RDE really does not take much time. In fact, it usually *saves a lot of time, effort, and money at the other end.* The important thing with RDE is that it forces you to *think about the problem,* not just react reflexively. The power of homework, or practice in school and in sports, is well known and acknowledged. RDE *is* that practice. Just thinking about the problem in the structured way required by RDE goes a long way toward solving the problem. Collecting and understanding the independent variables also helps, as does doing the experiment. Sometimes the most valuable part of RDE is the relaxed, up-front thinking time, and the insights you get from collecting the data and just looking at what pops.

But what about later? Does RDE work just because it forces you to think? Hardly. There's more. A lot of today's knowledge in corporations comes from unstructured observations. Sure, company files hold many reports— all sorts of databases, research, and more. Very little is systematic; often you can't go back to find what worked, what didn't, what rules hold, or whether there are any rules. Now let's look at all that we've done here. The words *rules* and *generalities* shout out to us again and again. RDE is all about rules, all about databases, all about going back with questions to see what facts from the one RDE exercise might help solve the *new* problem.

In short, the discipline works, whether at the beginning, to structure thinking; in the middle, to point out realities ("Chance favors the prepared mind," as Pasteur said in 1854); or later, when the data become a reference that is repeatedly consulted. Sometimes it is hard to believe that one project can find so many follow-ons, unexpected uses that delight. A little insight into today's corporation quickly answers that skepticism. Companies today run on knowledge. More than likely, when problems arise, someone in the company is given the task of rummaging through old corporate reports, research studies, and databases to find an answer. RDE data will come up, in the same way that lots of other data surfaces. The big difference is that the RDE data is already structured.

QUESTION 3: IS THERE ANY LIMIT TO WHAT RDE CAN DO?

What's the big idea behind RDE? Can it do what it says? Is RDE a magic bullet?

On one hand, in a world of guessing, systematic experimentation has to win in the long run simply because it is fact based. There's no reason for the universe to change its rules just because someone is making systematic observations. The odds are that RDE can do a lot—bounded, of course, by the ingenuity of the user. It will not make an artist out of a hack, it will not make a visionary out of an ignorant individual, and it will not reveal the secrets of the universe to someone who prefers guessing to measurement, and aimless hypotheses to disciplined fact-finding.

On the other hand, RDE inevitably will deliver consistent success simply because of the way it is structured. RDE forces the user to think about alternatives in a way that creates a discipline. Thinking is critical. No matter what people in corporations say, previous experience does not always predict what will win and what will fail. The business landscape is littered with the writings of pundits who were popular for a few years and then discarded as the crowd moved on to the next wisdom. The nice thing about RDE is that it does not let pundits take control. It forces the business to do the experiment, not just think about it (so-called "dry-labbing" in chemistry). When people think, take measurements, and actually look at what is happening, the rest happens like magic.

We saw how RDE produced foods and beverages, deconstructed competition, identified "hot button messages," innovated new products, and even moved into the realm of politics and the stock market. These are a few of the applications. Think about a topic in which human choice is involved and people's perceptions are important. Now think about systematic experimentation, providing the people with test stimuli, measuring responses, and discerning a pattern. If you can think of alternatives, think of vignettes or combinations, and think of responses to these vignettes, you've got another area where RDE can be applied.

And keep experimenting!

Epilogue

So, what happened to our protagonist, Allison-the-Entrepreneur? She dived head first into the RDE world without much hesitation. Where did it bring her? To answer this question, let's spend several moments with her family a few years later.

"Mom, let's play our game again! Which shelf do we start with?" asked her daughter in their local supermarket. The game is quite simple for the child: She turns away from a shelf and points to a random product. Her Mom tells her a short story related to that product. It is not a surprise that many items on the shelf by now have benefited from RDE applications—whether it be the optimized taste of the content, appearance, package, location, brand extension line, promotions, advertisements, and so on. The ones that did not use RDE have eventually lost their market share and have either disappeared or been moved to the lower shelves and to the bottom lines in ranking studies. Allison was at the forefront of the movement. She made her fortune using RDE and felt obligated to pass this "best hidden business secret" to others. She spent quite a bit of her time popularizing the idea among her business peers and the wider community. Now she can proudly point to the many items that resulted from these activities.

Allison quietly enjoys this game. Her daughter is much less impressed with her mom's professional, financial, and social status than with this game. Kids get used to their surroundings. Aren't their parents just "talking furniture?" "You did *this* as well? I saw *it* yesterday on TV!" "Well, I did not do it myself, John's company did.... But I remember showing John the advantages of RDE." "Who is John?" "He is a Fortune 500 CEO now.... Well, I'd say he is a very, very successful person."

Starting as a small entrepreneur, Allison has managed to position her novel product on the market by experimenting with the taste, appearance, packaging, and other attributes of a successful product. RDE helped her compete with "bigger guys" and win on multiple occasions. Even when her experiments did not produce the desired results at first, it was very easy to repeat them.

Allison's small startup grew into a multinational CPG corporation and is moving fast into other areas. Many of her friends in a prestigious business club are picking up the idea and extending it to TV programming, education, Web content optimization, and so on.

Try it yourself. You may find that even such a bizarre proposition as "selling blue elephants" is not that impossible for a prepared person.

If you want more hands-on experience with RDE, go to the RDE Web site, www.SellingBlueElephants.com.

INDEX

M